WORKING MEN'S COLLEGE.

## LIBRARY REGULATIONS.

The Library is open every week-day evening, from 6.30 to 10 o'clock, except on Saturdays, when it closes at 9.

This book may be kept for three weeks. If not returned within that period, the borrower wiill be liable to a fine of one penny per week.

If lost or damaged the borrower will be required to make good such loss or damage.

Only one book may be borrowed at a time

# HARVARD HISTORICAL STUDIES

PUBLISHED UNDER THE DIRECTION OF
THE DEPARTMENT OF HISTORY

FROM THE INCOME OF

THE HENRY WARREN TORREY FUND

VOLUME XXIX

# HARVARD HISTORICAL STUDIES

## HARVARD UNIVERSITY PRESS
### CAMBRIDGE, MASS., U. S. A.

# THE MONROE DOCTRINE

## 1823–1826

BY

### DEXTER PERKINS

WATSON PROFESSOR OF HISTORY IN THE
UNIVERSITY OF ROCHESTER

CAMBRIDGE

HARVARD UNIVERSITY PRESS

LONDON : HUMPHREY MILFORD

OXFORD UNIVERSITY PRESS

1927

PRINTED AT THE HARVARD UNIVERSITY PRESS
CAMBRIDGE, MASS., U.S.A.

# FOREWORD

ALTHOUGH it might seem a work of supererogation to add one more to the already numerous volumes on the Monroe Doctrine, there are several justifications for such a task. In the first place, even today, there is no really inclusive synthesis of the materials already known. Discussion of Monroe's famous message has tended to follow a beaten track; and the same events in the same order have been reproduced again and again. No doubt the essentials of the story must always remain the same; but were there nothing more to be discovered, there would be room for a new consideration of old materials, for a fresh interpretation of things already known. As a matter of fact, however, there are many phases of the message on which new light can and ought to be shed. The story of Monroe's declaration, as is the case with many another episode in American diplomatic history, has all too often been written from an exclusively American point of view. This not only gives it a provincial character, but renders it imperfect and inexact as an historical record. There is room for a better understanding of the events in Europe which accompanied the American pronouncement; for a study of the policy of the European powers toward South America; for an examination of the effects of the message on the attitude and activities of the powers of the Old World, and of the impression which it produced on the opinion of the time.

There are also other matters which deserve more emphasis than they have received. The evolution and underlying philosophy of the non-colonization principle have not yet been analyzed as fully as they deserve to be; we know very little of the reception of the message at home; and the story of its aftermath in the New World demands further consideration.

It is in the interests of a fuller understanding of what is perhaps the most important single document in American diplomatic history that the present study has been written. It was originally begun at the suggestion of Professor Archibald Cary Coolidge of

Harvard University, and owes much to his incisive criticism. His careful reading of the whole manuscript has been most helpful, and has improved both the structure and the substance of the work. I am also under obligations to Professor A. M. Schlesinger, whose scrutiny of the text has helped me greatly, and with whom frequent exchanges of view have been stimulating and profitable; and to Mr. Waldo G. Leland, always of great service to historical scholars, who read the first chapter. I wish to express my thanks to Mr. W. C. Ford for his kindness in examining the otherwise inaccessible J. Q. Adams papers for the answers to various questions which occurred in connection with this work. Finally, I am happy, too, to record my appreciation of illuminating discussions with Mr. H. W. V. Temperley of Peterhouse, Cambridge.

I desire also to express my appreciation to Mr. D. A. Salmon for the friendly reception which he has always given me at the Bureau of Indexes and Archives, and to Mrs. Maddin Summers for her aid and assistance in my work there. In all the European archives which I have consulted I have found courteous and friendly treatment which deserves to be given its word of recognition. Finally, I wish to thank Miss Irma H. Reed for her scholarly preparation of the manuscript for the press.

DEXTER PERKINS.

ROCHESTER, NEW YORK,
August, 1926.

# CONTENTS

## CHAPTER I

### THE NORTHWEST BOUNDARY CONTROVERSY AND THE NON–COLONIZATION PRINCIPLE

## CHAPTER II

### THE SPANISH AMERICAN PHASE OF THE MESSAGE. THE PRELUDE

## CHAPTER III

### THE WARNING TO EUROPE

# CHAPTER IV

## WHAT EUROPE INTENDED

# CHAPTER V

## THE RECEPTION OF THE MESSAGE

## CHAPTER VI

### THE AFTERMATH OF THE MESSAGE IN THE
### NEW WORLD

# CHAPTER VII

## THE AFTERMATH OF THE MESSAGE IN EUROPE

# LIST OF ABBREVIATIONS

*Alaskan Boundary Tribunal* .. *Proceedings of the Alaskan Boundary Tribunal. Senate Executive Documents*, Fifty-eighth Congress, Second Session, vol. ii. Washington, 1904.

*Am. Hist. Rev.* ............. *American Historical Review.* New York, 1895– .

*Ann. Report Amer. Hist. Assoc. Annual Reports of the American Historical Association.* Washington, 1902– .

Castlereagh, *Correspondence* .. *Correspondence, Despatches, and other Papers* of Viscount Castlereagh, edited by his brother, Charles Vane, Marquess of Londonderry. London, 1848–53. 12 vols.

Chile, *Sesiones* ............. *Sesiones de los cuerpos lejislativos de la República de Chile*, edited by Valentin Letelier. Santiago, 1887–1908. 37 vols.

*Eng. Hist. Rev.* ............. *English Historical Review.* London, 1886– .

Lockey .................... J. B. Lockey, *Pan-Americanism.* New York, 1920.

London. P. R. O., F. O. .... London. Public Record Office. Foreign Office.

*Mass. Hist. Soc. Proc.* ....... *Proceedings* of the Massachusetts Historical Society. Boston, 1791– .

Paris. Aff. Étr., Corr. Pol. .. Paris. Archives du Ministère des Affaires Étrangères, Correspondance Politique.

*Pol. Sci. Quart.* ............. *Political Science Quarterly.* New York, 1886– .

Rush, *Court of London* ...... Richard Rush, *Memoranda of a Residence at the Court of London.* Philadelphia, 1845.

St. Petersburg. F. O. ....... St. Petersburg. Foreign Office.

Wellington, *Despatches* ...... *Despatches, Correspondence, and Memoranda* of Arthur, Duke of Wellington, edited by his son. London, 1867–80. 8 vols.

Wellington, *Supplementary Despatches*............... *Supplementary Despatches and Memoranda* of Arthur, Duke of Wellington, edited by his son. London, 1858–72. 15 vols.

# THE MONROE DOCTRINE

# CHAPTER I

## THE NORTHWEST BOUNDARY CONTROVERSY AND THE NON-COLONIZATION PRINCIPLE. 1823-1824

THE famous declaration of December 2, 1823, which has come to be known as the Monroe Doctrine, had a dual origin and a dual purpose. On the one hand, it was the result of the advance of Russia on the northwest coast of America, and was designed to serve as a protest against this advance and to establish a general principle against Russian expansion. Referring to this question of the northwest, President Monroe laid down the principle in his message to Congress that "the American continents, by the free and independent condition which they have assumed and maintain, are henceforth not to be considered as subjects for future colonization by any European powers." On the other hand, the message was provoked by the fear of European intervention in South America to restore to Spain her revolted colonies, and was intended to give warning of the hostility of the United States to any such intervention. "With the governments [that is, of the Spanish-American republics] who have declared their independence, and maintained it," wrote the President, "and whose independence we have, on great consideration and just principles, acknowledged, we could not view any interposition for the purpose of oppressing them, or controlling in any other manner their destiny, by any European power, in any other light than as the manifestation of an unfriendly disposition toward the United States."

Of these two aspects of the message, it is no doubt the second which involves the more interesting and important questions. How far did the manifesto of December 2, 1823, actually check European designs on the New World? How great was its immediate influence? Did it lower or raise American prestige? Did it arouse resentment or command respect? These are only some of the more significant questions that suggest themselves in connection with the message in its South American aspects. An

3

examination of the Monroe Doctrine in the days of its origin must inevitably concern itself preponderantly with just these questions.

But, on the other hand, the non-colonization principle must not be neglected. It has a high importance in and of itself. It is indeed the most important *principle* connected with the declaration of 1823. The pregnant sentence directed against Russia was to have a wide influence as time went on. It was to play a rôle of ever-increasing importance. From it were to be deduced many of the corollaries of the Monroe Doctrine, and on it has been based more than one state paper of large significance. It is a matter of great interest, therefore, to study its origins, to understand its logic, and to analyze the effect which it produced at the time of its enunciation.

The introduction to such a study lies in an examination of the northwest controversy with Russia, in the course of which the non-colonization principle was to be laid down. Russian interest in the northwest coast of America goes back to the second quarter of the eighteenth century, to the days of the renowned navigator Vitus Behring, who discovered in 1727 the Straits that now bear his name,[1] and fourteen years later the Alaskan coast in the neighborhood of latitude 58.[2] Behring's explorations were followed by the voyages of fur traders and by the establishment of trading posts on the islands off the American mainland. After years of demoralizing competition on the part of private individuals, the Tsar determined to create a commercial monopoly for the exploitation of the rich fisheries to be found in that part of the world. By the ukase of July 8, 1799, the Russian-American Company was constituted, and to this company were granted exclusive trading rights and jurisdiction along the coast as far south as latitude 55, and the right to make settlements on either side of that line in territory not occupied by other powers.[3]

---

[1] H. H. Bancroft, *History of Alaska* (San Francisco, 1886), pp. 36 f.

[2] *Ibid.*, p. 78.

[3] J. C. Hildt, *Early Diplomatic Negotiations of the United States with Russia* (Baltimore, 1906), p. 157. Chap. ix of this book, pp. 157-192, deals with the northwest question as a whole, but without special reference to the evolution of the Monroe message.

From an early date the operations of this Russian corporation were impeded by interlopers, very largely American. American vessels sold arms and ammunition to the natives, and secured a considerable part of the fur trade. As early as 1808 and 1810 complaints on the part of the Russian government began to be made to the government at Washington. There was, obviously enough, a situation that might lead to serious friction.[4]

As time went on, moreover, the Russian-American Company manifested a distinct tendency toward the extension of its prerogatives. At the end of 1811, or early in 1812, it established a post, named Fort Ross, near Bodega Bay, and not fifty miles from the bay of San Francisco, in a region claimed by Spain.[5] The motives that prompted this action may have been, and in all likelihood were, commercial, rather than those of territorial expansion,[6] but the very existence of such a settlement was bound to cause disquietude. Such a step might easily prove to be the prelude to far-reaching designs of aggrandizement.

It is only recently that it has even been suggested that this Russian post in California might have some relation to the message of 1823.[7] The non-colonization clause of that message has

[4] J. C. Hildt, *op. cit.*, p. 158.

[5] For a brief account of the settlement at Fort Ross, see R. G. Cleland, *A History of California: The American Period* (New York, 1922), pp. 27 f. For a longer narrative, see H. H. Bancroft, *California*, vol. ii (San Francisco, 1885), especially chap. xiv, pp. 294–320. This work is vol. xiv of his *History of the Pacific States of North America*.

[6] The question of the motive behind the Ross settlement, though not strictly germane to the subject of this chapter, is interesting enough to deserve comment. Bancroft says that no territorial claim was made before 1817 (*op. cit.*, p. 314), and in 1820 the company was willing to waive whatever territorial rights it may have had, in exchange for trade privileges (*ibid.*, p. 320). It is interesting also to note that the most extreme claims ever put forward by a Russian minister to the American government never went beyond the Columbia, and these were speedily dropped. Furthermore, in the controversy which arose in 1821, as will appear, Russia limited her pretensions to the line of 51 degrees. All this time Fort Ross was still in her hands. (On Russian territorial claims see Hildt, *op. cit.*, p. 159.) In the light of these facts it seems improbable that the Russian government itself ever meditated taking possession of California, whatever some of its agents may have done. On general principles, it is difficult to believe that the Tsar Alexander would have attempted, or even connived at, the filching of California from Spain at a time when he was on terms of such cordial friendship with the government at Madrid.

[7] See Cleland, *op. cit.*, pp. 29–32. See also, by the same author, *One Hundred Years of the Monroe Doctrine* (Los Angeles, 1923), pp. 33 ff.

invariably been traced to another set of circumstances involving the northwest question, circumstances which we must soon examine. But the relation of the Bodega Bay settlement to Monroe's pronunciamiento is one that deserves a careful analysis.

There is no question that in some instances informed Americans watched with apprehension the Russian advance. Pinkney, the American representative in St. Petersburg, wrote warningly to Adams,[8] the Secretary of State, and so did his successor, Campbell.[9] J. H. Prevost, a commissioner sent to receive back Astoria from the British, after the peace of Ghent, saw designs of wide extent in the founding of the Russian settlement.[10] A writer in the St. Louis *Inquirer*, perhaps Senator Benton, expressed fears of the Russian advance.[11] And a committee of Congress, in 1821, commented jealously on the presence of the Russians in California.[12]

Whether Monroe and his advisers were much perturbed by the Bodega Bay settlement is, however, another question, and one difficult to decide with finality. The references to Fort Ross in the correspondence of the President or the Secretary of State are of the most meagre kind. We have no more than two allusions to the matter, both from the pen of John Quincy Adams. One is a mere passing comment.[13] The other is to be found in a dispatch to Middleton, the American minister at St. Petersburg. Writing on July 22, 1823, Adams declared that, if the motive of the establishment at Fort Ross

---

[8] Washington. State Dept. Despatches, Russia, vol. 6, July 17, 1817.

[9] Ibid., vol. 7, Mar. 25, 1820.

[10] Cleland, *op. cit.*, p. 29. "May we not infer views as to the early possession of this harbor, and ultimately to the sovereignty of all California? Surely the growth of a race on these shores, scarcely emerged from the savage state, guided by a chief who seeks not to emancipate, but to enthrall, is an event to be deprecated — an event, the mere apprehension of which ought to excite the jealousies of the United States, so far at least as to induce the cautionary measure of preserving a station which may serve as a barrier to a northern aggrandizement."

[11] *Ibid.*, p. 30.

[12] *Ibid.*, p. 31.

[13] In the cabinet meeting of June 28, 1823, Adams stated that "the Russians appear to have no settlement upon" this continent "except that in California." *Memoirs of John Quincy Adams*, edited by C. F. Adams (Philadelphia, 1874–77, 12 vols.), vi, 157.

was to lay the foundation for an exclusive territorial claim of Russia to the Northwest Coast, down to the very borders of California, and, founded thereon, to assert exclusive rights of trading with the natives of the Northwest Coast, and to navigation and fishery in the Pacific Ocean, it is time for the nations whose rights and interests are affected by this project effectually to interpose. There can, perhaps, be no better time for saying, frankly and explicitly, to the Russian Government, that the future peace of the world, and the interest of Russia herself, cannot be promoted by Russian settlements upon any part of the American Continent.[14]

From this comment it clearly appears that Bodega Bay had at least an incidental relationship to the famous paragraph on non-colonization. But the fact that this comment stands virtually alone tends to the conclusion that that relationship was not a very profound one, that it was of secondary, rather than of primary, importance. And it may be very definitely stated, as the mere matter of dates will demonstrate, that the establishment of the California trading-post was not the occasion for the enunciation of the Monroe Doctrine. In the eleven years from 1812 to 1823 the Russian government received no intimation of American displeasure. John Quincy Adams, who took office in 1817, did not mention Fort Ross in his correspondence till 1823. John Quincy Adams was not the man to wait six years to express himself if he felt strongly upon a subject.

It was a later act of overreaching on the part of the Russian-American Company which gave rise to the discussions in the course of which the non-colonization principle was definitely formulated. On September $^{4}/_{16}$, 1821, the Tsar Alexander I, acting at the instigation of the Russian monopoly, promulgated an imperial decree which renewed its privileges and confirmed its exclusive trading rights. This time the southern limit of these rights on the American coast was set, not at 55, but at 51 degrees. And in addition, all foreign vessels were forbidden, between Behring Straits and 51 degrees, to come within 100 Italian miles of the shore, on pain of confiscation.[15] A Russian warship

---

[14] *American State Papers*, Foreign Relations (Washington, 1832–59, 6 vols.), v, 445. Observations on the claim of Russia to territorial possessions on the continent of North America, communicated with Mr. Adams's letter to Mr. Middleton of July 22, 1823.

[15] This decree is quoted in Hildt, *op. cit.*, pp. 159 f. It is also to be found in the

was dispatched to the northwest coast to enforce this remarkable decree, and every intention was manifested of barring all other nations from any participation whatever in the trade or fisheries of the region. Such a course of action very naturally provoked a protest, not only on the part of the United States, but also on the part of Great Britain. At this time the two Anglo-Saxon powers had joint ownership, under the convention of 1818, of the territory north from 42 degrees to a line yet to be determined, and the Russian claims of exclusive jurisdiction as far south as 51 degrees could hardly fail to be disquieting. Both from London and from Washington, therefore, came strong diplomatic remonstrance, and thus began a controversy which was to have the closest relationship to the famous pronouncement of 1823.[16]

It is neither necessary nor desirable, in connection with this narrative, to trace the negotiations on the northwest question in all their details. What is of special interest here is the evolution of the non-colonization principle in the course of the discussions, the reception which it met at the hands of the interested powers, and the effect which it produced upon the diplomatic interchanges themselves.

It may be said at the outset that the development of the principle was due almost exclusively to the American Secretary of State, John Quincy Adams. With regard to that part of Monroe's pronouncement which refers to South America, there has been a tendency, since the appearance of Mr. W. C. Ford's significant articles, to overestimate the rôle played by the Massachusetts statesman. In this phase of the matter, it is well that fuller credit should be given to the President. But, on the northwest question, there can be little doubt that the Secretary of State was responsible for the position assumed, and that his chief did little more than ratify the principle formulated by his chief adviser in matters of foreign policy. Monroe himself was apparently not much concerned about the Russian problem. It

*Alaskan Boundary Tribunal Proceedings*, Senate Documents, Fifty-eighth Congress, Second Session (Washington, 1904, 7 vols.), ii, 25.

[16] The notes of protest are to be found in *Alaskan Boundary Tribunal*, ii, 32 and 104 f., respectively.

was certainly not the most important diplomatic question before the administration either in 1822 or in 1823. The Spanish-American question was of foremost importance. Neither in the President's correspondence, in the diary of Adams, nor in the later recollections of Calhoun, is there the slightest evidence that Monroe held very positive or definite views on the controversy with the Tsar. In all probability he gave Adams a very free hand in the matter.

The evidence on this point is negative, it is true; but it is re-inforced by the positive facts which relate to the Secretary of State's own rôle. For it is possible to trace the evolution of the non-colonization idea in his mind, and to find proof of his special interest in it in its revival at the time of the Panama Congress discussions of 1825 and 1826 during his presidency. How it took shape is well worth analysis.

There is some evidence that, at a date much earlier than 1823, Adams had begun to think of the American continents, especially the North American, as a special preserve of the United States, from which the rest of the world ought to be excluded. The world, he declared in a cabinet meeting of November, 1819, must be

familiarized with the idea of considering our proper dominion to be the continent of North America. From the time when we became an independent people it was as much a law of nature that this should become our pretension as that the Mississippi should flow to the sea. Spain had possessions upon our southern and Great Britain upon our northern border. It was impossible that centuries should elapse without finding them annexed to the United States. . . . Until Europe shall find it a settled geographical element that the United States and North America are identical, any effort on our part to reason the world out of a belief that we are ambitious will have no other effect than to convince them that we add to our ambition hypocrisy.[17]

This tendency to make very broad claims indeed for the United States was also exemplified in a heated colloquy with the British minister, Stratford Canning, in January, 1821. The two had been discussing the northwest question. The conversation is thus described by Adams in his diary.

[17] Adams, *Memoirs*, iv, 438 f.

"Have you any *claim*," said I, "to the mouth of the Columbia River?" "Why, do you not *know*," replied he, "that we have a claim?" "I do not *know*," said I, "what you claim nor what you do not claim. You claim India; you claim Africa; you claim — " "Perhaps," said he, "a piece of the moon." "No," said I; "I have not heard that you claim exclusively any part of the moon; but there is not a spot on *this* habitable globe that I could affirm you do not claim; and there is none which you may not claim with as much color of right as you can have to Columbia River or its mouth." "And how far would you consider," said he, "this exclusion of right to extend?" "To all the shores of the South Sea," said I. "We know of no right that you have there."

This extraordinary statement was no mere outburst of temper. Adams went on to stand by it, and amplify it. The diary continues,

"We certainly did suppose that the British Government had come to the conclusion that there would be neither policy nor profit in cavilling with us about territory on this North American continent." "And in this" said he [Canning], "you include our northern provinces on this continent?" "No," said I; "there the boundary is marked, and we have no disposition to encroach upon it. Keep what is yours, but *leave the rest of this continent to us*." [18]

Six months later we meet with a new outburst against Great Britain in which the same attitude is discernible. On July 4, 1821, at the invitation of citizens of the District of Columbia, Adams delivered an Independence Day oration.[19] For an American secretary of state it was an extraordinary document. A more ferocious assault upon the British policy under George III, a more jingo document, it would be difficult to imagine. But the interesting thing about it from the standpoint of this chapter is that it was a fierce attack upon the whole colonial principle. There is in it no reference to South America, no assertion of any general principle, but the trend of Adams's thought is apparent. It needed only a slight further step to produce a generalization on which a doctrine might be founded. It is no occasion for surprise, then, to find the secretary by November, 1822, informing the British minister with his usual downrightness that "the whole system of modern colonization was an abuse of govern-

[18] Adams, *Memoirs*, v, 252 f. The italics in the last sentence are mine. The other italicized passages are italicized in the *Memoirs* themselves.

[19] The complete text is ot be found in the *National Intelligencer* for July 11, 1821.

ment, and it was time that it should come to an end." [20] Here
was merely another step toward the assertion of a general theory,
a theory which he was finally to formulate in connection with the
discussions with the Russian government over the ukase of 1821.[21]

These discussions, begun in 1822, assumed little importance
till the late spring of 1823. By that time it had been agreed that
the question should be threshed out at St. Petersburg. In June
the cabinet discussed the instructions which were to be sent to
Mr. Middleton, American minister at the court of the Tsar. The
Secretary of State declared it to be his conviction that the
United States ought to contest the right of the Russian government to any territorial establishment on the American continents.
Apparently this point of view did not pass unchallenged. It was
pointed out that Russia would have little reason to accept such
drastic doctrine. The United States, in maintaining it, would be
asking everything, and conceding virtually nothing. A compromise was suggested and agreed upon by which this country
would recognize the territorial claims of the Tsar north of 55 degrees.[22] On this basis, the negotiations were actually to be conducted.

But Adams, with a curious inconsistency, did not on this account surrender the principle which was taking shape in his mind.
At the very moment when he was perfecting the instructions to
Middleton along the lines agreed upon in the cabinet, he declared
himself to Tuyll, the Russian minister at Washington, in language very much more sweeping.

I told him specially [he writes in his diary, alluding to an interview of
July 17, 1823], that we should contest the right of Russia to *any* territorial
establishment on this continent, and that we should assume distinctly the
principle that the American continents are no longer subjects for *any* new
European colonial establishments.[23]

---

[20] Adams, *Memoirs*, vi, 104.

[21] The principal published sources for this Russo-American negotiation are in
*American State Papers*, Foreign Relations, v, 432–471, in *Alaskan Boundary Tribunal*, ii, 1–93, and in *Am. Hist. Rev.* (Jan. and Apr., 1913), xviii, 309–345, and
537–562.

[22] Adams, *Memoirs*, vi, 157 f.

[23] *Ibid.*, p. 163.

In this statement, almost five months before the appearance of the President's message, we have the non-colonization principle full-fledged, no longer merely a subject of cabinet debate, but explicitly put forward to the minister of another power, to the minister of the power perhaps most concerned in denying it. One might expect that such a declaration would have been most distasteful to Tuyll. But such evidence as we have leads to a contrary conclusion. There are no indications that the Russian minister challenged or controverted Adams. In his dispatch to St. Petersburg reporting the conversation of July 17, he contented himself with the following allusion to the matter: "The American government will avail itself of the present occasion to ask the acceptance of a general principle by which foreign powers will definitely and finally renounce the right of establishing new colonies in either of the Americas." [24]   This is underlined in the text itself, but the Russian minister goes on to say that he sees no great difficulty in the way of a settlement of the northwest question. He clearly did not regard the language of Adams as a serious obstacle to understanding. There was nothing in his attitude which might lead the Secretary of State to modify his position.

We have another statement of the non-colonization dogma almost contemporaneous with the interview with Tuyll. This is found in the instructions to Richard Rush, American minister at the Court of Saint James's. As England had an interest in the northwest controversy, it was obviously desirable that the diplomatic representative of the United States at London should be informed of the views of his government on the subject. Accordingly, on July 22, Adams sent forward a long and careful dispatch, in which he set forth his new theory in greater detail than at any other time. [25]   That dispatch will claim our special attention later.

Curiously enough, the instructions to Middleton, of the same date, contain no such clear reference to the non-colonization

<hr/>

[24] St. Petersburg. F. O., Reçus, no. 20,122, July 24, 1823. It is interesting to observe that Tuyll waited seven days after his talk with Adams before writing.

[25] *Alaskan Boundary Proceedings*, ii, 52–56.

principle. They do, of course, contest the Russian claims to territorial sovereignty on the northwest coast. They even go so far as to declare that "there can, perhaps, be no better time for saying, frankly and explicitly, to the Russian government that the future peace of the world, and the interest of Russia herself, cannot be promoted by Russian settlements upon any part of the American Continent." [26] This is strong and definite language. But there is, it may fairly be asserted, at least a shade of difference between such language and the enunciation of a general proposition of universal application.

It must, therefore, be a little doubtful just how far Adams intended to push his new theory at this time. Certainly he did not intend to make it the central point in the pending negotiations. He did not specifically direct either Rush or Middleton to press for its positive recognition. He did not develop it at all, as a general diplomatic maxim, in his correspondence with the latter. As a dogma of general purport, Middleton was first to learn of it through the publication of the President's message in the European newspapers.

The process by which it got into that important document was a very simple one.

Adams secured Monroe's assent to his new principle in July, at the time of sending the dispatches just alluded to.[27] Whether that assent was cordial and positive, or whether it was given as a mere matter of routine, we have no way of knowing. The President may have warmly approved the non-colonization doctrine; he may, on the other hand, have been little aware of its significance or its implications. On this point his writings provide us with no illumination. But at any rate, he *did* accept it. When, therefore, the Secretary of State drew up in November, the customary sketch of the topics of foreign policy which might interest the President in connection with the preparation of the forthcoming message, he naturally included in the paragraph on the Russian negotiations a reference to the new dogma. That paragraph was taken over almost without verbal change by Monroe,

---

[26] *American State Papers*, Foreign Relations, v, 445.
[27] Adams, *Memoirs*, xii, 218.

and thus it appeared in his communication to the Congress. These facts are clear, for we have the actual manuscript of Adams's outline of the diplomatic matters which he wished to draw to the attention of the President,[28] and the language of that outline, so far as the non-colonization principle is concerned, corresponds almost exactly with the language of the message itself.

There was, apparently, no consideration of the principle in the cabinet discussion preceding the publication of the President's declaration.[29] On this point Calhoun, then Secretary of War, was to testify many years later, and the silence of Adams's diary at the time confirms this testimony. There is, after all, nothing strange in such a circumstance. For the question of the hour, in November, 1823, was not the dispute with Russia, but the menace offered by the Holy Alliance to the independence of the States of South America. It was on these problems that all the debates turned; so, very naturally, the other problem was crowded out.

Perhaps, however, the fact that Monroe did not call the attention of his official family to the non-colonization dogma may

[28] New York Public Library, Manuscript Division. Monroe Papers.

[29] *Works* of J. C. Calhoun (New York, 1853–55, 6 vols.), iv, 462 f., from a speech of May 15, 1848. "Mr. Adams, then, in speaking of the whole as one, must have reference to the declaration relative to colonization. As respects this, his memory does not differ much from mine. My impression is, that it never became a subject of deliberation in the cabinet. I so stated when the Oregon question was before the Senate. I stated it in order that Mr. Adams might have an opportunity of denying it, or asserting the real state of the facts. He remained silent, and I presume that my statement is correct — that this declaration was inserted after the cabinet deliberation. It originated entirely with Mr. Adams, without being submitted to the cabinet, and it is, in my opinion, owing to this fact that it is not made with the precision and clearness with which the two former are. . . . I will venture to say that if that declaration had come before that cautious cabinet — for Mr. Monroe was among the wisest and most cautious men I have ever known — it would have been modified, and expressed with a far greater degree of precision." Calhoun here seems to intimate that even the President was hardly aware of the presence of the clause in the message. But there is no reason for believing that Adams smuggled the non-colonization principle into the message. Monroe may not have paid much attention to it, but he was certainly not wholly ignorant of its existence. In his own notes in preparation for the declaration of 1823, Adams's doctrine appears, no less than in the Secretary of State's sketch. (New York Public Library, Manuscript Division. Monroe Papers.)

serve to indicate that he did not attach to it the importance which it has since assumed. In all probability, the words which have exercised so great an influence on American thought, on American public opinion, and on American policy, were pronounced, like many another important declaration, with little realization of the great rôle which they were to play in the future. Even Adams, with his insight and experience, could hardly have realized how great would be the future of the doctrine which he brought forward in 1823.

In this connection, moreover, it is interesting to note the reception which the non-colonization principle met in the American press. By far the greater number of the newspapers of the time seem to have passed it by unnoticed. Out of the nineteen papers which I have examined, which comment more or less fully on the President's message, only three have anything to say of the famous lines whose evolution we have been examining. Of these three, the *National Gazette and Literary Register* of Philadelphia was enthusiastic in its praise. The principle asserted, this journal declared,

has a very comprehensive meaning; forms quite an epoch in our relations with Europe, and cannot fail to have produced a new sensation in all the leading courts. . . . The Russian minister of state must have been somewhat surprised, even startled, when he read [it]. We do not know [it sceptically added] whether it be expected that Russia will renounce any of her pretensions in regard to the Northwest coast; but if she do, it will be the first instance of her retracting a claim of right, real or fictitious, in the whole course of her history since the era of the great Peter's reign.[30]

The New York *Spectator* attempted to justify and explain the language of the President.

The principle assumed [it wrote] appears to be a broad one at first, but no one on reflection will doubt its justice, or hesitate to commend the President for the intrepidity of its annunciation. We presume the existing rights of the Russian and British Fur Companies are not embraced in the "principle," because they are not exactly in the nature of colonies, and the question is still further narrowed by a subsequent part of the message, where the President avows the neutral course the administration will pursue in the event of any renewed attempt that may be made by Spain and Portugal (unaided by other Powers) upon the revolted American colonies. In this

---

[30] December 6.

view of the case, what cause can any European nation have of complaint?
The British cannot of course be dispossessed of their American colonies,
except by conquest or purchase. And the remaining part of the continents
of right belong to the civilized independent nations who possess them.
We are persuaded that the principle adopted will be sustained by Congress,
and the nation.[31]

The third paper which commented on the message, the *Albion*, of
New York, a sheet edited by an Englishman, was almost hostile
to Monroe's new principle. It regretted that his language was
not "more explicit," and added,

We cannot for a moment suppose that the American cabinet entertains
the preposterous notion of regulating matters in the South American States,
or to set limits to the extension of the British settlements in Canada. Such
an assumption could not only apply to any future Selkirk, but would also
go to prohibit the Northwest Fur Company from making a settlement on
their own hunting ground in New Caledonia, or elsewhere in their extensive
territories. In fact the principle would even knock up Macgregor and his
Poyais settlement.[32]

Outside of these few comments, the non-colonization dogma
seems to have been passed over in silence by the press of the
nation. Speaking generally, it cannot be said to have been hailed
with enthusiasm, or even with interest; its large and sweeping
implications were for the most part unsuspected, and so, for the
moment, with few exceptions, neither warmly supported nor
seriously challenged.

Having thus examined the origins of the non-colonization
clause in the message of 1823, we must now turn back to discuss
the viewpoint and the reasoning which lay behind it. What was
the motive in promulgating such a sweeping theory? What was
the logic by which it might be supported?

In later interpretations of this part of the President's declaration, the emphasis has frequently been laid on the dangers involved in bringing the intrigues and conflicting territorial ambitions of Europe across the seas and into the New World. The
United States, the argument has run, would thus be swept into
the vortex of European politics, and exposed to the wicked influences for which those politics are notorious. Or it has been main-

[31] December 6.      [32] December 5.

tained that new European territorial establishments would endanger American security, and ought to be opposed on these grounds.

These were not the bases, however, on which John Quincy Adams, in 1823, rested his opposition to colonization. The territorial aspects of colonization were not uppermost in his mind. He was thinking (and the point has been all too little emphasized) primarily of the commercial interests of the United States. In the history of American diplomacy, the principle of non-colonization has a certain affinity with the principle of the open door, asserted three quarters of a century later. It was based on immediate economic factors, not on vague fears of the future. It was because the colonial system meant commercial exclusion that the Secretary of State proclaimed its banishment from the American continents.

A close examination of Adams's point of view makes this clear. The principle of equality of commercial opportunity was one for which he contended with the utmost vigor, not only in the northwest controversy, but in other fields. He fought vigorously against the narrow policy of Great Britain in the British West Indies. He instructed the ministers to the South American states, when they set out in 1823, to contend for the principle that the new republics should treat all nations on the same footing, and that they should give no preferences, not even to their former mother country.[33] The right to which he held most tenaciously in the dispute with Russia was not the right to full possession of the territory on the northwest (on this, as we have seen, it had been agreed to compromise on the line of 55 degrees); the right which he deemed of most importance was the right to trade, and this Middleton was instructed stoutly to maintain.[34] In

[33] *Writings of John Quincy Adams*, edited by W. C. Ford (New York, 1913–17, 7 vols.), vol. vii. See the instructions to Rodney (pp. 437 ff.), in which Adams alludes to the "principle of mutual treatment upon a footing of equality with the most favored nation" as "the great foundation of our foreign policy," and declares that it must be "assumed as the basis of negotiation." Also the instructions to Anderson (pp. 457–461), in which the object of a commercial treaty is said to be "the sanction by solemn compact of the broad and liberal principles of *independence, equal favors,* and *reciprocity.*"

[34] *Alaskan Boundary Tribunal,* ii, 50 f.

Adams's opinion the notion of European colonization was flatly opposed to the maintenance of these economic interests. The colonizing methods of the Old World, he told Stratford Canning in November, 1822, had always involved a more or less complete commercial monopoly. "Spain had set the example. She had forbidden foreigners from setting a foot in her Colonies, upon pain of death, and the other colonizing states of Europe had imitated the exclusion, though not the rigor of the penalty." [35] From the very beginning, therefore, the Adams doctrine was knit up with the commercial interests of the United States. And so it remained throughout this early period of its development. Nothing shows this more clearly than the important dispatch of July 22, 1823, to Richard Rush, in which the whole theory of the doctrine found most careful expression. After declaring that the American continents will henceforth no longer be subjects for colonization, the American Secretary of State goes on to say:

Occupied by civilized independent nations, they will be accessible to Europeans and to each other on that footing alone, and the Pacific Ocean in every part of it will remain open to the navigation of all nations, in like manner with the Atlantic. . . . The application of colonial principles of exclusion, therefore, cannot be admitted by the United States as lawful upon any part of the northwest coast of America, or as belonging to any European nation.[36]

In these clear-cut and precise phrases, the innermost connection of the new dogma with American trading rights stands revealed.

It need not be contended, of course, that there was no more to it than this. It would be a clear exaggeration to say that Adams was contending for trading rights alone. He was thinking also of territorial settlement, as the very dispatch just quoted helps to make clear.

It is not imaginable [he declared] that, in the present condition of the world, *any* European nation should entertain the project of settling a *colony* on the northwest coast of America. That the United States should form establishments there, with views of absolute territorial right and inland communication, is not only to be expected, but is pointed out by the finger of nature.[37]

---

[35] Adams, *Memoirs*, vi, 104.
[36] *Alaskan Boundary Tribunal*, ii, 55 f.
[37] *Ibid.*, p. 54.

But these comments were made with an eye to the future. What was interesting in the immediate sense, "the only useful purpose to which the northwest coast of America" had been or could be made "subservient to the settlement of civilized men," was that of trade and of the fishery.[38] The rights of the United States in this regard it was vital to maintain. On the territorial question there might be compromise; this we have already seen. But on the commercial question there ought to be none. "The right of carrying on trade with the natives throughout the northwest coast they [the United States] cannot renounce." [39] Clearly, it was antagonism to commercial restriction that lay at the basis of the Secretary of State's famous dictum.

So much for the viewpoint which underlay the assertion of the non-colonization principle. But what of the validity of the principle itself? Was it based upon a sound hypothesis? Was its truth demonstrable by careful and solid reasoning?

The answer to these questions must certainly be given in the negative. Such a proposition as the Secretary of State set out to maintain could be logically valid only if based on the fact that the whole of the American continent was, in 1823, actually in the possession of civilized powers. As Dana has well said, the matter was one of political geography.[40] If the new doctrine were true, it must rest upon the thesis stated by Adams

[38] *Alaskan Boundary Tribunal*, ii, 54.

[39] *Ibid.*, p. 56. The trade with the northwest coast, it is worth pointing out, was largely of New England origin; indeed, most of it seems to have been carried on in New England ships. S. E. Morison, *The Maritime History of Massachusetts* (Boston, 1921), p. 53. I have been unable, however, to trace any direct connection between the New England merchants and Adams's attitude. It is to be noted, moreover, that the trade was declining. Amounting to a half-million in 1818, the first year for which statistics are available, it had declined to less than $40,000 in 1824. The figures are as follows: 1818, $504,110; 1819, $242,652; 1820, $234,431; 1821, $376,-998; 1822, $165,589; 1823, no return; 1824, $39,378. George Watterston and N. B. Van Zandt, *Tabular Statistical Views of the Population, Commerce, Navigation, Public Lands, Post Office Establishment, Revenue, Mint, Military and Naval Establishments, Expenditures, and Public Debt of the United States* (Washington, 1828), pp. 83 f. These are export figures; there were practically no imports. The concrete economic interest at stake, it will be seen, was not a large one.

[40] Henry Wheaton, *Elements of International Law*, edited by R. H. Dana, 8th ed. (London and Boston, 1866), p. 99.

in his despatch to Rush,[41] and reiterated more fully at a later date, that "the two continents consisted of several sovereign and independent nations, whose territories covered their whole surface," [42] that they were not *ferae naturae*, and were therefore not open to colonization. But such a thesis, in 1823, was very difficult to maintain, in the light of the facts or by accepted maxims of international law.

With regard to South America, perhaps, it might be contended that Adams was right. It is true that the "independent nations" of which he spoke had not, in 1823, been recognized by any European power, and that they were, therefore, in the eyes of European public law, nothing more or less than provinces of Spain. But whether independent or dependent, the territories of the Southern continent might reasonably be said to belong to some one, and to be no longer subject to appropriation. They were certainly not *res nullius*, or no man's land. America and Europe might disagree as to just who enjoyed the legal title to these regions, but they both might admit that they were closed to the colonial enterprise of the future.

And yet, in thus doing justice to the view of the American Secretary of State, one thinks irresistibly of the dispute between Great Britain and Venezuela in 1895 over the boundaries of British Guiana, and of the obvious fact, illumined by that dispute, that there were, three quarters of a century after Adams promulgated his theory, portions of America the ownership of which was doubtful, and which might reasonably be claimed by a European power. It is hardly just, perhaps, to describe a controversy over boundaries as involving any question of colonization in the exact sense of the term; but it is at least interesting to observe that there were boundaries still undetermined long after Monroe's pronouncement, and questions of title still to be solved, in which European claims and interests might play a part.

But whether or not it might be contended in 1823 that all the

[41] "Occupied by civilized independent nations," wrote Adams to the American minister, "they [that is, the American continents] will be accessible to each other and to Europeans on that footing alone." *Alaskan Boundary Tribunal*, ii, 55.

[42] J. D. Richardson, *A Compilation of the Messages and Papers of the Presidents* (Washington, 1896–99, 10 vols.), ii, 334.

South American continent was in the possession of some civilized power, it is entirely clear that by Adams's own reasoning no such proposition could stand in the case of North America. The Russian title to Alaska Adams was unwilling to concede. There were, he declared, only a few scattering settlements on the islands of the coast, the two principal ones being at Kodiack and Sitka.[43] These, he maintained, could never give title to the vast interior. He wrote in the despatch to Rush,

> It has never been admitted by the various European nations which have formed settlements in this hemisphere, that the occupation of an island gave any claim whatever to territorial possessions on the continent. . . . The recognized principle has been rather the reverse, as, by the law of nature, islands must be considered as appendages to continents [rather] than continents to islands.[44]

Yet if Alaska did not belong to Russia, to whom could it belong? Was it not clearly *res nullius,* and did it not therefore invalidate the theory that the whole surface of North America was in the possession of some civilized state?

What, too, of the vast reaches of territory that now fall within what is known as the Northwest Territories and the Yukon? There were no settlements in these regions, and north of 56 degrees only the trading posts of the Hudson Bay Company on the Mackenzie River.[45] Would Adams have been willing to admit that all this country belonged to Great Britain? Yet, if it did not, was it not, like Alaska, still to be taken into possession?

Turn from these unsettled and unoccupied districts of the remotest parts of the continent to the region between 55 degrees, which we may take as the southern border of Alaska, and 42 degrees, the northern border of the Mexican province of California, and eastward to the mountains. In this whole territory there were still only a few trading posts. The only American post was that at Astoria, near the mouth of the Columbia. From the presence of this post, it is true, and from certain other facts, Adams deduced the American right of ownership to 51 degrees.[46]

---

[43] *Alaskan Boundary Tribunal,* ii, 49.     [44] *Ibid.,* ii, 53.

[45] See the statement of the Hudson Bay Company in *ibid.,* ii, 109 f.

[46] *Ibid.,* pp. 52 f.  On the question of settlements, see H. H. Bancroft, *History of the Northwest Coast* (San Francisco, 1884, 2 vols.), ii, 328–332.

But who was the possessor, then, of the territory between 51 and 55 degrees? Adams himself would have been forced to admit that in 1823 this question could not be definitely answered, and that three nations, Great Britain, Russia, and the United States, all put forward more or less convincing arguments in favor of their title. But how, if this were true, could it be asserted that the whole surface of the continent was in the possession of independent civilized nations?

The truth of the matter is that any such assertion was clearly contrary to fact, and that the non-colonization principle, if it rested upon such an assertion, would inevitably fall to the ground.

There was, however, another method of reasoning by which it was sought to sustain the Adams doctrine. We cannot be sure that it is reasoning which Adams himself fully approved; yet it is clearly drawn from his own language, and is meant to be the expression of his point of view.[47] It is to be found in the language used by Rush, acting on the basis of his instructions, in the discussions of 1824 with the British government with regard to the Oregon question. In the course of these discussions the American minister declared that

the independence of the late Spanish Provinces precluded any new settlement within the limits of their respective jurisdictions; that the United States claimed the exclusive sovereignty of all the territory within the parallels of latitude which include as well the mouth of the Columbia, as the heads of that river, and of all its tributary streams; and that, with respect to the whole of the remainder of that continent not actually occupied, the Powers of Europe were debarred from making new settlements, by the claim of the United States, as derived under their title from Spain.[48]

---

[47] Adams's viewpoint with regard to the matter about to be discussed, the claims of the United States on the northwest coast, as derived from Spain, is not absolutely clear. A careful reading of the dispatches to Rush and Middleton leads to the conclusion that he did not baldly put forward a pretension to territorial sovereignty north of 51 degrees. He rather relied upon the Spanish rights to *deny* the sovereignty of other nations, and to justify his favorite thesis of equality of trading rights. But a flat claim of this more extreme character *was* put forward in the report of a committee of Congress in 1821. *American State Papers*, Miscellaneous (Washington, 1834), ii, 630 f.

[48] This protocol is most easily found in Richard Rush, *Memoranda of a Residence at the Court of London* (Philadelphia, 1845), pp. 628 f. Protocol of the twentieth conference of the American and British Plenipotentiaries, held at the Board of Trade, on June 29, 1824.

These words must represent a considered view of the matter, for they were incorporated in a formal protocol.

With regard to the American contention so far as the late Spanish colonies are concerned, we need add nothing to what has been said; and since the claim to the Columbia basin could not, in and of itself, establish any general principle as regards non-colonization, we may also omit examining the complicated question of the conflicting rights of the United States and Great Britain in that territory. But the rights of the American government with regard to the title derived from Spain are worth examination.

That title was based on the cession by Spain, in the Florida treaty of 1819, of all her claims to land north of the forty-second parallel. These claims, so Adams asserted in his July correspondence with Rush and Middleton, extended to latitude 61. Spanish documents of 1790, of the period of the Nootka Sound controversy, attested that they had been so recognized by Russia.[49] The Nootka Sound convention of 1790 with Great Britain [50] recognized for both parties the rights of trade, and of making settlements for the purpose of trade, along the northwest coast (presumably within the limits recognized by Russia). As the successor to Spain, the United States enjoyed all the rights formerly enjoyed by that power. This, in brief, is Adams's own view of the matter.

Even as an argument for commercial equality, this argument has its weaknesses. In setting the upper limit of Spanish pretensions, Adams was relying on the *ex parte* evidence of Spanish authorities; and the recognition by Russia of Spanish claims of exclusive navigation up to 61 degrees might fairly be contended to have been qualified by the ukase of 1799, which conceded to the Russian-American Company on the part of the Tsar special privileges of trade and settlement as far south as 55 degrees. But these flaws in the reasoning are as nothing compared with those which exist from the standpoint of the non-colonization prin-

---

[49] The document particularly relied on was a despatch of the Count Fernan Nuñez to the Count de Montmorin, the French Minister for Foreign Affairs, dated June 16, 1790. It is to be found in *American State Papers*, Foreign Relations, v, 444 f.

[50] Quoted, *ibid.*, p. 445.

ciple. What was there in the Spanish claim which gave to the
United States the right to debar European powers from making
new settlements? Such a right could be based only upon the
theory that Spain had given the American government positive
sovereignty over the whole of the northwest. But to claim this
was virtually to claim an absurdity. It was to claim that title
could rest upon discovery alone. There were no Spanish settlements north of San Francisco, and never had been, save for the
short-lived venture at Nootka Sound, established in 1790 and
abandoned in 1795. But if there was one point clearer than another in 1823, it was that discovery alone could not be made the
legal basis of territorial claims. The rules of international law
on this matter had then been clearly defined. They are to be
found very definitely set forth in the writings of the contemporary
jurists, in the works of Martens,[51] Günther,[52] Klüber,[53] and Vat-

[51] G. F. De Martens, *Précis du droit des gens moderne de l'Europe* (Paris, 1831,
2 vols.), i, 118 ff. "Supposé que l'occupation soit possible, il faut encore qu'elle ait
lieu effectivement; que le fait de la prise de possession ait concouru avec la volonté
manifeste de s'en approprier l'objet. La simple déclaration de volonté d'une nation
ne suffit pas, non plus qu'une donation papale, ou qu'une convention entre deux
nations, pour imposer à d'autres le devoir de s'abstenir de l'usage ou de l'occupation
de l'objet en question. Le simple fait d'avoir été le premier à découvrir ou à visiter
une île, etc., abandonnée ensuite, semble insuffisant. . . . A défaut de limites cer-
taines, le droit d'une nation d'exclure des nations étrangères des terres ou îles
voisines ne s'étend pas au delà du district qu'elle cultive ou duquel du moins elle
peut prouver l'occupation."

[52] K. G. Günther, *Europaisches Völkerrecht* (Altenburg, 1787–92, 2 vols.), ii,
section 9: "Um das Eigenthum dergleichen Länder [that is, newly-discovered
lands], zu erlangen, ist es nicht hinlänglich, sie entdeckt zu haben, oder blos die
Absicht der Bemächtigung an den Tag zu legen. Sie müssen . . . wirklich in Besitz
genommen werden. Das besitzergreifende Volk muss, z. B. auf der Insel wirklich
landen, gewisse Grenzen abstecken, und sie entweder gleich mit Mannschaft be-
setzen, oder wenigstens solche Veranstaltungen zurücklassen, voraus andere, die
nachher dahin kommen, sogleich abnehmen können, das sie einen Eigenthümer
habe, und nicht mehr herrnlos sei. Die Anbauung muss nachher auch wirklich
erfolgen, denn wenn dieses nicht geschieht, so sind andere Nazionen nicht ver-
bunden."

[53] J. L. Klüber, *Droit des gens moderne de l'Europe* (Paris, 1874), section 126.
"L'occupation d'une partie inhabitée et sans maître du globe de la terre, ne peut
donc s'étendre que sur les territoires dont la prise de possession effective, dans
l'intention de s'attribuer la propriété, est constante. On peut faire servir comme
preuves d'une pareille prise de possession ainsi que de la continuation de la possession, à titre de propriétaire, tous les signes extérieurs qui marquent l'occupation

tel.[54] The judgment of textbook writers, moreover, was reinforced by the practice of nations. Spain's extended and overreaching claims had been contested, as is well known, from the
earliest period, and the criterion of occupation had been set up
even as early as the end of the sixteenth century. Even Adams
himself declared, arguing against the Russian claims to the northwest, that there was no part of the globe where the mere fact of
discovery could be held to give weaker rights. In the light of all
these facts, it was utterly impossible to invoke the rights in-
herited by the United States from Spain as a justification for
barring European powers from further colonization in this part
of the world.

The reasoning, then, by which it was sought to sustain the
Adams doctrine must be pronounced fallacious. It rested on one
of two propositions, each equally indefensible — on the notion
that exclusive rights in the northwest had been acquired from
Spain, or on the theory that the whole surface of the American
continents was occupied by independent civilized nations. Both
were untenable from the standpoint of the facts and of international law, and both must be unhesitatingly rejected. The new
principle promulgated by the American Secretary of State could
have no valid claims to acceptance.

The declaration of Monroe [declares one of the most acute students of the
Monroe Doctrine] applied in part to territory discovered and claimed by
Great Britain and Russia; in part, to territory presumed to be in the possession of insurgents whom the United States alone had recognized as independent; and in part, to any additional territory which the progress of ex-

---

et la possession continue. . . . La simple découverte, p. e., d'une île, ne suffirait-elle
pas."
    [54] Emerich de Vattel, *Law of Nations* (Dublin, 1787), pp. 163 f. "These things
[that is, unoccupied lands] belong to the first possessor. . . . Navigators going on the
discovery, furnished with a commission from their sovereign, and meeting with
islands, or other desert countries, have taken possession of them in the name of
their nation: and this title has been commonly respected, provided it was soon
after followed by a real possession. . . . Such a pretension [that is, to more land than
is naturally occupied] would be absolutely contrary to the law of nature, and opposite to the views of nature. . . . The law of nations then only acknowledges the
property and sovereignty of a nation over uninhabited countries, of which they
shall really, and in fact, take possession, in which they shall form settlements, or
of which they shall make actual use."

ploration might reveal. In the view of public law, then, it was worthless. The United States could not by a declaration affect the international status of lands claimed, ruled, or discovered by other powers. They might proclaim in advance the policy which they would adopt when such questions should arise, but no unilateral act could change the Law of Nations. . . . The Law of Nations could be changed only by the renunciation, made tacitly or expressly, by every civilized power of its right to colonize any unoccupied part of the western hemisphere.[55]

We should, of course, be perfectly clear as to the implications of the conclusions just reached. Those conclusions should not be misinterpreted or extended beyond their just range. They indicate merely this, that the reasoning on which Adams based his new doctrine was fallacious; they do not indicate anything whatsoever as to the good or bad policy of making such a declaration, or as to the cogency of the non-colonization principle as a matter of American interest, and not of law. It might be wholly wise and desirable to warn European powers off the American continents. Nothing in the facts we have just outlined necessarily leads to the contrary conclusion. But if, as Dana avers, the American Secretary of State intended merely to assert a fact, then it must be confessed that he asserted a fact that was subject, to say the least, to very serious challenge.

The question of the *policy* of such a pronouncement is as interesting, however, as that of its legal justification. No one who examines the statement of the non-colonization principle in the President's message can deny that it is worded extremely judiciously, from the standpoint of the diplomat. It commits to no positive action of any kind; it does not even intimate what steps the United States will take to defend the new doctrine; it leaves the way entirely open for a diplomatic retreat, while at the same time giving the impression of great definiteness. But, however adroitly the principle was stated, was it sound diplomacy to put forward such a pretension on the verge of important, and perhaps delicate, negotiations? Was it wise to make such sweeping claims? This is certainly a debatable question. We have already seen that the cabinet did not approve of denying Russia's right to any territory whatsoever on the northwest coast. Adams himself

[55] W. F. Reddaway, *The Monroe Doctrine*, 2d ed. (New York, 1905), pp. 101 f.

recognized the justice of this view, and yielded to it in practice. Nay, more, he toned down his own dogma in his instructions to Middleton, and did not press for the recognition of the non-colonization principle. Under the safe cover of a domestic document, like the President's message, he was again to put it forward vigorously, but he seems, none the less, to have had some little misgiving about pressing it too far. This, too, was very obviously the attitude of both Rush and Middleton. They said just as little about it as they conveniently could in the discussions of 1824. Both of them were clearly of the opinion that nothing could be gained by pressing such dangerous doctrine.

Moreover, there was something to be said against the new dogma from the standpoint of the general diplomatic situation. The United States at that time feared the intervention of the Holy Alliance in South America. Against such intervention it could find no better ally than Great Britain. Indeed, the British government had suggested coöperative action, and these proposals were already known at Washington. In the northwest question itself, in resisting the extreme pretensions of Russia, this country might also expect to count on the support of the British government. By putting forward such extravagant claims of its own, it ran the risk of alienating the very power with which its interests would lead it to coöperate,[56] and all this for no tangible gain, and with very little hope that the doctrine which was thus put forward would be recognized.

Theoretically, at any rate, the expediency of the Adams dogma

---

[56] This view was put forward with much force by Calhoun in 1848. "The declaration," he stated, "was broader than the fact, and exhibits precipitancy and want of due reflection. Besides, there was an impropriety in it when viewed in conjunction with the foregoing declarations [that is, those on South America]. I speak not in the language of censure. We were, as to them, acting in concert with England, on a proposition coming from herself — a proposition of the utmost magnitude, and which we felt at the time to be essentially connected with our peace and safety; and of course it was due to propriety as well as policy that this declaration should be strictly in accordance with British feeling. Our power then was not what it is now, and we had to rely upon her coöperation to sustain the ground we had taken. We had then only about six or seven millions of people, scattered, and without such means of communication as we now possess to bring us together in a short period of time." *Works*, iv, 462 f.

in 1823 may well be questioned.  And yet, if we examine the actual course of the northwest controversy after its enunciation, we shall not find that the language of the American government produced any very appreciable effect upon the negotiations, or made them in any sense more difficult or less successful.  The non-colonization principle was indeed hardly mentioned in the conversations which preceded the final settlement.  These conversations opened in February, 1824, some time after the message had reached St. Petersburg.  In the first conference, on February 9, Count Nesselrode, the Russian Foreign Minister, began by observing (obviously with the Adams doctrine in mind), that "it would be best for us to waive all discussion upon abstract principles of *right* and upon the actual state of *facts*," and that "we must endeavor to settle the differences which had arisen between our Governments 'on the basis which might be found most conformable to our *mutual interests*.'" [57]  To this observation the cautious Middleton made no reply.  He knew enough to let sleeping dogs lie.  Nothing in his instructions compelled him to press the Secretary of State's new theory.  Accordingly, the discussions which followed, and which culminated in the treaty of 1824, were entirely concerned with the practical details of the settlement, and not at all with general theories.  They ended in a considerable diplomatic success for the United States.  The treaty of April 17 conceded virtually the whole American claim on land, with the fixing of the line of 54 degrees 40 minutes as the southern limit of Russian territory; and it granted to American citizens for a period of ten years the right of trading with the natives on that part of the coast which was recognized as belonging to Russia. [58]  There is no indication whatever that the language of the President's message influenced these concessions in the slightest degree, either for better or worse.  It certainly did not impede the negotiations.

The truth of the matter seems to be, indeed, that from the

[57] *Alaskan Boundary Tribunal*, ii, 71 f.

[58] The convention's most important articles are to be found in Hildt, *op. cit.*, p. 186.  For the full text see *Treaties and Conventions Concluded between the United States of America, and other Powers since July 4, 1776* (Washington, 1889), pp. 931 ff.

very beginning the Russian government showed a most conciliatory attitude. The terms of the imperial decree of 1821 had, in
all probability, been suggested by the Russian-American Company in its own interest, and had received very little consideration. Middleton even speaks of the ukase as "having been
surreptitiously obtained." [59] From the time of the earliest diplomatic protests, Alexander showed no desire to execute it in practice. As early as July, 1822, he withdrew in part from his previous
position. An order of that date was issued to Russian vessels of
war, directing them to restrict their activities to the coast, and
to exercise surveillance only over the prohibited commerce with
actual Russian settlements.[60] At the same time the directors of
the trade monopoly were directed to transmit to the ministry
such information as would serve to indicate "the parallel of latitude which can be fixed as the furthest limit of our dominions,
without giving rise to remonstrances and pretensions such as
those which have lately been invoked." [61] For Baron Tuyll,
about to set forth for Washington, were penned instructions of
the most conciliatory character. "The true and only object of
the decree of the $^4/_{16}$ September," wrote the Russian Chancellor,
"was to put a stop to enterprises which the laws of all nations
recognize as unjust, and to protect interests, whose legality no
one can contest." [62] More significant still, when Middleton, on
July 24, 1822, read to Capodistrias, Nesselrode's associate in the
conduct of foreign affairs, a vigorous note of protest which he
intended later to present to the Chancellor, he received this interesting counsel: "If you want this affair settled, do not present
your note. The Emperor has already had the good sense to see
that this matter has been pressed too far. We are not disposed to
follow it up." [63] From the beginning of the discussions, the Tsar
intended to renounce the extreme claims put forward in the famous decree of 1821. And his intention of so doing was not

[59] *Alaskan Boundary Tribunal*, ii, 42.
[60] St. Petersburg. F. O., Expédiés, no. 5559 (encl. B.), July 15, 1822.
[61] *Alaskan Boundary Tribunal*, ii, 41.
[62] St. Petersburg. F. O., Expédiés, no. 5559, July 15, 1822. See also *Am. Hist. Rev.*, xviii (Jan., 1913), 335–344, especially p. 337.
[63] *Alaskan Boundary Tribunal*, ii, 43.

altered or modified by the equally extreme pretensions embodied in the language of Adams and Monroe.

In the Russian negotiations, it may safely be asserted, the new American doctrine played no important part. But what of the attitude of other governments toward the President's declaration? How did the rest of Europe react to the non-colonization principle?

On the Continent the paragraphs that refer to the northwest controversy appear to have attracted relatively little attention, except at Paris. In Austria and Prussia they were hardly commented upon at all, by statesmen or in the press.[64] But in the French capital they attracted fully as much attention as that part of the President's declaration which related to South America. The *Étoile*, the ministerial journal, was highly indignant at the language of Monroe.

> Mr. Monroe, who is not a sovereign [it wrote in its issue of January 4] has assumed in his message the tone of a powerful monarch, whose armies and fleets are ready to march at the first signal. He has done more; he has prescribed to the potentates of Europe the conduct which they will observe under certain circumstances, if they do not wish to incur their own disgrace. Such is the prohibition laid upon them never even to think of any new colony in the two Americas. . . . Mr. Monroe is the temporary President of a Republic situated on the east coast of North America. This republic is bounded on the south by the possessions of the King of Spain, and on the north by those of the King of England. Its independence was only recognized forty years ago; by what right then would the two Americas today be under its immediate sway from Hudson's Bay to Cape Horn? What clamors rose in the United States last year when the emperor of Russia attempted to define the boundaries of the territory which he claims on the northwest coast as discovered by his subjects. But this monarch did not pretend to dictate laws to any of the states which have establishments on the same coast. It was reserved to Mr. Monroe to show us a dictator armed with a right of suzerainty over the entire New World.

On the other hand, the liberal journals took up the cudgels for the President. In the judgment of the *Constitutionnel* the "wise Monroe" had "firmly traced the limits of the New World."

> Today for the first time the new continent says to the old, "I am no longer land for occupation; here men are masters of the soil which they

---

[64] They were, so far as I am aware, quoted only in the Berlin *Allgemeine Staats-Zeitung*.

occupy, and the equals of the people from whom they came, and resolved not to treat with them except on the basis of the most exact justice." The new continent is right.[65]

The *Tablettes Universelles* expressed much the same view. The President had spoken "with all the calm and force of a sage," it declared, in proclaiming that the New World was no longer subject to occupation.[66]

In the government itself the new principle was, of course, hardly likely to arouse enthusiasm. Chateaubriand, the French foreign minister, at first seems to have meditated a protest against it. He probably had this part of the message in mind when he told Stuart, the British ambassador, that the Monroe declaration "ought to be resisted by all the powers possessing either territory or commercial interests in that hemisphere." [67] But later he declared that "the prohibition of future colonization on the Continent of America . . . was satisfactorily accounted for by the presumption that it was brought forward by the President with a view to meeting the unwarranted pretensions of the Russian ukase," and indicated that he had abandoned all idea of challenging it.[68, 69]

It was in Great Britain that the non-colonization principle attracted the greatest attention, and was of most diplomatic significance. There it was that it met with the most vigorous criti-

[65] Jan. 2.  [66] Jan. 3.

[67] London. P. R. O., F. O., France, vol. 305, no. 8, Jan. 12, 1824.

[68] Ibid., no. 13, Jan. 13, 1824.

[69] It is worth noting, however, that Polignac discussed the non-colonization principle with Rush at a dinner at the French embassy given on February 15. The conversation is thus reported in Rush's *Court of London*, pp. 486 f. "He says that there are rumors about the extent of our demands. I ask of what nature. He does not know, or draws back from telling; and only refers to our principle of non-colonization on the American continents. He asks if I have understood how France views that principle. I answer in the negative, and express a hope that France may not intervene on such a principle, considering all the circumstances now surrounding it in the hands of the United States; whose Plenipotentiary had to meet the known opposition of the whole British Cabinet to it, and the probable influence of Russia superadded. He said, that his impression was, that France also had objected to it, or would." It is an interesting query where Polignac got his impressions on this subject. Certainly not from the instructions of Chateaubriand. Was he expressing a personal view? Had Canning sought to stir up a little bad blood between France and the United States?

cism, both in the public press and from the government. The London *Times* described Monroe's new formula as "a grave and novel doctrine," [70] and *Bell's Weekly* criticized it in some detail.

It is scarcely necessary to observe [it declared] that this is a most important principle, and one which the English Government in particular will have great difficulty in admitting. For example, suppose Franklin or Captain Parry had got behind the northwest point of America, and upon coming upon the back of that continent had discovered a vast uninhabited tract of fertile wilderness — suppose the back parts of Canada (the extreme back parts) should invite future settlement. It is needless to multiply examples to which the above principle will apply. So far as regards Russia we should be happy to see the principle established, and we should be satisfied if our own government would concede it. But we fear it is in vain to expect it.[71]

The moderation of this criticism was hardly matched by the tone in which George Canning, the British Foreign Secretary, was to express himself on the new doctrine. Some time before the arrival of the message in Europe, Canning had received intimations of what was in the wind. Addington, the British chargé at Washington, describing an interview of September 19, with Adams, wrote that the American Secretary of State had spoken to him of a new and important principle, already asserted in the negotiations with Russia, which would bar European nations from further colonizing in the New World.[72] And Rush, the American minister at London, in a conversation of December 17, told the British Foreign Secretary that the United States no longer regarded any part of the northwest coast as open to European colonization.[73] But these advance notices of American policy could hardly have made any more palatable to Canning the assertion in the President's message of a dogma on the formulation of which Great Britain had never been consulted, and which was so directly opposed to her interests. It is easy to understand why

[70] Dec. 27, 1823.                    [71] Dec. 28, 1823.

[72] London. P. R. O., F. O., America, vol. 177, no. 25, Confidential, Dec. 1, 1823. "He [that is, Adams] spoke loftily," wrote Addington, "of the announcement which had already, on a former occasion, been made to some of the European Powers, more especially Russia, of the United States considering the whole American Continent to be composed of independent Nations, and of the intention of this Country to oppose any future attempts at colonizing any part of North or South America by European Powers."

[73] *Alaskan Boundary Tribunal*, ii, 66.

he expressed himself in terms of irritation with regard to it. To Lieven, the Russian minister at London, he declared that the new principle was no less extreme than that laid down by Russia, that it would certainly be necessary to require an explanation of its meaning, and that it seemed to him to interpose a very serious difficulty in the way of the negotiations between Russia and the United States.[74] To Rush he set forth his views very positively indeed. The new doctrine, he declared,

is laid down broadly and generally, without qualification or distinction. We cannot acknowledge the right of any power to proclaim such a principle; much less to bind other countries to the observance of it. If we were to be repelled from the shores of America it would not matter to us whether that expulsion were effected by the ukase of Russia, excluding us from the sea, or the new doctrine of the President prohibiting us from the land. But we cannot yield obedience to either. . . . Suppose [added the British minister] that Captain Parry's expedition had ended, or that any new British expedition were to end, in the discovery of land approximate to either part of the American continent, north or south, would the United States object to our planting a colony there? [75]

To this Rush had little to reply. When such a case arose, he said, it might be considered. For the present, he declared, he was without instructions on the principle since it had been laid down in the President's message, but he would be prepared to support it in any discussion which might take place on the northwest question.[76]

These observations could hardly have been very satisfactory to Canning. They were scarcely of a nature to allay his resentment at the American attitude. And that resentment he was soon to show in a very practical form. Great Britain, it will be remembered, had, like the United States, protested against the Russian ukase of September, 1821. The two Anglo-Saxon powers had a

[74] St. Petersburg. F. O., Reçus, no. 21,304, Jan. 2, 1824. The attempt thus to sow dissension between Russia and the United States was not very successful. Lieven answered, "Les deux Gouvernements s'étant déjà entendu sur les principes à suivre dans les négociations rélative à l'Oukase précité, il n'était pas à supposer qu'on voulût par des récriminations compliquer une question sur laquelle on était prêt à s'entendre."

[75] London. P. R. O., F. O., America, vol. 194, Draft to Mr. Rush, Jan., 1824. Not sent, nor read to him, but the substance stated in conversation.

[76] Rush, *Court of London*, pp. 471 f.

common interest in opposing it.  Accordingly, in May, 1823, Adams suggested to Stratford Canning, the British minister at Washington, the possibility of a joint negotiation.[77]  This suggestion was, at first, well received by the British Foreign Office, especially as regards coöperation against the maritime pretensions of Russia.[78]  On the territorial question there was more hesitation, but in November, 1823, Canning indicated to Lieven that on this matter, too, he might be ready to yield to the request of the United States, and consent to act in concert with the American government.[79]  But by January, with the receipt of the President's message, the situation had changed.  On January 2, in the interview with Rush from which we have already quoted, Canning declared that he would be under the necessity either of addressing an official note to the American minister on the subject of the non-colonization principle, or of declining to coöperate with the American government in the negotiations about to take place at St. Petersburg.  He added that he should prefer the latter course.  To these observations Rush made no immediate reply. But he was acute enough to see that there was a good deal to be said for the second of Canning's alternatives, that is, the abandonment of the concerted action of the two governments at St. Petersburg.  The assertion of the non-colonization principle, he believed, would tend to align Russia and Great Britain together against the United States.  And such an alignment ought, of course, to be avoided.[80]  Accordingly, on January 5, Rush told

[77] *Alaskan Boundary Commission*, ii, 120.

[78] *Ibid.*, p. 124.  Canning wrote to Bagot, British minister at St. Petersburg, as follows, under date of July 12, 1823: "Upon this point [that is, the maritime question], such a concert as the United States are understood to desire will be peculiarly advantageous; because, supposing the disavowal made, there is no disposition on the part of His Majesty to press hard upon the feelings of the Emperor of Russia, and it would certainly be more easy for His Majesty to insist lightly on what may be considered as a point of national dignity, if he acted in this respect in concert with another maritime power, than to enact any less degree, either of excuse for the past or of security for the future, than that other power might think necessary." He gave Bagot no specific instructions, however, awaiting more definite word from the American government.

[79] St. Petersburg.  F. O., Reçus, no. 20,695, Nov. 30, 1823.  Lieven to Nesselrode.

[80] Rush, *Court of London*, pp. 471 f.

Canning that it would be just as well to give up the idea of a joint negotiation,[81] and on the fifteenth the British Foreign Secretary instructed Sir Charles Bagot, his minister at the Russian capital, that the future conversations on the northwest question between England and Russia were to take place without the participation of the United States.[82]

Thus Monroe's declaration undoubtedly influenced the policy of the British government. It played a part in preventing the coöperation of the two Anglo-Saxon powers in the negotiations at St. Petersburg. It would be too much, however, to say that it was the single factor which made coöperation impossible. On the territorial question Canning had always been reluctant to associate Great Britain with the United States. In November, it is true, he had spoken to Lieven as if he might consent to such a proposal. But this was before he fully understood the views of the United States. He and Rush had their first important discussion on the northwest question on December 17.[83] The result was decidedly disquieting to Canning. The American minister told him that the United States would "agree to make no settlement north of fifty-one, on Great Britain agreeing to make none south of that line or *north of fifty-five*." This latter phrase seemed particularly ominous. "What can this intend?" wrote Canning. "Do the United States mean to travel *north* to get *between* us and Russia? and do they mean to stipulate against Great Britain, in favor of Russia, or reserve to themselves whatever Russia may not want?" Precisely so, was Rush's instant reply.[84]

No doubt Canning, from this time onward, though he did not commit himself, was little inclined to coöperate with the United States. He was suspicious of the motives of the American government. The choice of the line 55 degrees for the southern limit of Russian settlement, the very line which the Tsar's government appeared to desire, seemed to argue a previous understanding between Washington and St. Petersburg, or at least a disposition on the part of the former to gratify the viewpoint of Alexander.

[81] Rush, *Court of London*, p. 472.
[82] *Alaskan Boundary Tribunal*, ii, 144–149.
[83] Rush, *Court of London*, pp. 467 f.
[84] *Ibid.*, pp. 468 f.

The choice of the line 51 degrees as the southern limit for Great Britain, the precise point where Russian pretensions terminated, was additional evidence of a wish to avoid collision with Russia, while maintaining vigorously the American claims against England. Moreover, it would be distinctly inconvenient to discuss the American claims to the line 51 degrees along with those of Russia, especially since the convention of 1818 for the joint occupation of the regions in dispute had yet some time to run, and was, for the present, entirely satisfactory to Great Britain. All these reasons induced the British Foreign Secretary to hesitate very much, as he wrote Bagot, to accept the idea of coöperation with the United States. And then came the President's message, "decisive in itself, and susceptible of being stated to Mr. Rush with more explicitness" than any other reason "for our not mixing ourselves in a negotiation between two parties whose opposite pretensions are so extravagant in their several ways as to be subject not so much of practical adjustment as of reciprocal disavowal." [85]

So far, then, as the territorial question was concerned, the Monroe Doctrine seems to have crystallized the opinion and point of view already forming in Canning's mind rather than to have produced an abrupt change in his attitude. But on the question of Russia's maritime pretensions, the British Foreign Secretary had previously been entirely favorable to a joint negotiation. He threw over this plan in his instructions of January 15, 1824, to Bagot.

The principle put forth by the President of the United States [he wrote] has introduced a difference between the respective situations of the United States and Great Britain with respect to Russia which did not exist before. In the former state of things it might have been expedient, both for ourselves and for the United States, as well as less distasteful to Russia, to return an answer common to us both; but, as things stand now, Russia might naturally wish to qualify her answer to the United States with some reciprocal demand of explanation.[86]

From these lines it would appear that the message was, in this respect, responsible for a decided change in Canning's attitude. It may be that, in the maritime as in the territorial problem, the

[85] *Alaskan Boundary Tribunal*, ii, 146 f.        [86] *Ibid.*, p. 149.

December interview with Rush was also an influence. But it seems tolerably certain that the message was the decisive factor.

The first effects, then, of the assertion of the non-colonization principle were to make coöperation with Great Britain against Russia extremely difficult. But at the same time Rush, by assenting to Canning's proposal that the idea of a joint negotiation be dropped, had forestalled further discussion of the new doctrine on the part of the British government. He was, very clearly, desirous of doing just this. For, as he wrote Adams, "a preliminary and detached discussion of so great a principle, against which England protested *in limine*, brought on by me when her Foreign Secretary was content to waive" the matter, might readily prejudice a decision on other matters of "more immediate and practical interest." [87] "By abstaining from discussing it," he added, "nothing was given up. The principle as promulgated in the President's message would remain undiminished, as notice to other nations, and a guide to me in the general negotiation with England when that came on." [88]

"The general negotiation" of which Rush here speaks was an effort on the part of the two powers to settle a considerable number of subjects of dispute between them — disputes with regard to American trade with the British West Indies, with regard to the eastern boundary between the United States and Canada, with regard to the suppression of the slave trade, with regard to Oregon, to mention some of the more important matters. From February to July, 1824, Stratford Canning and William Huskisson for Great Britain, and Rush for the United States, wrestled with these various problems. And in the course of the discussions on Oregon, we meet once more with the famous principle enunciated by President Monroe. It does not appear that the American minister had received any further instructions from his government with regard to the principle in question. But he brought it forward in the course of the complex discussions as to the sovereignty of the contested region between 42 degrees and 55 degrees. I have already quoted his words on the subject,[89] and do not need to repeat them here. It will be

---

[87] Rush, *Court of London*, p. 473.    [88] *Ibid.*    [89] See p. 22, above.

sufficient to observe that the American contention now met with a formal and categorical denial, a denial incorporated in the protocol of June 29, 1824.

The British Plenipotentiaries asserted, in utter denial of the above principle, that they considered the unoccupied parts of America just as much open as heretofore to colonization by Great Britain, as well as by other European Powers, agreeably to the Convention of 1790, between the British and Spanish Governments, and that the United States would have no right whatever to take umbrage at the establishment of new colonies from Europe in any such parts of the American continent.[90]

The language of this denial could hardly have been more definite and explicit. But it is interesting to note that the British negotiators rested their case, not, as they might have done, on the general maxims of international law, but on the Nootka Sound convention with Spain. They had, as that convention demonstrated, been unwilling to concede exclusive rights to Spain; they must now, by the same token, refuse to concede such rights to Spain's successor. This, no doubt, is well enough as far as it goes; but why was not the argument pressed further?

The reason, no doubt, is that neither side wished to prolong discussion on an abstract point of principle. In the English as in the Russian negotiations, there were more practical matters afoot than altercation over a dogma the test of whose validity would probably be found, in the long run, in deeds rather than words. Neither Rush nor his antagonists returned to the conflict after this first engagement.

Nor, so far as we can see, did the introduction of the Adams doctrine into the negotiations have any influence on their result. There was a failure to arrive at an agreement; but the failure was due to an inability to find common ground with regard to the partition of the Oregon territory, not to any difference of theory. The United States would not concede more than the line 49 degrees as its northern boundary. Great Britain, on her side, insisted on the line of the Columbia. It was on this point that the discussions broke down.[91]

[90] Rush, *Court of London*, p. 629.

[91] See Rush's discussion of the matter, in his despatch to Adams, published in *Court of London*, pp. 592–611, especially pp. 607 f.

And thus, with the discussion of June, 1824, the non-colonization principle drops for a brief time out of sight. When we meet
with it again, it no longer has anything to do with the northwest
controversy. It becomes a point of discussion in the relations of
the United States with South America. This phase of its existence we may well postpone until we have examined some of the
earlier aspects of those relations, and some other phases of the
complex and interesting story of the Monroe Doctrine.

# CHAPTER II

## THE SPANISH–AMERICAN PHASE OF THE MESSAGE —
## THE PRELUDE

THE revolt of the Spanish-American colonies followed hard upon the Napoleonic conquest of Spain. From the very beginning, the sympathies of the United States appear to have been engaged upon the side of the revolutionists.[1] American sentiment was distinctly favorable to a movement for independence which had at least a superficial resemblance to that of 1776, and which could easily be regarded as an effort to throw off an odious tyranny and establish throughout the greater part of the New World the blessings of republican government. Fellow feeling in a struggle for liberty and independence was an essential element in forming the policy of the United States with regard to South America.

It was indeed, to all appearances, a far more important element than any hope of material gain. In the formative period of this country's relations with the new states of South America, certainly down to 1822, there is little evidence of the working of economic interest. In the absence of exact statistics for much of the period, and in view of the paucity of references to trade with the Spanish colonies, it is difficult to speak with precision. But certain general observations may safely be made. In the first place, the trade with Cuba and with Spain itself was far more important than the trade with the new republics of the South.[2] A diplomatic policy favorable to the South-American states might jeopardize or even sacrifice commercial interests superior to those which it would promote. If economic reasons

---

[1] The best summary of American policy down to 1822 is to be found in F. L. Paxson, *The Independence of the South American Republics*, 2d ed. (Philadelphia, 1916). See also J. B. Lockey, *Pan-Americanism* (New York, 1920), especially chap. iv, "United States and Hispanic American Independence," pp. 134–171.

[2] Watterston and Van Zandt, *Tabular Statistical Views*, p. 45.

were to be regarded as shaping political developments, there were more reasons for a cautious than for an active line of policy. In the second place, there was not, as in the case of Great Britain, any powerful pressure from the commercial classes in favor of colonial independence. The evidence on this point is partly negative, it is true, but it is negative evidence of the strongest kind. One can hardly imagine that the existence of such pressure would pass unnoticed in the debates in Congress, and in such contemporary records as the diary and writings of Adams, and the correspondence of Monroe. But it is not necessary to depend upon this fact alone. Statistics indicate that as late as 1821 only 2.3 per cent of American exports and 1.6 per cent of American imports were South American in destination or origin.[3] In March of the same year Adams could tell Henry Clay that he had little expectation of any commercial advantages from the recognition of the new states.[4] And even later, in 1823, the Secretary of State speaks of commercial development as a matter of hope for the future rather than a present accomplishment.[5] That hope may, of course, have counted for something from the beginning. But, all things considered, it seems highly probable that political sympathy, not economic self-interest, lay at the root of American policy so far as it revealed itself as favorable to the new states of South America.

From the very beginnings of the South American struggle this sympathy asserts itself. As early as 1810, the American government, then headed by Madison, sent agents to South America — Joel R. Poinsett to La Plata and Chile, and Robert Lowry to Venezuela.[6] At the end of 1811, James Monroe, then Secretary of State, thought seriously of raising the question of the recognition of the new states, and of exerting American influence in Europe to secure like action from the principal European powers.[7] He also entered into informal relations with agents from at least

---

[3] Watterston and Van Zandt, *Tabular Statistical Views*, p. 45.

[4] Adams, *Memoirs*, v, 325.

[5] Adams, *Writings*, vii, 433, 456.

[6] Lockey, pp. 142, 145.

[7] *The Writings of James Monroe*, edited by S. M. Hamilton (New York and London, 1898–1903, 7 vols.), v, 364.

one of the revolted provinces.[8] And in Congress, at the same time, in response to the sympathetic language of the President's message, a resolution was passed, expressing a friendly solicitude in the welfare of these communities, and a readiness, when they should become nations by a just exercise of their rights, to unite with the Executive in establishing such relations with them as might be necessary.[9] Thus, very early in the course of the colonial struggle, the general bent of American policy was made plain.

But it was some time before the South-American question became a matter of really first-rate importance. In the years 1810 to 1815, the prime concern of the administration at Washington lay in the preservation of American neutral rights, and, from 1812 to 1814, in the prosecution of the war with Great Britain. Moreover, the course of events in the overseas dominions of Spain was for some time hardly favorable to the revolutionists. In 1814 and 1815, indeed, it seemed entirely possible that the revolutionary movements might be snuffed out. In the north, in Venezuela and Colombia, the army of the Spanish general, Morillo, won victory on victory, and drove the leader of the revolutionists, Bolívar, into exile. In the south, in Chile, Osorio reëstablished the power of the mother country, and in Buenos Aires the struggles of contending factions weakened the new government that had been set up. Under such circumstances, prudence would have dictated a policy of reserve on the part of the United States, even if its government had not been preoccupied with other and more pressing matters.

With the year 1817, however, a change takes place in the status of the colonial question. In the case of one, at any rate, of the new states, the struggle was virtually over. The republic of La Plata had declared its independence and successfully maintained it, so that not a Spanish soldier remained upon its territory; even more, it had dispatched its great general, San Martín, across the Andes, and, with the victory of Chacabuca, taken a great step toward the final liberation of Chile. Perhaps as a result of these

[8] See especially the article by I. J. Cox, "Monroe and the Early Mexican Revolutionary Agents," in *Ann. Report Amer. Hist. Assoc.* i (1911), 199–228.

[9] Lockey, p. 145.

developments, interest in favor of the recognition of the new state began to develop in the United States; there were numerous newspaper articles in the summer of 1817, notably the discussions of Lautaro in the Richmond *Enquirer;* and the affairs of South America became a matter of debate both in the councils of the administration and in the halls of Congress.

It is interesting, in the light of later events, to examine these developments. So far as the administration was concerned, the point especially to be emphasized is the warm sympathy of the President himself with the South American cause. There has been a tendency in some quarters, in connection with the evolution of the Monroe Doctrine, to ascribe a very slight importance to the views of the very man who promulgated it. Mr. Monroe has been pictured as "slow-moving and lethargic," as prodded forward only by the more vigorous mind and more determined will of John Quincy Adams, his Secretary of State.[10] But as a matter of fact, Monroe was at all times quite as much interested in the colonial cause, and in as full sympathy with it, as Adams. From the very beginning of his presidency, he showed his concern with regard to it. As early as May, 1817, some months before Adams took office, the President had determined upon a mission of inquiry to the provinces of La Plata,[11] and as early as October he questioned his cabinet on the expediency of recognizing the government of that region.[12] He raised the problem again in the succeeding May, even suggesting the possibility of sending an armed force to the coast of South America, to protect American commerce, "and to countenance the patriots."[13] His views, it is true, were to be overruled or modified by his advisers. But his interest in positive action was very real, and is quite consistent with the character of the man whose flaming sympathy with French republicanism had been so obvious in his earlier career.

Adams, on the other hand, expressed a very conservative view

[10] J. B. Angell, "The European Concert and the Monroe Doctrine," *Harvard Graduates' Magazine* (Sept. 1905), xiv, 13–24, especially p. 21.
[11] Monroe, *Writings*, vi, 31.
[12] *Ibid.*
[13] Adams, *Memoirs*, iv, 91.

of the South American question. He was swayed by no theoretical devotion to republicanism, and had no particular confidence in the capacity of the new states for self-government. In
a letter to Alexander Hill Everett, written in December, 1817,
he expressed in some detail his doubts as to the similarity of the
South- and North-American revolutions, and as to the whole trend
of revolutionary activities.[14] Long afterwards, as late as March,
1821, he told Henry Clay that he saw no prospects that the new
states would establish free or liberal institutions of government.
"They are," he declared, "not likely to promote the spirit either
of freedom or order by their example. They have not the first
elements of good or free government. Arbitrary power, military
and ecclesiastical, was stamped upon their education, upon their
habits, and upon all their institutions. . . . I had little expectation," Adams added, "of any beneficial result to this country

---

[14] Adams, *Writings*, vi, 281 f. Adams says that he would like to see the question
raised as to what "the cause of the South Americans is, and whether it really be,
as their partisans here allege, the same as our own cause in the war of our Revolution? Whether for instance, if Buenos Ayres has formally offered to accept the
Infant Don Carlos as their absolute monarch, upon condition of being politically
independent of Spain, their cause is the same as ours was? Whether if Bolívar,
being at the head of the republic of Venezuela, has solemnly proclaimed the absolute and total emancipation of the slaves, the cause of Venezuela is precisely the
same as ours was? Whether, in short, there is any other feature of identity between
their cause and ours, than that they are, as we were, colonies fighting for independence?" He goes on to describe the situation as follows: "In South America
civil rights, if not entirely out of the question, appear to have been equally disregarded and trampled upon by all parties. Buenos Ayres has no constitution, and
its present rulers are establishing [themselves] only by the arbitrary banishment of
their predecessors. Venezuela, though it has emancipated all its slaves, has been
constantly alternating between an absolute military government, a capitulation to
Spanish authority, and guerillas black and white, of which every petty chief has
acted for purposes of war and rapine as an independent sovereign. There is finally
in South America, neither unity of cause nor unity of effort, as there was in our
Revolution."

It is amusing to note that the temper of this criticism is much the same as that
of a leading European reactionary of the period, who plays a prominent rôle in the
events to be examined in this volume. Pozzo di Borgo instituted a contrast of much
the same kind between North and South America. The North American colonists,
he declared, were exclusively European, and had not been fused with the aboriginal
population. They had the civil and administrative institutions of Great Britain; they
had political institutions of their own; their revolt merely substituted one political
sovereignty for another. Such could not possibly be the case in South America. The
races there are as varied as the plants of its soil; and political philosophies as op-

from any future connection with them, political or commercial." [15]

Observations such as these do not, of course, indicate a fundamental antagonism to the movement of independence in South America. So great a lover of liberty, so theoretical a republican, as Thomas Jefferson, is to be found expressing much the same view. But Adams's interest in the new states was not based on any doctrinaire notions as to theories of government. He wished them well, as he told Clay, because they were contending for independence. He wished them well because he hated colonialism in all its guises. But he was not the man to be swept off his feet by enthusiasm, or by the superficial resemblance of South American institutions to those of the United States. In the cabinet meeting of October 30, 1817, he opposed the recognition of La Plata with his usual definiteness.[16] And in the discussions of the next year, he counselled caution in dealing with the whole problem.[17] Far from advancing beyond the ground taken by the President, he exercised a restraining influence upon his chief. At no time can it fairly be said that he outstripped Monroe in zeal for the welfare of the new republics.

There was, however, outside the cabinet, a more doughty champion of the South American cause than either the President or any of his advisers. That champion was Henry Clay, the Speaker of the House of Representatives. Clay had early given evidence of his sympathy with the patriots, and in 1817 he had voted against the neutrality act. On March 24, 1818, he introduced an amendment to the appropriation bill for the fitting out

posed to one another as the colors of those who profess them. "The leaders who excite and direct the colonists have the power to arm them; but in the last five years, there is practically no example of success in establishing a civil government. As things are going, the Spanish supremacy may indeed be destroyed, but there will be substituted therefor a number of petty tyrants bent only on destroying one another." Сборникъ Русскаго Историческаго Общества (St. Petersburg, 1904), cxix, 228–231. Published separately as A. A. Polovtsov, *Correspondance diplomatique des ambassadeurs et ministres de Russie en France et de France en Russie* (St. Petersburg, 1902–07, 3 vols.), ii, 228–232. To most of this Adams apparently could have subscribed. See also his comment to Clay, mentioned in the text.

[15] Adams *Memoirs*, v. 325.          [16] *Ibid.*, iv, 15 f.

[17] *Ibid.*, iv, 167.

of a public minister to La Plata.[18]  This amendment came up for
debate on the next day, and was supported by him in a three-
days speech which may fairly be called one of the great oratorical
efforts of his career.[19]

The importance of this speech, indeed of Clay's whole rôle in
the colonial question, has been too little realized.  The Speaker's
action in urging recognition of Buenos Aires in 1818 and thereafter has been set down to factious opposition to the Monroe
administration.  This cynical interpretation of his conduct is
largely due to the diary of John Quincy Adams.  The American
Secretary of State was always unsparing in his judgment of public
men, and never by temperament in the least sympathetic with
Henry Clay, and he judged his activities accordingly.  Now,
there may well be some truth in his view of the matter.  No one
who studies the career of the Kentucky statesman can fail to see
how often he was influenced by personal and political motives
of no very exalted type.  But Clay's advocacy of the South
American cause accords perfectly well with his convictions and
his sympathies, and his notions of sound policy.  In executive
office he was to exhibit much the same temper that he did in
earlier years in the House of Representatives.  It is no fairer
to accuse him of purely partisan motives than it would be to
accuse Webster of a like purpose when he introduced a resolution in favor of Greek independence in 1824.  And in any case,
whether factious critic or generous patriot, Clay, in his advocacy
of the South American cause in 1818, laid down principles that
were later to find expression in the declaration of Monroe.  When
we come to discuss the general theories that underlay the Monroe
doctrine, we shall have to give no small meed of credit to the
great Kentuckian.

Clay's agitation was, however, without any immediate practical consequences.  His resolution was voted down by the House
by the decisive vote of 115 to 45.[20]  Toward the end of 1817, the
President had dispatched commissioners to the new states on a

[18] *Annals of Congress*, Fifteenth Congress, First Session (Washington, 1854,
2 vols.), vol. ii, cols. 1468 f.

[19] *Ibid.*, cols. 1474–1500, 1606–1620.        [20] *Ibid.*, col. 1646.

mission of information.[21] It was thought to be desirable to await their return and their report before taking action. And in any case, it was not desired to embarrass or hurry the administration. Monroe and Adams were left a free hand to deal with their diplomatic problem.

There were, indeed, for some time to come, cogent reasons against a departure from the policy of neutrality to which the government had adhered from the beginning of the colonial struggle. In January, 1818, Adams learned from the British minister, Bagot, of a projected mediation by the European powers between Spain and the new states.[22] Two months later he received confirmatory evidence of some such plan from the commissioners sent to La Plata.[23] In the light of such information it seemed wise to await the outcome of the European discussions of the whole problem, and to see what success these projects of reconciliation might have, before embarking upon a policy of recognition. These reasons for delay were no longer controlling by the end of the year, for the efforts of the Tsar and of the French to promote a solution of the colonial question at the Congress of Aix-la-Chapelle ended in complete failure. But a new motive for delay speedily appeared. On February 22, 1819, was signed the treaty providing for the cession of Florida to the United States. While ratification was pending, it was obviously unwise to give any cause of umbrage to the government at Madrid. For the next two years, therefore, the policy of the United States was prudence itself. The annual messages of President Monroe confined themselves to a sketch of events and to an expression of the hope that Spain would find a way to make peace with her former subjects.[24] Though Clay's motion for the fitting out of a minister to La Plata, defeated in 1818, actually passed in 1820, the administration took no action. Its hands were tied until the news of Spain's tardy adhesion to the Florida treaty arrived in the United States in the spring of 1821. Even then there was no immediate recognition. John Quincy Adams was still very far from enthusiastic for the

---

[21] Lockey, p. 160.   [22] Adams, *Memoirs*, iv, 49.   [23] Adams, *Writings*, vi, 315.
[24] These messages are to be found in J. D. Richardson, *Messages and Papers of the Presidents*, ii, 59, 77, 105.

cause of the South Americans.[25]  And if, with regard to La Plata, it might fairly be contended that the results of the revolutionary struggle were no longer doubtful, in the north Bolívar was still too far removed from a decisive victory to make recognition expedient.  The Secretary of State had long before laid it down as a legal maxim that acknowledgment of national independence must wait on the triumph of the national cause.[26]  His influence, therefore, was still exerted for caution and delay.

In the summer and fall of 1821, however, there occurred events of high importance.  Henry Clay, still ardent for the colonial cause, brought up a new resolution in the House of Representatives.  It declared that "the House join with the people of the United States in their sympathy with the South Americans; and that it was ready to support the President whenever he should think it expedient to recognize their governments."  The first part of this resolution passed by a vote of 134 to 12; and the second, by a vote of 86 to 68.[27]  The trend of opinion in Congress was clearly for action, and the hands of the administration were strengthened by this expression of opinion.  Meanwhile, events of the greatest importance occurred in South America.  In June, Bolívar inflicted a severe defeat upon the army of Morillo at Carabobo.  In July, his great rival and associate, San Martín, had entered Lima, bringing the revolution to Peru, the last and most faithful of Spain's American provinces.  In August, the Spanish acting viceroy in Mexico, General O'Donoju, signed a treaty with the revolutionary forces in that province on the basis of independence.  The facts of the situation pointed toward the complete success of the revolutionists.  In March, 1822, the President finally sent to Congress a message recommending that the independence of the new states be acknowledged, and that provision for the sending of ministers be made.[28]

In a sense, the policy of the American government had been prudence itself.  Yet in another sense, the recognition of colonial

[25] See p. 44, antea.

[26] See the famous statement in Adams, Writings, vi, 442, and in J. B. Moore, A Digest of International Law (Washington, 1906, 7 vols.), i, 78 f.

[27] Lockey, p. 167.

[28] J. D. Richardson, Messages and Papers of the Presidents, ii, 116 ff.

independence was a bold and decisive act, when considered in relation to the past policy of the United States, and to the political
situation in 1822.  In the earlier period of the discussion of the
South American question there was a distinct desire to conciliate
European opinion, and even to strengthen the position of the
government by active coöperation with European powers.  This
attitude was never carried to the point of subserviency.  The
American government never concealed its sympathy with the
colonial cause, or its conviction that the only solution of the colonial question lay in the recognition of colonial independence.
The language of Adams on this point is unequivocal.  "We can
neither accede to nor approve of any interference to restore any
part of the Spanish supremacy in any of the Spanish American
provinces," he wrote to Gallatin, the minister of the United States
at Paris, in his instructions of May, 1818, with the pending Congress of Aix-la-Chapelle in mind.[29]  "We cannot approve any
interposition of other powers, unless it be to promote the total independence, political and commercial, of the colonies," he declared to Campbell, American minister at St. Petersburg, at about
the same time.[30]  There is nothing of the tone of undue deference in
such declarations.  But, although the United States thus clearly
avowed its views, there was, none the less, great reluctance on the
part of the administration to act alone, and in opposition to
Europe.  In May, 1818, Monroe suggested to his cabinet the possibility of a concert of action with Great Britain to promote the
independence of the new states,[31] and he renewed the proposal
to Adams two months later.[32]  His point of view in regard to the
matter had the ardent support of Calhoun.[33]  As for Adams himself, his first instincts were to oppose such a policy.[34]  The American Secretary of State was not by instinct a coöperator.  And

---

[29] Adams, *Writings* (May 19), vi, 318.    [30] *Ibid.* (June 28), p. 379.
[31] Adams, *Memoirs*, iv, 92.    [32] *Ibid.*, p. 118.    [33] *Ibid.*, p. 207.
[34] *Ibid.*, p. 92. "I thought . . . particularly that no proposal should be made to
Great Britain for concerted measures with her to promote the independence of
South America. First, because it would be a departure from neutrality. Secondly,
because Great Britain, though she will readily acquiesce in the South American
Independence, will cautiously avoid having the appearance of supporting it; and
thirdly, because she would at once decline our overture, and make it an engine to
injure us with the other European powers."

yet, despite his temperamental preference for independent action, his policy in 1818 was not based on that preference. His instructions to Gallatin and Campbell professed a desire to act in harmony with the allied powers.[35] In December, 1818, he directly suggested to Bagot, the British minister, concerted action for the recognition of La Plata;[36] at about the same time he told Hyde de Neuville that he hoped France would be prepared to move with the United States; [37] and considerably later, toward the end of 1819, he assured the Russian minister, Poletica, that his desire in these earlier overtures had been to lay the foundations of a general understanding on the colonial question.[38]

When these facts are considered in their entirety, the recognition of the colonies in 1822 assumes a new significance. It required a considerable alteration of American policy to ignore the attitude of the powers of the Old World, and base American action on American interests and sympathies, and nothing else.

This is particularly true when the general European situation is considered. The tendencies of European politics at the close of the Napoleonic wars are too well known to require more than the briefest summary here. They were characterized by the efforts of the Tsar Alexander to found a world alliance for the maintenance of European order. They were characterized by the effort to transact European business in congresses dominated by the great powers. They were characterized by a strong attachment to order, and a strong aversion to revolution. From the time of the Congress of Vienna, the tide of events in the Old World flowed strongly toward reaction. But the events of 1820 and 1821 accentuated that tendency. It needed the actual outbreak of revolution in Spain and in Naples and in Piedmont

---

[35] See notes 28 and 29 *antea*.       [36] Adams, *Memoirs*, iv, 186 f.

[37] *Ibid.*, p. 190.

[38] *Ibid.*, p. 442. Adams, in an interview of November, 1819, told Poletica of the proposal of joint action made to Great Britain, and declared "that the only reason why it was not at the same time made to the Emperor was, the reason we had to suppose that the proposition itself would not only have been unacceptable to him, but that it would not have been agreeable to him that it should be made. . . . I said I wished him to assure his Government that it was made to Great Britain alone, not with the purpose of a partial concert with her, but of a general concert of all the European powers with us."

to develop the new gospel of order to its full. In the Troppau protocol of October, 1820, the three Eastern courts, Russia, Prussia, and Austria, committed themselves to the doctrine that it was the sacred duty of the great states of Europe, in case of danger, to put down pernicious uprisings by force of arms. In the course of the next year, the constitutional movements in Naples and Piedmont were snuffed out summarily, and there was already talk of similar action in Spain. At a time when, in the Old World, the detestation of revolution was finding deeper and deeper expression, it was an act of no equivocal character on the part of the United States to proclaim to the world its recognition of the republics of South America, and to set the seal of its approval on governments which in Continental Europe were regarded by the constituted authorities as fit subjects of moral odium.

Moreover, the administration, when it acted, acted with the most striking independence. It consulted with no European power; it gave no warning to any European chancellery of what was coming; and it paid no attention whatsoever to the situation which existed in Spain. It reckoned not at all with the fact that Ferdinand was in the power of his revolutionary subjects, and that recognition under such circumstances would be particularly distasteful to the legitimists of the Old World; it reckoned no more with the fact that the Spanish constitutionalists were making, or at least professing to make, new efforts at the reconciliation of the colonies with the mother country. Its action was taken on a purely American basis, and from a purely American point of view. It is thus inevitably a fact of profound significance; and its whole character makes it a fitting presage for the still more striking declaration of 1823.

As yet, however, the distrust of Europe, and dislike of its reactionary purposes, which were to play so large a part in the evolution of Monroe's declaration, were only half developed. The United States, in the recognition of the colonies, acted independently of, but not in professed hostility to, the point of view of the Holy Alliance. It needed the events of the next eighteen months to work a further change in the whole aspect of the Spanish-

American question, and to deepen the rift between the United States and the powers of Continental Europe.

The fall of 1822 and the winter of 1823 were to furnish new and striking evidence of the strength of the reaction in the Old World. In October was held the Congress of Verona. At this Congress, the allied powers, not content with the suppression of revolution in Piedmont and Naples, had moved on toward intervention in Spain. In this instance, France, not Austria, was to be the agent of their repressive designs. Great Britain dissenting, it was agreed by the representatives of the great Continental states that they should follow a common policy with respect to Spain, and should morally support the French government if it found it necessary to march its armies into the Peninsula.

At Verona, too, it has sometimes been assumed, the allied powers signed a new pact against constitutional government. This pact, which first appeared in the London *Morning Chronicle* of June 11, 1823, was published in the United States in *Niles' Register* on August 2, and has frequently been quoted by commentators on the Monroe Doctrine.[39] There seems, however, every

[39] For example, in J. B. Henderson, *American Diplomatic Questions* (New York, 1901), p. 314, and also in D. Y. Thomas, *One Hundred Years of the Monroe Doctrine* (New York, 1923), p. 22, and A. B. Hart, *The Monroe Doctrine: An Interpretation* (Boston, 1916), p. 46. The most relevant parts of the treaty are the first two articles, which run as follows:

"ARTICLE I. The high contracting powers, being convinced that the system of representative government is equally as incompatible with the monarchical principles as the maxim of the sovereignty of the people with the divine right, engage mutually, in the most solemn manner, to use all their efforts to put an end to the system of representative governments, in whatever country it may exist in Europe, and to prevent its being introduced in those countries where it is not yet known.

"ARTICLE II. As it cannot be doubted that the liberty of the press is the most powerful means used by the pretended supporters of the rights of nations, to the detriment of those of Princes, the high contracting parties promise reciprocally to adopt all proper measures to suppress it, not only in their own states, but also in the rest of Europe."

The treaty purports to be signed by Metternich, Chateaubriand, Bernstorff, and Nesselrode. The absurdity of Chateaubriand's putting his signature to a document which would have meant the abolition of the *Charte* would seem to be tolerably clear. It is also worth noting that, though it is possible to construe Article I as applying to both the New World and the Old, the general tenor of the document would seem to make it apply to Europe alone.

reason to believe that it is spurious. It is apparently unknown to European historians, and unmentioned in contemporary records like those of Metternich, Nesselrode, or Chateaubriand. It is not to be found, so far as I am aware, in any of the principal European archives. It is not cited in any of the great European treaty collections, such as that of Martens; and Tétot in his *Répertoire* declares its authenticity to be more than doubtful.[40] Even in the newspapers noted above, though the correspondent who communicated it is said to "have ground for believing" in its authoritative character, it is published "without giving any positive opinion" on the matter. As an episode in the events leading up to Monroe's declaration, it certainly deserves a less prominent place than it has sometimes received.

Yet, however unlikely is the signing of any such agreement at Verona, the deliberations of the Congress, as has been seen, certainly mark a further step in the direction of legitimist reaction. And they were soon followed by intervention in Spain. In January, after a struggle in the bosom of the cabinet, the French ministry of Villèle virtually determined upon war, and recalled its ambassador from Madrid. In April, the forces of Louis XVIII, under the command of the Duc d'Angoulême, crossed the Pyrenees and began their victorious march on Madrid. The opposition of the revolutionists rapidly crumbled; in a few months the French were in almost complete possession of the country, with the exception of Cadiz, whither the liberal leaders had fled with Ferdinand as their captive. Order had been restored in Europe. Only the New World remained in revolution. Was the next step in the triumphal progress of reaction to be the suppression of the new governments of Spanish America?

Throughout the winter and spring of 1822–23, the President and Adams seem to have remained tolerably calm as to the danger of any such intervention. Monroe's message of 1822 does, it is true, allude to the course of events in Europe in a tone of forebod-

[40] M. Tétot, *Répertoire des traités de paix, de commerce, d'alliance* (Paris, 1866), p. 203. Tétot cites the treaty itself as published in Jonathan Elliot, *The American Diplomatic Code* (Washington, 1834, 2 vols.), ii, 179. This is, of course, an American treaty collection, and Elliot probably got the document from Niles.

ing.[41] But he does not speak specifically of the Spanish colonial question, and his words, standing as they do in close relation to an appeal for increased military expenditures, seem to have something of the character of special pleading.[42] They are a slender basis on which to build any theory whatever. The effort to connect them specifically with the Monroe Doctrine seems to be lacking in logic.[43] Nothing else in the correspondence of the President indicates that he was as yet seriously concerned as to the peril in which the new states stood.

Adams, too, even in the spring of 1823, after French interference in Spain had become certain, does not seem to have been disturbed as to the possibility of allied intervention in the New World. What did disturb him, beyond a doubt, was the fate of the island of Cuba. The dispatch of April 28, 1823, in which he set forth to Hugh Nelson, the new American minister to Spain, his views on the subject, has often been quoted in connection with the evolution of the Monroe Doctrine.[44] In reality, it stands a little aside from the main line of events which led up to the President's message. There is only one sentence which alludes to the possibilities of intervention on the South-American continent, and that sentence declares that the purposes of the Continental powers have "not been sufficiently disclosed."[45] Even

---

[41] The language of the message is as follows: "Whether we reason from the late wars [in Europe], or from those menacing symptoms which now appear in Europe, it is manifest that if a convulsion should take place in any of those countries it will proceed from causes which have no existence and are utterly unknown in these States, in which there is but one order, that of the people, to whom the sovereignty exclusively belongs. Should war break out in any of those countries, who can foretell the extent to which it may be carried or the desolation which it may spread? Exempt as we are from these causes, our internal tranquillity is secure; and distant as we are from the troubled scene, and faithful to first principles in regard to other powers, we might reasonably presume that we should not be molested by them. This, however, ought not to be calculated on as certain. Unprovoked injuries are often inflicted, and even the peculiar felicity of our situation might with some be a cause for excitement and aggression." J. D. Richardson, *Messages and Papers of the Presidents*, ii, 193 f.

[42] This was the view of Stratford Canning, the British minister. London. P. R. O., F. O., America, vol. 164. Stratford Canning to George Canning, Dec. 5, 1822.

[43] Compare, however, J. B. Henderson, *American Diplomatic Questions*, part iv, "The Monroe Doctrine," pp. 289–448. See especially pp. 305 f.

[44] Adams, *Writings*, vii, 369–421, for the dispatch itself.      [45] *Ibid.*, p. 374.

those portions of the dispatch which refer to Cuba are filled with distrust, not of France and her allies, but of Great Britain. The conquest of the island by France, Adams did not regard as likely, on account of the "probable incompetency of the French maritime force to effect the conquest, and the probability that its accomplishment would be resisted by Great Britain." [46] In case of successful intervention in Spain, there would be, he thought, "no disposition, either in Ferdinand or his allies, to transfer the only remaining colonies of Spain to another power." [47] What he dreaded was that Great Britain would take advantage of the situation to secure the cession of the island, perhaps as the price of her aid to the Spanish constitutionalists against the French.[48] This view he developed at great length and with much force. But there is nothing in the dispatch to Nelson which indicates a growing fear and suspicion of the designs of the Holy Alliance in the New World.

As a matter of fact, in the spring and early summer of 1823 the administration had as yet no reason for serious disquietude. The dispatches from abroad, from London, from Madrid, from St. Petersburg, contained nothing that was alarming. And from Paris came information which, whether taken at its face value or not, was reassuring rather than disturbing. On June 24, Gallatin, American minister at Paris, reported to the Secretary of State the gist of conversations with Chateaubriand, the French Foreign Minister, and Pozzo di Borgo, Russian ambassador at the court of Louis XVIII.[49]

I did not leave Mr. de Chateaubriand [he wrote] without adverting to the affairs of Spain. That our sympathies were entirely on her side, and that we considered the war made on her by France as unjust, I did not pretend to conceal; but I added that the United States would undoubtedly preserve their neutrality, provided it was respected, and avoid every interference with the politics of Europe. Even in the questions connected with South America they had not interfered, and, although their wishes were not doubtful, they had neither excited nor assisted the Spanish colonies. But I had every reason to believe that, on the other hand, they would not suffer others

---

[46] Adams, *Writings*, vii, 372–382, 384 ff., 411 ff., 420 f.

[47] *Ibid.*, p. 382.        [48] *Ibid.*, pp. 379 ff.

[49] Gallatin had returned to the United States at this time. His letter was written from New York on his arrival.

to interfere against the emancipation of America. If France was successful in her attack on Spain, and afterwards attempted either to take possession of some of her colonies or to assist her in reducing them under their former yoke, I was of opinion that the United States would oppose every undertaking of this kind, and it might force them into an alliance with Great Britain. Mr. de Chateaubriand answered in the most explicit manner that France would not make any attempt whatever of that kind or in any manner interfere in the American questions.[50]

To Pozzo, Gallatin had spoken in much the same manner as to the French Foreign Minister, and the Russian, he reported to Adams, "seemed to coincide with me in opinion." [51]

So far, then, as the views of Europe on the colonial question were known in the summer of 1823, they were not a matter of great concern. At the end of August, the American Secretary of State left Washington for a month and a half's visit to his home at Quincy, an almost certain indication that he did not anticipate a diplomatic crisis.[52] There was, as yet, hardly an intimation of the momentous problems that were soon to engage the attention of the administration. The events that were to create an entirely new atmosphere at Washington and produce the Monroe Doctrine are, first, the historic interviews of George Canning with Richard Rush, and, second, two fateful communications from the Tsar.

To understand the interviews between Rush and Canning, it is necessary to say a word as to British policy in the colonial question.

From the very beginnings of the revolutionary movement in South America, British commerce had flowed into the new states, and created an interest of vital importance which the government could hardly ignore. None the less, under the conservative guidance of Lord Castlereagh, the ministry had abstained for a considerable period from positive action in behalf of the patriots. Down to 1818, it cherished at least a faint hope that the quarrel of Spain with her colonies might be settled by some kind

---

[50] *Writings of Albert Gallatin*, edited by Henry Adams (Philadelphia, 1879, 3 vols.), ii, 271.

[51] *Ibid.*, p. 272.

[52] Adams, *Memoirs*, vi, 175. Adams had returned to Washington by October 9.

of compromise, which would leave the ports of the New World open to British commerce, and permit at least the nominal restoration of Spanish control. Such a settlement would have been perfectly acceptable to a government that was hardly less conservative than those that existed at the same time upon the Continent.[53]

On the other hand, any project of intervention in South America by force of arms Great Britain from the beginning flatly opposed. Castlereagh laid down the views of England in this regard in a great memorandum of August 28, 1817, and reiterated them with equal force at the Congress of Aix-la-Chapelle. After Aix-la-Chapelle, moreover, he began to feel that even proposals of mediation were fruitless, and to gravitate toward recognition of the new states. If England had to make her election between conservative principles and practical trading interests, she would inevitably choose the latter. Devotion to abstract theory is not an English quality, nor has it as a rule been characteristic of English diplomacy. Accordingly, in 1822, stimulated, very probably, by American recognition of colonial independence, Lord Castlereagh made overtures to France looking to joint acknowledgment of the new states,[54] and at the same time entered into direct relations with the South American agents in London. The overtures to France were not favorably received, and the British ministry was not yet ready to act alone. But in July, just before his death, the British Foreign Secretary drew up instructions for the Duke of Wellington, who was to represent Great Britain at the Congress of Verona, directing him to raise the question of recognition at that forthcoming meeting of the great states of Europe.[55] Great Britain, repelled by their policy of intervention, had for some time been drawing away from the Continental

---

[53] British policy during the Castlereagh régime has been perspicuously set forth in two articles by C. K. Webster in *Eng. Hist. Rev.*, xxvii (1912), 78–95, and xxx (1915), 631–645. See also his book, *The Foreign Policy of Castlereagh* (London, 1925), pp. 405–437.

[54] Dexter Perkins, "Europe, Spanish America, and the Monroe Doctrine," in *Am. Hist. Rev.* (Jan., 1922), xxvii, 209.

[55] *Despatches, Correspondence, and Memoranda* of Arthur, Duke of Wellington, edited by his son (London, 1867–80, 8 vols.), i, 286 f.

powers. The Spanish colonial question did much to incline the scales more and more definitely in favor of independent action.

The death of Castlereagh accentuated this tendency. To the Foreign Office succeeded George Canning, a frank sceptic as to the value of international conference, an enemy of the European Areopagus, an exponent of a purely British policy. In Parliament he sat for Liverpool, the centre of the trading interests which were more and more making their voice heard with regard to the South-American question.[56] Far more than Castlereagh, he was able to understand and sympathize with the views of the opposition, led by Brougham and Mackintosh, which was sponsoring more and more definitely the cause of colonial independence. Indeed, there is every reason for believing that if Canning had been able to sway the conservative cabinet of Lord Liverpool according to his own desires, the new states might have been recognized much earlier than they were, perhaps even in the late autumn of 1822.[57]

Canning watched, then, with anything but a favorable eye, the course of events on the Continent in the early months of 1823. The intervention of France in Spain seriously disquieted him. He feared that it would be only the prelude to a like intervention in the colonies, to the establishment of a predominant French influence in the New World, perhaps to a cession of some part of Spain's late possessions as the reward for the reëstablishment of Ferdinand's authority. He took occasion, therefore, to set forth British policy with great explicitness at an early date, indeed a day or two before the French armies crossed the Pyrenees on their crusade in behalf of legitimacy.

With respect to the Provinces in America [he wrote to Sir Charles Stuart], time and the course of events appear to have substantially decided their separation from the mother-country; although the formal recognition of these Provinces, as Independent States, by his Majesty, may be hastened or retarded by various external circumstances, as well as by the more or

---

[56] For Britain's commercial interest, see Paxson, *The Independence of the South American Republics*, pp. 184 ff., 189, 198, 203, and L. A. Lawson, *The Relation of British Policy to the Declaration of the Monroe Doctrine* (New York, 1922) (*Columbia University Studies*, ciii, no. 1), chap. iv, pp. 76–103.

[57] Wellington, *Despatches*, i, 413–417.

less satisfactory progress, in each State, toward a regular and settled form of government. Disclaiming in the most solemn manner any intention of appropriating to Himself the smallest portion of the *late* Spanish possessions in America, his Majesty is satisfied that no attempt will be made by France to bring under her dominion any of those possessions, either by conquest, or by cession, from Spain.[58]

To this veiled threat of recognition in case of intervention in the New World, the French government made no reply. Its silence could hardly be entirely reassuring. Canning's suspicions were certainly not allayed; on the contrary, they seem to have been increased. The British Foreign Secretary was thus led in the direction of an understanding with the only power which, in this important question, could be trusted to see, to some extent at least, eye to eye with Great Britain.

Canning's overtures to the United States, however, were not without an important prelude. They have all too commonly been treated as if they came out of a clear sky. As a matter of fact, they have both an immediate and a more remote background that deserve to be emphasized. Their more remote background is to be found in the distinctly manifested desire of the American government in 1818 and 1819 to come to terms with Great Britain on the South American question; their more immediate background is to be found in extraordinary manifestations of cordiality toward England on the part of the Washington government in the spring of 1823, and, indeed, in pretty definite intimations of a desire for a closer understanding.

The increasing friendliness of American sentiment toward Great Britain in the months preceding the interviews between Rush and Canning is not difficult to understand.

With regard to the course of events in Europe, the United States and Great Britain were on a similar footing. Both held much the same views concerning the new doctrines by which the great Continental powers assumed a right of intervention in the interests of European order. From the first, Great Britain had balked at any such principle, refusing to associate herself with the decisions of Troppau and Laybach, and earning thereby the commen-

[58] London. P. R. O., F. O., France, vol. 284, no. 29, March 31, 1823.

dation of the American Secretary of State.[59] Still more, as we have seen, had the British government objected to the French invasion of Spain. And here again, its objections were fully shared by the administration at Washington. Monroe, under the influence of the events of the spring of 1823, began to consider if the time had not come to speak out against the pernicious doctrines of the Old World. In a too little noticed letter to Thomas Jefferson, of June 2, 1823, he wrote as follows: "Our relation to it [the state of Europe] is pretty much the same, as it was, in the commencement of the French revolution. Can we, in any form, take a bolder attitude in regard to it, in favor of liberty, than we then did? Can we afford greater aid to that cause, by assuming any such attitude, than we now do, by the form of our example?"[60] And Adams, despite his natural asperity, found himself admitting to Stratford Canning, the British minister, that England's attitude on the Spanish question was highly gratifying to American opinion, "more particularly as it affected the great principle of national independence, which he seemed to consider as brought into immediate danger by what he termed, the impending conflict, between 'autocracy and parliamentary government.'"[61]

The course which you have taken in the great politics of Europe [wrote Stratford Canning to his cousin in a private letter of May 8, 1823] has had the effect of making the English almost popular in the United States. The improved tone of public feeling is very perceptible, and even Adams has caught a something of the soft infection. The communication of your correspondence with France has also had its effect. On the whole, I question whether for a long time there has been so favorable an opportunity — as far as general disposition and good will are concerned, — to bring the two Countries nearer together. France for the moment is quite out of fashion. It may possibly be worth your while to give this a turn in your thoughts.[62]

Stratford Canning's intimation that "even Adams had caught a something of the soft infection" was soon most strikingly borne out by the tone and bearing of the Secretary of State.

[59] Adams, *Memoirs*, v, 194.

[60] Monroe Manuscripts, Library of Congress, quoted in W. A. McCorkle, *The Personal Genesis of the Monroe Doctrine* (New York and London, 1923), p. 64.

[61] Reddaway, *The Monroe Doctrine*, pp. 36 f.

[62] London. P. R. O., F. O. 352, vol. 8. Stratford Canning Papers. Stratford Canning to George Canning.

Great Britain [he told the British minister] had separated herself from the councils and measures of the alliance. She avowed the principles which were emphatically those of this country, and she disapproved the principles of the alliance, which this country abhorred. The coincidence of principle, connected with the great changes in the affairs of the world, passing before us, seemed to me a suitable occasion for the United States and Great Britain to compare their ideas and purposes together, with a view to the accommodation of great interests upon which they had heretofore differed.[63]

These observations, considering the stiffness of Adams's diplomatic manners, were cordial indeed. They were accompanied by concrete suggestions for an agreement, not only on such questions as the slave trade, and the terms of intercourse with the British-American colonies, but also on such more remote matters as the principles of maritime law and neutral rights. The Secretary furthermore pointed out the identity of views between the two governments on the South American question, and, though he very definitely disavowed any notion of or desire for an alliance, his tone seemed to indicate that he was not unready for a diplomatic rapprochement.[64] By the summer of 1823, therefore, George Canning might logically have assumed that any overtures on his part for common action in the South American question would meet with success. He was not acting without foreknowledge when he made the famous proposals to Richard Rush which had so much to do with the Monroe Doctrine. In view of the change of tone at Washington, what more natural than that he should turn to the United States for support in his South American policy? Were not the circumstances highly favorable to an understanding between the two governments? [65]

Other motives, moreover, less friendly to this country, prompted the British Foreign Secretary to an exchange of views

[63] Adams, *Memoirs*, vi, 152.

[64] London. P. R. O., F. O., America, vol. 176, no. 56, June 6, 1823. See also Adams, *Memoirs*, vi, 152 ff.

[65] Canning's relations with Rush were already quite cordial, as an incident of the spring of 1823 may serve to illustrate. At a diplomatic dinner party the American minister gave the toast, "Success to neutrals!" "Good," said Canning, and followed up this praise with a reference to the neutral doctrines of 1793. When Rush thanked him for this allusion to the doctrines of Jefferson, the British Foreign Secretary added, "I spoke sincerely. They are admirable." Monroe Manuscripts, Library of Congress. Rush to Monroe, Apr. 4, 1823.

with the American minister. From the autumn of the previous year, Canning had been extremely nervous with regard to Cuba. There were all sorts of disquieting rumors afloat concerning the future of the island. In September, 1822, a secret agent of Cuban revolutionary interests had appeared at Washington to seek aid in the struggle for independence, and eventual admission to the American Union, and these facts had become known in Europe.[66] In November, Canning wrote to Wellington at Verona, "I hope I may not have to tell you, before your return, that the Yankees have occupied Cuba; a blow which I do not know how we can prevent, but which as a government I hardly know how we should survive." [67] These suspicions probably persisted, and to some extent shaped British policy in 1823. But they only made more desirable an understanding with the American government. Why should not Great Britain seek to secure from the United States some pledge with regard to the island? Why would it not be feasible — by declaring Great Britain's opposition to the transfer of Cuba to any other power, and by inviting the support of the administration at Washington to a common declaration of disinterestedness — to ascertain the purposes of the United States, and tie its hands for the future, while at the same time concerting common measures against the aggression of Continental Europe in Cuba or any other part of the New World?

These considerations played a part in Canning's mind, and no doubt colored his interviews with Richard Rush. His purpose in those interviews was a double one. He wished to limit the action of the United States with regard to Cuba, but he also wished to secure the support of the American government against the possible aggression of France. In the evolution of the Monroe Doctrine, it is obviously the second of these purposes which is the more important.

The occasion for an exchange of views with regard to French designs on South America was in the first instance furnished, not by Canning, but by the American minister. On August 16,

[66] J. M. Callahan, *Cuba and International Relations* (Baltimore, 1899), pp. 124 f.
[67] E. M. Lloyd, "Canning and Spanish America," in *Transactions of the Royal Historical Society*, xviii, 89.

in a conference with the British Foreign Secretary, Rush "transiently asked him" concerning the course of events upon the Continent, and remarked that "should France ultimately effect her purpose of overthrowing the constitutional government in Spain, there was at least the consolation left, that Great Britain would not allow her to go farther and stop the progress of emancipation in the colonies." [68] He also mentioned the British note of March 31, and observed that he considered it as "sufficiently distinct in its import, that England would not remain passive," under any attempt on the part of France to acquire territory in America, "either by conquest or by cession from Spain." To these observations, Canning replied with a proposal for a common understanding, asking Rush what he thought his government would say to going hand in hand with England in such a policy. He did not think that concert of action would become necessary, but believed that "the simple fact of our two countries being known to hold the same opinion" would check the French government in any ambitious enterprise it might entertain.[69] "This belief was founded, he said, upon the large share of the maritime power of the world which Great Britain and the United States held, and the consequent influence which the knowledge of their common policy, on a question involving such important maritime interests, present and future, could not fail to produce everywhere." [70]

To these overtures Richard Rush returned a noncommittal reply. He had no instructions on the subject, and to take, without instructions, a step so decisive as that proposed would have been rash indeed. The danger of intervention in the colonies was as yet vague and indefinite; there was no concrete information in the possession of either the British or the American minister to justify precipitate action, action which might imperil the relations of the United States with France, and involve them in "the federative system of Europe." Moreover, and it is immensely to the credit of the American minister that he perceived this fact, the relations of Great Britain and the United States with the colonies did not rest upon an identical footing.

[68] Rush, *Court of London*, p. 399.   [69] *Ibid.*, p. 400.   [70] *Ibid.*, p. 401.

The United States had recognized their independence; Great Britain had not. The United States was irrevocably committed; Great Britain, even in case of temporary coöperation with the United States, would still be free to alter her policy, and to bring it into harmony with that of the Continental allies. Common action ought to rest upon a common basis. The American minister, therefore, while declining to commit himself, questioned Canning as to "the precise situation in which England stood in relation to those new communities, and especially on the material point of acknowledging their independence." [71] He thus hinted, in the very first exchange of views, at the necessity of recognition of the new republics by Great Britain as indispensable to joint action, a point of view which was later to be expressed with great vigor by his chief at Washington.

On the twentieth, Canning again raised the question of coöperation. He now wrote a note to Rush setting forth the principles of British policy with regard to the colonies, and suggesting the adhesion of the United States to these principles. "England," he wrote, "had no disguise on the subject."

"She conceived the recovery of the colonies by Spain, to be hopeless.

"That the question of their recognition as Independent States, was one of time and of circumstances.

"That England was not disposed, however, to throw any impediment in the way of an arrangement between the colonies and the mother country, by amicable negotiation.

"That she aimed at the possession of no portion of the colonies for herself.

"That she could not see the transfer of any portion of them to any other Power, with indifference."

Holding these views, Great Britain would be very ready to declare them in concert with the United States. Could Rush sign a convention on the subject? Or, if this were not possible, could he consent to an exchange of ministerial notes? "Nothing could be more gratifying to me than to join with you in such a work," wrote Canning, "and, I am persuaded, there has seldom,

[71] Rush, *Court of London*, p. 401.

in the history of the world, occurred an opportunity when so small an effort of two friendly Governments might produce so unequivocal a good and prevent such extensive calamities." [72]

Three days after making this overture the British Foreign Secretary received further information, which led him to press even more eagerly for an understanding with the American government. The French Foreign Minister, Chateaubriand, informed Sir Charles Stuart, British ambassador at Paris, that on the termination of the war in Spain a congress would probably be called to deal with the colonial question.[73] This information, speedily transmitted to Canning at Liverpool, led him to write Rush again on August 23, apprising him of the posture of affairs, and urging that the proposal of a congress formed

an additional motive for wishing that we might be able to come to some understanding on the part of our respective Governments on the subject of my letter; to come to it soon, and to be at liberty to announce it to the world. . . . I need not point out to you [he added] all the complications to which this proposal, however dealt with by us, may lead.[74]

Rush replied to these communications of Canning's with an interesting exposition of the general point of view of the United States. In a note of August 23, he emphasized the anxiety of the American government to see the colonies "received into the family of nations by the powers of Europe, and especially by Great Britain." He stated his entire concurrence in the principles laid down in the note of August 20, barring the matter of recognition on which the United States had already made its decision.[75] In a note of the twenty-sixth he indicated that his country "desired to see the Independence of the late Spanish Provinces in America permanently maintained," and that it "would view as unjust and improper any attempt on the part of the Powers of Europe to intrench upon that Independence." He added that the United States "would regard as alike objectionable any interference whatever in the affairs of Spanish America, unsolicited by

[72] Rush, *Court of London*, pp. 412 ff. The text of Canning's note is to be found in T. B. Edgington, *The Monroe Doctrine* (Boston, 1905), pp. 7 ff.

[73] London. P. R. O., F. O., France, vol. 291, Aug. 18, 1823.

[74] Rush, *Court of London*, p. 418. Edgington, *op. cit.*, p. 9.

[75] Rush, *Court of London*, p. 414.

the late Provinces themselves, and against their will; that it would regard the convening of a Congress to deliberate upon their affairs, as a measure uncalled for, and indicative of a policy highly unfriendly to the tranquillity of the world; that it could never look with insensibility upon such an exercise of European jurisdiction over communities now of right exempt from it, and entitled to regulate their own concerns unmolested from abroad." With regard to the possibility of coöperation the American minister went further than in his previous communication. Indeed, he intimated the possibility of accepting Canning's offer.

I further said [writes Rush, in his *Memoranda*] that if he supposed any of these sentiments, or those expressed in my first note, might be moulded by me into a form promising to accomplish the object he proposed, I would be happy to receive and take into consideration whatever suggestions he would favor me with to that end, either in writing, or in the full and unreserved intercourse of conversation when he returned to town. Lastly, I said, that could England see fit to consider the time as now arrived for fully acknowledging the independence of the new communities, I believed, that not only would it accelerate the steps of my Government, but that it would naturally place *me* in a new position in my further course with him on the whole subject.[76]

Rush thus broadly hinted at the possibility of Anglo-American coöperation if Great Britain would recognize the new republics of South America.

The British Foreign Secretary was not ready, however, for coöperation on such terms. He was, perhaps, anxious to sound his fellow members of the cabinet on such a proposition. Furthermore, he was on the point of leaving London. On August 31 he wrote Rush that, pending more definite information on the American viewpoint, he did not wish to tie the hands of Great Britain, and went on to request him to treat his previous communication "*not* as a proposition already made, but as evidence of the nature of one which it would have been his desire to make, had he found me provided with authority to entertain it." [77]

There was, however, a temporary suspension rather than a cessation of the exchange of views between Canning and the American minister. In September, at the request of the former, new conversations took place, and once again joint action was

[76] Rush, *Court of London*, pp. 418 ff.     [77] *Ibid.*, p. 425.

urged by the British Foreign Secretary. Never, perhaps, in our early history, was the coöperation of the United States so earnestly besought as it was in 1823. When Rush raised objections to such coöperation on the grounds of America's general policy of avoiding European entanglements, the British minister replied in language that shows the strength of his feeling. The United States, he declared, "were the first Power established on that [the American] continent, and now confessedly the leading Power. They were connected with Spanish America by their position, as with Europe by their relations; and they also stood connected with these new states by political relations. Was it possible that they could see with indifference their fate decided upon by Europe? Could Europe expect this indifference? Had not a new epoch arrived in the relative position of the United States toward Europe, which Europe must acknowledge? Were the great political and commercial interests which hung upon the destinies of the new continent, to be canvassed and adjusted in this hemisphere, without the coöperation or even knowledge of the United States? Were they to be canvassed and adjusted, he would even add, without some proper understanding between the United States and Great Britain, as the two chief commercial and maritime states of both worlds? He hoped not, he would wish to persuade himself not." [78] "Could higher motives exist to coöperation, and immediately?" Let it be delayed until Rush could receive specific powers, "and the day might go by; the progress of events was rapid; the public evil might come on. A portion of it might, and probably would be, consummated; and even admitting that Great Britain could, by herself, afterwards arrest it, preventive measures among nations were always preferable, whether on the score of humanity or policy, to those that were remedial. Why then, should the United States, whose institutions resembled those of Great Britain more than they did those of the other Powers in Europe, and whose policy upon this occasion was closely approximated to hers, hesitate to act with her to promote a common object, approved alike by both, and achieve a common good, estimated alike by both?" [79]

[78] Rush, *Court of London*, pp. 431 f.     [79] *Ibid.*, pp. 434 f.

This eloquent appeal did not move Rush from his previous decision to consent to joint action only on the basis of immediate British recognition of the colonies, and such terms Canning could not accept. Though, personally, he might have been disposed to acknowledge the new states, he could not possibly have carried the cabinet with him at this early date. But, even so, he was not yet willing to forego the possibility of coöperation. The interview just cited took place on September 18; on the twenty-sixth the British Foreign Secretary again took up the matter. Sir Charles Stuart had written him from Paris that the American chargé there, Mr. Sheldon, had declared that the United States knew of the projects of the Continental powers, and disapproved of them. Did this statement, Canning asked Rush, rest upon new instructions, in which Rush shared? Was there a new hope of agreement? [80] When the answer to these questions was given in the negative, Canning inquired whether "a promise by England of *future* acknowledgement" of the South American states would alter the American minister's position, and make coöperation possible. Once again, however, the reply left no hope of common action. [81] Yet even then he did not despair. There is reason for believing that, having failed in London, he renewed his efforts at Washington. There is, it is true, no direct evidence on this point in the form of instructions to Addington, the British chargé. But there is highly interesting circumstantial evidence, which has been brought to light by one of the most acute students of the Monroe Doctrine, Mr. W. F. Reddaway. [82] This evidence lies in a note of Canning's of early December, in which the British Foreign Secretary directs Addington to put into the form of a private letter a dispatch, no. 18, written in the first days of November. [83] On the margin of this instruction are the words, "joint manifesto on Spanish America." [84] Now, it is possible that the suppressed

---

[80] Rush, *Court of London*, p. 444.                    [81] *Ibid.*, p. 445.

[82] Reddaway, *The Monroe Doctrine*, p. 53.

[83] London. P. R. O., F. O., America, vol. 177. Private and Confidential. Dec. 8, 1823.

[84] *Ibid.* The date of the suppressed despatch must be about November 1–3, for Addington's no. 17 is dated simply November, and the despatch which became no. 18 is dated November 3.

dispatch merely refers to Adams's conversations with Addington, in which the American Secretary of State revealed and discussed with the British chargé the despatches from Rush describing the exchanges of views in early August. But if this were the case, it seems strange that subsequent communications from Addington upon the same subject were left in the files. It is likely, then, that the no. 18 to which Canning referred contained some data of a more special character. It is at least a plausible conjecture that that reference was to an overture initiated by the British Foreign Secretary at Washington after the failure of his efforts to bring Rush to common action.

At any rate, the fact that Canning was desirous of coöperating with the United States in the matter of Spanish America was clearly understood in Washington early in October, with the receipt of the dispatches from the American minister in London. For the first time, grave suspicions began to be felt by President Monroe as to the motives and purposes of the Continental powers in the New World. A definite purpose on the part of the allies to reconquer Spanish America had not been alleged by the British Foreign Secretary. But there had been allusions to a congress to discuss the colonial problem, and Rush himself had been led to believe that serious dangers were impending. In the face of such facts, it was necessary seriously to consider what should be the attitude of the United States.

The news of the British overtures, therefore, stimulated an earnest discussion of the colonial question at Washington. In the course of the next two months, after the most careful consideration, Monroe and Adams were to prepare and launch a warning to Europe against interference across seas, and to challenge the reigning doctrines by which the sovereigns of the Old World affected to be guided. This more intensive period in the genesis of the message deserves a chapter to itself.

# CHAPTER III

## THE WARNING TO EUROPE

THE arrival at Washington of the news of Canning's first interviews with Rush was speedily followed by other events of high importance. On October 16, Baron Tuyll called on the Secretary of State and informed him that the Tsar Alexander would not receive any minister or agent from any one of the states just formed in the New World. He also expressed the satisfaction of the Russian government at the attitude of neutrality that had been observed by the United States in the colonial conflict, and at its declared intention to continue to maintain that neutrality.

The views thus more or less informally expressed were embodied in an official note that was transmitted on the same day.

His Imperial Majesty [it stated] . . . faithful to the political principles which he follows in concert with his Allies, cannot under any circumstances receive any agent whatsoever, either from the Regency of Colombia, or from any of the other governments, which owe their existence to the events of which the New World has been for some years the stage.[1]

This declaration of policy on the part of Alexander had been entirely unsolicited by the United States. It came at a time when its exact purpose was extremely difficult to fathom. It was like lightning from a clear sky. True, there was nothing necessarily sinister about it. On its face it was no more than a declaration of the Russian viewpoint on South America, and a commendation of the neutral attitude of the United States. But did it indicate a reviving interest on the part of the Tsar in the colonial question? Why compliment the United States on its neutrality? What political principles were those to which the note alluded? Was there here a veiled reference to the right of intervention in behalf of legitimacy? So the President, at any rate, may have feared,

[1] W. C. Ford, "John Quincy Adams and the Monroe Doctrine," I, in *Am. Hist. Rev.* (July, 1902), vii, 685 f.

for he directed Adams to seek an explanation of the phrase from Tuyll.[2]

A month later came a communication even more disturbing. It was a note written by Nesselrode, dated August 30, 1823, and dealing with the recent intervention in Spain. It was framed, Adams sets down in his diary, in "a tone of passionate exultation," and was

an "*Io Triumphe*" over the fallen cause of revolution, with sturdy promises of determination to keep it down; disclaimers of all intention of making conquests; bitter complaints of being calumniated, and one paragraph of compunctions, acknowledging that an apology is yet due to mankind for the invasion of Spain, which it is in the power only of Ferdinand to furnish, by making his people happy.[3]

There was nothing in this state paper which directly menaced the liberties of the New World, as a careful reading of its full text [4] will serve to show. The Tsar Alexander, indeed, may well have regarded it as a reassuring explanation of the benevolent intentions of the allied powers. In the main, it was a homily on purely Continental affairs, and contained hardly a reference to the New World. The only phrase which could even by the closest construction be taken to hint at a purpose to intervene in the Spanish colonies is that in which the Tsar speaks of a policy, "whose only object is to guarantee the tranquillity of all the states of which the civilized world is composed." But to anyone aware of Alexander's penchant for sonorous phrase, and sweeping generalization, such a sentence was hardly to be taken too seriously. And yet the principles which the note professed, and the tone in which they were set forth, could hardly fail to be disturbing to the government at Washington, and to furnish an addi-

[2] Adams, *Memoirs*, vi, 182. "I had also received a note from the President just before I met the Baron, in which he had suggested the idea of inquiring of the Baron what was the import of the term 'political principles' in his note. I accordingly asked him. He said they were used in the instructions of the Government to him, and he understood them to have reference to the right of supremacy of Spain over her colonies. I had so understood them myself, and had not entertained a moment's doubt as to their meaning." Adams was evidently less perturbed than Monroe.

[3] Adams, *Memoirs*, vi, 190.

[4] Published in W. C. Ford, "John Quincy Adams and the Monroe Doctrine," II, in *Am. Hist. Rev.* (Oct., 1902), viii, 30 ff.

tional reason for setting forth, without delay and in the most explicit terms, the opposition of the United States to the doctrine of intervention, and to interference by the European powers with the affairs of the New World.[5]

Before Tuyll had presented this dispatch to Adams, however, Monroe and his advisers had already discussed the dangers in which the Spanish colonies stood. From the beginning of the cabinet discussions of November, 1823, the President and John C. Calhoun, the Secretary of War, were wholly convinced that the Holy Alliance would soon act to restore the colonies to Spain. The President, wrote Adams, "is alarmed far beyond anything that I could have conceived possible," and "the news that Cadiz has surrendered to the French has so affected him that he appeared entirely to despair of the cause of South America."[6] Calhoun, in Adams's phrase, was "perfectly moonstruck" at the danger.[7]

[5] In addition to these official representations which aroused the disquietude of the President, worth noting, also, is a letter from G. W. Erving, then travelling in Europe, to Crawford, the Secretary of the Treasury. "Without supposing it to be true that this government [i.e., the French] has made a treaty with the actual regency at Madrid by which she engages to bring the Spanish colonies in South America to submission by force, as has been said," wrote Erving, "this is evident, that all the influence of Russia as well as of France, will be employed in that object; the obvious policy of Russia in this respect will be reinforced by considerations growing out of the termination of the Spanish revolution (should it terminate according to her desire) — considerations belonging to the common cause of the Holy Alliance. But will any means of negotiation or force (or corruption) be able to bring about the reunion of the colonies with Spain — I think affirmatively as to most of them. Shall we find it necessary to do anything in favor of the independence we have already acknowledged? I apprehend so. Shall we act in this matter in unison with Great Britain? I fear so." Monroe Manuscripts, Library of Congress. This letter was written September 25, 1823, and was certainly made known to the President by Crawford. It is impossible to estimate its importance, though, in any case, it must have been a distinctly secondary consideration as compared with the overtures of Canning and the language of Tuyll. Monroe mentioned it to Adams on November 21; the Secretary declared that he "put very little reliance on anything written by G. W. Erving. It might or might not eventuate as he said; but he knew nothing about the matter more than was known to the world, and had views of his own in whatever he wrote." Adams, Memoirs, vi, 196.

[6] Adams, Memoirs, vi, 185. In the quotation the pronoun "him" has been substituted for Adams's "the President" to avoid repetition of the latter phrase in the same sentence.

[7] Ibid., p. 186.

The Secretary of State himself refused to be thus terrified. It is, indeed, not the least striking evidence of his ability as a diplomat that he viewed the situation without panic, and with superb sense of proportion. Five years before, at the time of the deliberations at Aix-La-Chapelle, he had pointed out that the allies had no interest whatsoever in the reconquest of the colonies.[8] This was still his viewpoint in 1823. He believed that the Holy Alliance "would not ultimately invade South America." If they should actually do so, "they might make a temporary impression for three, four, or five years," said Adams in the cabinet meeting of November 15, but "I no more believe that the Holy Allies will restore the Spanish dominion upon the American continent than that the Chimborazo will sink beneath the ocean."[9] They would have no conceivable reason to restore the old exclusive system of the past. Spain could never maintain herself in the New World alone, and "was it in human absurdity to imagine that they [the allied powers] should waste their blood and treasure to prohibit their own subjects upon pain of death to set foot upon those territories?"[10] If they took action at all, the ultimate result would be to partition the colonies among themselves. But was it reasonable to suppose that they could agree upon any principle of partition?[11] And even if they were able to do so, what inducement could they offer to Great Britain to acquiesce in any such scheme? "The only possible bait they could offer . . . was Cuba, which neither they nor Spain would consent to give her."[12]

But though Adams was very far indeed from the panic fear that the Holy Alliance would reconquer South America, and was strongly inclined to the opinion that no intervention would even be attempted, he was by no means inclined to let the situation pass without an expression of the views of the United

---

[8] Adams, *Writings*, vi, 317. "There is no discernible motive of justice or of interest, which can induce the allied sovereigns to interpose for the restoration of the Spanish colonial dominion in South America. There is none even of policy; for if all the organized power of Europe is combined to maintain the authority of each sovereign over his own people, it is hardly supposable that the sober senses of the allied cabinets will permit them to extend the application of this principle of union to the maintenance of colonial dominion beyond the Atlantic and the Equator."

[9] Adams, *Memoirs*, vi, 186.        [10] *Ibid.*, p. 207.
[11] *Ibid.*, p. 203.        [12] *Loc. cit.*

States. He believed that the situation required a very definite assertion of American policy. And so, for the matter of that, did all the other members of the cabinet and the President himself. There was not even a disposition to delay action until Canning's overtures could be accepted, and a concert of action established with Great Britain. When Adams, in one of the first of the cabinet meetings, that of November 7, declared that "it would be more candid as well as more dignified, to avow our principles explicitly to Russia and France, than to come in as a cock-boat in the wake of the British man-of-war," his idea "was acquiesced in on all sides." [13] President Monroe himself, who leaned toward the acceptance of the British proposals, was heartily averse to taking any attitude that might be regarded as "subordinate," and was ready to make the position of the United States entirely clear.[14] There was to be no dependence on Great Britain.

The question was not whether action should be taken, but in what form. What answer should be given to Rush? What answer should be given to Tuyll? And, finally, how should the colonial question be treated in the forthcoming communication to Congress? All these matters taken together engaged the attention of the cabinet during the momentous sessions of November, 1823. All of them have a direct relation to the enunciation of the Monroe Doctrine. But it will be best to begin with a discussion of the evolution of the actual message itself.

From the moment when the President set about the preparation of that document he seems to have intended that some reference to the colonial question should be made. The idea — and this fact is of the first importance — was almost certainly his own. There are several reasons for so believing. In the first place, in the sketch prepared by Mr. Adams for his chief, summarizing the matters of foreign policy which might be treated in the message, there is no mention of South American affairs at all. Nowhere in his diary does the Secretary so much as intimate that he wished to see a public declaration of the kind which the President actually penned. He was occupied, as we shall see, with the answer to Rush, and the reply to Tuyll, the latter of which docu-

---

[13] Adams, *Memoirs*, vi, 179.          [14] *Ibid.*, p. 178.

ments, as he himself records, was modelled on the language of
Monroe. There is no positive evidence whatsoever to show that
he suggested that the colonial problem should be treated in the
message, and the negative evidence tends strongly in the other direction. Furthermore, the place of the paragraphs on South America in the President's communication to Congress strongly suggests a separate origin from the other sections dealing with foreign
affairs. These latter come near the beginning, and closely follow
Adams's sketch. The Monroe Doctrine comes near the end, entirely apart from all other diplomatic matters.[15] Standing by itself,
it was, to all appearances, a pronouncement independent of all
others, and the special pronouncement of the President himself.

The motives for its insertion Monroe himself explained in a
letter to Jefferson written shortly after the sending of the message.

By taking the step here [he wrote] it is done in a manner more conciliatory
with, and respectful to Russia, and the other powers, than if taken in England, and as it is thought with more credit to our govt. Had we moved in
the first instance in England, separated as she is in part, from those powers,
our union with her, being marked, might have produced irritation with
them. We know that Russia dreads a connection between the United States
and G. Britain, or harmony in policy. Moving on our own ground, the apprehension that unless she retreats, that affect may be produced, may be a
motive with her for retreating. Had we mov'd in England, it is probable
that it would have been inferr'd that we acted under her influence, & at her
instigation, & thus have lost credit as well with our Southern neighbors, as
with the allied powers.[16]

Acting under some such considerations as these, then, on November 21 Monroe presented the first draft of the forthcoming
communication to the cabinet. Far from being a timid document,
it was in some respects too advanced for his Secretary of State. It
was couched in a tone of "deep solemnity and of high alarm." It
alluded to the recent events in Spain and Portugal, speaking in terms of the
most pointed reprobation of the late invasion of Spain by France, and of the
principles upon which it was undertaken by the open avowal of the King of

---

[15] Monroe apparently originally intended to put the pronouncement at the
beginning of the message. See Adams, *Memoirs*, vi, 194.

[16] Monroe Manuscripts. Library of Congress. Monroe to Jefferson, Dec. —,
1823.

France. It also contained a broad acknowledgment of the Greeks as an independent nation, and a recommendation to Congress to make an appropriation for sending a Minister to them.[17]

The President was evidently anxious to carry his republican principles to the furthest possible extreme. Influenced, no doubt, by his own fears, by the course of events in Europe, and by the communications of the Tsar, he was willing to defy the powers of the Old World, to condemn unequivocally the basic principle of their policy, the principle of intervention, and to associate the United States with republicanism wherever it showed itself, in Greece no less than in South America.[18] This was not the desire of the Secretary of State. He wished to make no such provocative declaration. The message, in the form in which the President had written it, he declared,

would be a summons to arms — to arms against all Europe, and for objects of policy exclusively European — Greece and Spain. It would be as new, too, in our policy as it would be surprising. For more than thirty years Europe had been in convulsions; every nation almost of which it is composed alternately invading and invaded. Empires, kingdoms, principalities, had been overthrown, revolutionized, and counter-revolutionized, and we had looked on safe in our distance beyond an intervening ocean, and avowing a total forbearance to interfere in any of the combinations of European politics. This message would at once buckle on the harness and throw down the gauntlet. It would have the air of open defiance to all Europe, and I should not be surprised if the first answer to it from Spain and France, and even Russia, should be to break off their diplomatic intercourse with us. I did not expect that the quiet which we had enjoyed for six or seven years would last much longer. The aspect of things was portentous; but if we must come to an issue with Europe, let us keep it off as long as possible.[19]

These views of Adams's, we have already said, were expressed in the cabinet meeting of November 21. In a private interview with the President the next day the American Secretary of State urged them again very warmly.

[17] Adams, *Memoirs*, vi, 194.

[18] The President may have been influenced also by Madison's reply to his transmission of the Rush correspondence. "Will it not be honorable to our country & possibly not altogether in vain," the ex-President had written, "to invite the British Govt to extend the avowed disapprobation of the project agst the Spanish Colonies, to the enterprise of France agst Spain herself; and even to join in some declaratory act in behalf of the Greeks?" (Monroe, *Writings*, vi, 395.)

[19] Adams, *Memoirs*, vi, 195.

If the Holy Alliance were determined to make up an issue with us [he said] it was our policy to meet, and not to make it. . . . If they intend now to interpose by force, we shall have as much as we can do to prevent them without going to bid them defiance in the heart of Europe. . . . The ground that I wish to take is that of earnest remonstrance against the interference of the European powers by force with South America, but to disclaim all interference on our part with Europe; to make an American cause, and adhere inflexibly to that.[20]

At first the President seems to have been a little doubtful about the validity of Adams's criticism. He had mentioned Greece and Spain in the message of last year, he remarked, and saw no objection to doing so now.[21] His viewpoint was supported by Calhoun, who thought, in common with his chief, that

there was a material difference in the wars and revolutions which since the year 1789 to this time have been raging in Europe, and this last invasion of Spain by France; that this was a more direct attack upon the popular principle; and that although no former message ever censured those overthrows and conquests before, yet it might be very proper to censure this now.[22]

But Adams stood firm on his own ground. He was ready to accept "general terms," pledging nothing, but wished "to avoid anything" which might "be construed as hostility to the Allies." The upshot of the matter was that the President declared that he would draw up a revised draft for consideration,[23] and on November 24 he read a new sketch to Adams, which was "entirely conformable to the system of policy" which the latter had recommended.[24] In these modifications of his original draft, the critics of the President have often professed to find weakness; but why might it not be equally well maintained that they demonstrate his sagacity and largemindedness, and his willingness to profit from constructive criticism?

On November 25 and 26 there came new cabinet meetings to consider the message. The discussion on those eventful afternoons centred around the question whether, in all coolness and reflection, any positive and unequivocal statement of the policy of the United States was desirable.

The sentiment of the earlier meetings had certainly favored a positive course. But the question was not one to be decided

---

[20] Adams, *Memoirs*, vi, 197 f.     [21] *Ibid.*, p. 196.     [22] *Ibid.*
[23] *Ibid.*, p. 198.               [24] *Ibid.*, p. 199.

lightly. The language of the message was very emphatic. It was certainly necessary to consider maturely the dangers in such a stand. It was, as the Secretary of State wrote in his diary, a "fearful question." [25]

The "fearful question" was raised by William Wirt, the Attorney General. In the meeting of November 25 Mr. Wirt "remarked upon the danger of assuming the attitude of menace without meaning to strike, and asked, if the Holy Allies *should* act in direct hostility against South America, whether this country would oppose them by war?" [26] The next day he resumed his objections, and enlarged upon them. "He said he did not think this country would support the Government in a war for the independence of South America. There had never been much general excitement in their favor. Some part of the people of the interior had felt warmly for them, but it never had been general, and never had there been a moment when the people thought of supporting them by war. To menace without intending to strike was neither consistent with the honor nor the dignity of the country. It was possible that the proposals of Mr. Canning themselves were traps laid to snare us into public declarations against the Holy Allies, without intending even to take part against them; that if we were to be so far committed, all the documents ought to be communicated to Congress, and they ought to manifest their sentiments in the form of resolutions, and that the Executive ought not to pledge the honor of the nation to war without taking the sense of the country with them." [27]

This conservative point of view on the whole colonial question was combated vigorously by the Secretary of State. It was extremely doubtful, he told the President, whether, in any case, the Holy Allies were inclined to attack Spanish America. But if they were to attempt any such thing,

it was impossible, in the nature of things, that they should do it to restore the old exclusive dominion of Spain. . . . The ultimate result of their undertaking would be to recolonize them [i.e., the colonies], partitioned out among themselves. Russia might take California, Peru, Chili; France, Mexico — where we know she has been intriguing to get a monarchy under a Prince of

---

[25] Adams, *Memoirs*, vi, 202.        [26] *Ibid.*        [27] *Ibid.*, p. 205.

the House of Bourbon, as well as at Buenos Ayres. And Great Britain, as
her last resort, if she could not resist this course of things, would take at
least the island of Cuba for her share of the scramble. . . . The danger therefore was brought to our own doors, and I thought we could not too soon take
our stand to repel it.[28]

There was another point of view, which the President had in part suggested, and which I thought highly important [continues Adams in his diary].
Suppose the Holy Allies should attack South America, and Great Britain
should resist them alone and without our coöperation. I thought this not
an improbable contingency, and I believed in such a struggle the allies
would be defeated and Great Britain would be victorious, by her command
of the sea. But, as the independence of the South Americans would then be
only protected by the guarantee of Great Britain, it would throw them completely into her arms, and in the result make them her Colonies instead of
those of Spain. My opinion was, therefore, that we must act promptly and
decisively.[29]

In any case, added the Secretary of State, the course taken by
the Executive could not definitely commit the country to war.

From quite a different standpoint, John C. Calhoun, Monroe's
Secretary of War, set forth, along with Adams, the argument for
a vigorous policy. Calhoun took the whole crisis far more melo-
dramatically than Adams. The latter hardly believed that intervention was likely, though he was convinced that it was well to
be prepared for the emergency. The South Carolinian statesman,
on the other hand, was convinced that not only South America
but the United States itself was in danger.

Great Britain would not, could not, resist them [the Holy Alliance] alone,
we remaining neutral. She would fall eventually into their views, and the
South Americans would be subdued. The next step the allies would then take
would be against ourselves — to put down what had been called the first
example of successful democratic rebellion.

In such a contingency Calhoun believed that it was necessary to
act with decision. The peril was too serious to admit of equi-
vocation. Hesitation would only postpone the day when the
United States might be compelled to fight upon its own shores
for its own institutions.[30]

The objections of Mr. Wirt to the language of the President's
message were thus overborne. Monroe himself, as has been seen,
had from the beginning taken the crisis very seriously indeed and

---

[28] Adams, *Memoirs*, vi, 207 f.     [29] *Ibid.*, p. 208.     [30] *Ibid.*, p. 206.

believed in the necessity of vigorous action. The arguments of
Adams and Calhoun accorded with his own views. After the
cabinet meetings of November 25 and November 26 it seems
definitely to have been determined that the forthcoming communication to Congress should take a clear and decisive tone on
the Spanish colonial question.

In looking back at these debates, so full of interest to the
student of American diplomatic history, one fact seems particularly worth noting.  It is the fact of their preponderantly political
character.  In the discussions upon the northwest controversy, as
has been seen, trading influences contributed very materially to
the stand which was taken by the administration.  But it would
be difficult to prove anything of the kind with regard to the warning given to Europe against intervention in South America.  This
is not to say that such influences necessarily played no rôle at all.
John Quincy Adams, of course, came from the great shipping
section of the Union.  In his instructions to the American ministers sent out to Colombia and La Plata in the spring of 1823, he
had laid a very considerable emphasis upon freedom of commercial
opportunity,[31] though he was by no means exuberantly optimistic
as to the possibilities of the South American trade.  In the cabinet discussions of November, he had, on one occasion, brought
forward as a reason for action the fact that if the United States
stood aside and Great Britain alone vetoed the designs of the
Continental powers, the latter country would gain great commercial advantages.[32]  It is worth noting, too, that our commerce with the Spanish-American states was considerably more
important in 1823 than it had been two or three years before.[33]
But these facts would be a slender foundation on which to base
an "economic interpretation" of the Monroe Doctrine.  And they

---

[31] See Chapter I, note 33.          [32] Adams, Memoirs, vi, 208.

[33] In 1821 the Spanish-American trade was almost negligible. Only 2.3 per cent
of American exports and 1.6 per cent of American imports were Spanish American
in destination or origin. But in 1822 and 1823, the figures are 7 and 3 per cent,
and 9.7 and 5.8 per cent, respectively. (Watterston and Van Zandt, Tabular Statistical Views, pp. 45 and 97, provide the figures for this calculation.) But was the
growth of this trade certainly known to Adams? There is, so far as I know, no
way of answering this question.

are offset by many others. Whoever reads the pages of Adams's diary will find it hard to believe that trading considerations played a very considerable rôle in his mind. The distaste produced by the homilies of the Tsar, a genuine and robust disapproval of the trend of European politics, a desire to set forth the political doctrines of the United States in opposition to those of the Alliance, these are the factors that bulked largest in his thought. Economic considerations there may have been in the background. But it was a profound political antagonism that gave force to the action which he advocated in the councils of President Monroe.

With the President himself, this antagonism was even more keenly felt. The letter to Jefferson, written early in June, seems to express his point of view pretty accurately. He was anxious to strike a blow for liberty, and the situation in the fall of 1823 offered him an excellent opportunity. To this must be added the fact that Monroe, like Calhoun, feared that an assault upon the liberties of the Spanish Americans would be dangerous to the safety of the United States itself. It was these considerations, beyond a doubt, that sharpened his pen as he wrote the declaration of December 2.

Monroe's decision, it may fairly be contended, took a measurable amount of courage. This has sometimes been questioned on the ground that the warning to Europe was launched in the certainty that the greatest naval power in the world stood behind it. But in reality, though British coöperation in maintaining the principles of the message might be assumed, it could not be regarded as beyond all question. There was always the possibility that Great Britain would play a double game, negotiating with both sides, accommodating her policy, as Adams phrased it, to "those distributions of power, and partitions of territory which have for the last half century been the ultima ratio of all European political arrangements." [34] There was, indeed, something suspicious in the way in which Canning had handled the whole matter. The President himself, and Richard Rush, as well as Adams, were

[34] W. C. Ford, "John Quincy Adams and the Monroe Doctrine," *Am. Hist. Rev.*, (Oct., 1902), viii, 47.

quick to question his motives.[35]  Calhoun, too, remarked upon the circumstance that the British minister had not confided to Rush the grounds for his suspicions with regard to intervention.  To cap all this, in September the overtures of Canning, as the cabinet knew, had suddenly ceased.  Such behavior on the part of the British Foreign Secretary was bound to be disquieting.  From the standpoint of Monroe and his advisers, therefore, the message, it may reasonably be contended, was not a mere *brutum fulmen*, launched in the secure knowledge that it would be made good by the British navy.  It was a serious attempt to deal with a really threatening diplomatic situation, one which Monroe regarded as portentous, one which even the cooler Adams could not regard as of light importance.

Of course, as Adams pointed out in the cabinet debates, the Executive could not commit the country to war, and might take shelter behind that fact, if circumstances dictated such action.  But to do so, after so vigorous a pronouncement, would have been neither easy nor dignified.  There was a measure of hazard, a measure of courage, in the President's decision.

[35] Rush wrote: "I am bound to own, that I shall not be able to avoid, at bottom, some distrust of the motives of all such advances to me, whether directly or indirectly, by this government, at this particular juncture of the world. . . . The estimate which I have formed of the genius of this government, as well as of the characters who direct, or who influence, all its operations, would lead me to fear that we are not as yet likely to witness any very material changes in the part which Britain has acted in the world for the past fifty years, when the cause of freedom has been at stake; the part which she acted in 1774 in America, which she has since acted in Europe, and is now acting in Ireland.  I shall therefore find it hard to keep from my mind the suspicion that the approaches of her ministers to me at this portentous juncture for a concert of policy which they have not heretofore courted with the United States, are bottomed on their own calculations." Quoted in *Mass. Hist. Soc. Proc.*, 2d series, xv, 420 ff.  Monroe told Adams that the British government "were in a dilemma between their anti-Jacobin policy, the dread of their internal reformers, which made them sympathize with the Holy Allies, and the necessities of their commerce and revenue, with the pressure of their debts and taxes, which compelled them to side with South American independence for the sake of South American trade.  He believed they must ultimately take this side, but if we should shock and alarm them upon the political side of the question, and the Holy Allies could hold out to them anything to appease the craving of their commercial and fiscal interest, they might go back to the allies — as Portugal has gone back — insignificant and despised, but leaving us in the lurch, with all Europe against us." Adams, *Memoirs*, vi, 203.

So seriously, in fact, did Monroe take the situation, that he may, at the last moment, have wavered a little at the heavy responsibility that he was assuming. According to the journal of William Plumer, Jr., a few days before the actual sending of the message the President expressed to Adams his "doubts about that part of it which related to the interference of the Holy Alliance with Spanish America," and "said he believed it had better be omitted, & asked him if he did not think so, too? Adams replied, 'You have my sentiments on the subject already, & I see no reason to alter them.' 'Well,' said the President, 'it is written, & I will not change it now.'" [36]

This interesting anecdote certainly ought not to be taken too literally. Plumer was a personal supporter of the Secretary of State. He got his information from Adams himself, and Adams was not the most objective person in the world in describing the events around him. That Monroe seriously proposed to strike out the paragraphs on South America it is not easy to believe. But that he hesitated a little before taking the decisive step of sending the message is entirely possible.[37]

But, none the less, the paragraphs stood, and on December 2 were made known to the Congress and the people of the United States. Often as they have been quoted, they deserve requotation, since they form the very centre around which this study revolves.

It was stated at the commencement of the last session [begin the relevant passages of the message] that a great effort was then making in Spain and Portugal to improve the condition of the people of those countries, and that it appeared to be conducted with extraordinary moderation. It need scarcely be remarked that the result has been, so far, very different from what was then anticipated. Of events in that quarter of the globe, with which we have so much intercourse and from which we derive our origin, we have always been anxious and interested spectators. The citizens of the United States cherish sentiments the most friendly in favor of the liberty and happiness of their fellow-men on that side of the Atlantic. In the wars of the European powers in matters relating to themselves we have never taken

---

[36] *Pennsylvania Magazine of History*, vi (1882), 358.

[37] London. P. R. O., F. O., America, vol. 177, no. 25, Dec. 1, 1823. "I judged from Mr. Adams' expressions that the President felt a little nervous in making his final decision on what the Secretary of State characterized as the most delicate and important measure of his administration," writes Addington.

any part, nor does it comport with our policy so to do. It is only when our rights are invaded or seriously menaced that we resent injuries or make preparation for our defense. With the movements in this hemisphere we are, of necessity, more immediately connected, and by causes which must be obvious to all enlightened and impartial observers. The political system of the allied powers is essentially different in this respect from that of America. This difference proceeds from that which exists in their respective Governments; and to the defense of our own, which has been achieved by the loss of so much blood and treasure, and matured by the wisdom of their most enlightened citizens, and under which we have enjoyed unexampled felicity, this whole nation is devoted. We owe it, therefore, to candor, and to the amicable relations existing between the United States and those powers, to declare that we should consider any attempt on their part to extend their system to any portion of this hemisphere as dangerous to our peace and safety. With the existing colonies or dependencies of any European power we have not interfered and shall not interfere. But with the Governments who have declared their independence and maintained it, and whose independence we have, on great consideration and on just principles, acknowledged, we could not view any interposition for the purpose of oppressing them, or controlling in any other manner their destiny, by any European power, in any other light than as the manifestation of an unfriendly disposition toward the United States. In the war between these new Governments and Spain we declared our neutrality at the time of their recognition, and to this we have adhered and shall continue to adhere, provided no change shall occur which, in the judgment of the competent authorities of this Government, shall make a corresponding change on the part of the United States indispensable to their security.

The late events in Spain and Portugal show that Europe is still unsettled. Of this important fact no stronger proof can be adduced than that the allied powers should have thought it proper, on any principle satisfactory to themselves, to have interposed by force in the internal concerns of Spain. To what extent such interposition may be carried, on the same principle, is a question in which all independent powers whose governments differ from theirs are interested, even those most remote, and surely none more so than the United States. Our policy in regard to Europe, which was adopted at an early stage of the wars which have so long agitated that quarter of the globe, nevertheless remains the same, which is, not to interfere in the internal concerns of any of its powers; to consider the government *de facto* as the legitimate government for us; to cultivate friendly relations with it, and to preserve those relations by a frank, firm, and manly policy, meeting, in all instances, the just claims of every power, submitting to injuries from none. But in regard to those continents, circumstances are eminently and conspicuously different. It is impossible that the allied powers should extend their political system to any portion of either continent without endangering our peace and happiness; nor can anyone believe that our southern brethren, if left to themselves, would adopt it of their own accord. It is equally impossible, therefore, that we should behold such interposition, in any form, with indifference. If we look to the comparative strength and resources of

Spain and those new Governments, and their distance from each other, it must be obvious that she can never subdue them. It is still the true policy of the United States to leave the parties to themselves, in the hope that other powers will pursue the same course.

The well-known paragraphs just quoted seem rather the expression of a faith than a closely reasoned justification of American opposition to intervention in the New World. Monroe's belief in the superiority of American institutions, his conviction that the extension of European dominion would be dangerous to our peace and safety — these are propositions that are hardly capable of rigorous demonstration. Perhaps their strength lies in just that fact. Yet there is, I think, one thing more to be said for them. In resting his opposition to European intermeddling in Spanish America on the "peace and safety" of the United States, the President was taking up a strong position from the legal and moral point of view. For he was basing American policy on the right of self-preservation, a right that is and always has been recognized as fundamental in international law. If in very truth the interposition of the Holy Alliance in South America imperilled the peace and safety of the United States, then the President's right to protest against it was obvious. Nor was it to be expected that as to the reality of the peril he would accept the conclusions of European statesmen. He stood secure in his own conviction and on his own ground.

The practical wisdom and the immediate effectiveness of his declaration are matters that will become clearer as this narrative proceeds. But before passing to a study of the aftermath of the Doctrine, it is necessary to study certain documents which run parallel with the message.

The first is the answer to the Russian communication of November 16, an answer which did directly what the message did indirectly, fully apprising Alexander of the viewpoint of the United States.[38] The question of preparing such an answer had come up

[38] Tuyll's earlier communication of October 16 had already been answered both verbally and in writing. The Secretary of State's note in reply to it had been toned down by the President until it had become, in Adams's view, the "tamest of all state papers." But, on the presentation of the note, and again with the authorization of the President on November 8, Adams had the satisfaction of declaring to

very early in the discussions of the cabinet. Even before Tuyll's note of December 16 hrd been sent, Adams had been of the opinion, in the meeting of November 7, that "we ought to avow our principles explicitly to Russia and France." On November 21 he pressed the point home.

My purpose would be [he explained], in a moderate and conciliatory manner, but with a firm and determined spirit, to declare our dissent from the principles avowed in those [the Russian] communications; to assert those upon which our own Government is founded, and, while disclaiming all intention of attempting to propagate them by force, and all interference with the political affairs of Europe, to declare our expectation and hope that the European powers will equally abstain from the attempt to spread their principles in the American hemisphere, or to subjugate by force any part of these continents to their will.[39]

The American Secretary of State was obviously eager to exercise his dialectical and diplomatic skill upon the Tsar and his representative. The President approved his desires, and Adams set about the preparation of a state paper which was certainly one of the most remarkable he ever penned, and which parallels the language of the Monroe message.

The dispatch, in the form in which it was first drawn up, began with an exposition of the principles of the United States. Those principles, Adams declared, were as follows:

1 that the Institution of Government to be lawful must be pacific, that is, founded upon the consent, and by the agreement of those that are governed; and 2 that each nation is exclusively the judge of the Government best suited to itself, and that no other Nation can justly interfere by force to impose a different Government upon it.

The United States, Adams continued, recognized in other nations the right which they claim and exercise for themselves, of establishing and modifying their own governments. It had never had any quarrel with monarchical governments as such, or any desire to interfere or intermeddle in the policy of Europe. With regard to the Spanish-American colonies it had long pursued a policy of neutrality, and had recognized the new governments only when

the Russian minister that the continuance of American neutrality in the colonial struggle was based on "the observance of a like neutrality by the European Powers in the same contest." See W. C. Ford's presentation of this episode in full in *Mass. Hist. Soc. Proc.*, 2d series, xv, especially pp. 373-436.

[39] Adams, *Memoirs*, vi, 194.

no rational doubt could remain that the dominion of Spain was irrevocably lost. The neutrality which they had observed, they expected from others.

> With regard to the communications of the Tsar [Adams wrote], the President indulges the hope that they are not intended either to mark an era of change in the friendly disposition of the Emperor towards the United States or of hostility to the principles upon which their Governments are founded; or of deviation from the system of neutrality hitherto observed by him and his allies, in the contest between Spain and America.

The Secretary of State then proceeded to answer the two communications of the Tsar: the note of October 16 in which Alexander expressed his determination not to receive agents from the new states, and in which he expressed the hope that the United States would remain neutral, and the note transmitted a month later, in which the principles of the Alliance with regard to Spain were so fully developed. In reply to the first, Adams restated a viewpoint already expressed to Tuyll on October 16 and November 8, to the effect that American neutrality was based upon a like neutrality on the part of the allies.[40] In reply to the second he expressed himself at greater length, as follows:

> So far as it [i.e., the note transmitted on November 16] relates to the affairs of Spain and Portugal, the only remark which it is thought necessary to make, is of the great satisfaction with which the President has noticed *that* paragraph, which contains the frank and solemn admission that "*the undertaking of the Allies yet demands a last Apology to the eyes of Europe.*" In the general declarations that the allied Monarchs will never compound, and never will even treat with the *Revolution* and that their policy has only for its object by *forcible* interposition to guaranty the tranquillity of *all the States of which the civilized world is composed*, the President wishes to perceive sentiments, the application of which is limited, and intended in their results to be limited to the Affairs of Europe,

and, furthermore,

> that the United States of America, and their Government, could not see with indifference, the forcible interposition of any European Power, other than Spain, either to restore the dominion of Spain over her emancipated Colonies in America, or to establish Monarchical Governments in those Countries, or to transfer any of the possessions heretofore or yet subject to Spain in the American Hemisphere, to any other European Power.[41]

---

[40] See note 38, above.

[41] This note is published in full in W. C. Ford's "John Quincy Adams and the Monroe Doctrine," II, in *Am. Hist. Rev.* (Oct., 1902), viii, 43 f.

There are many aspects of this remarkable document which may well command the attention of the historian. In the first place, it may be observed, it reveals some of the natural defects of the Adams manner. The sarcastic reference to the Tsar's allusion to the intervention in Spain, and the didactic exposition of principles with which it begins, are a little revealing of the limitations of the Secretary of State. He had a masterly vigor, and a genuine directness of manner; in many respects he knew how to phrase what he had to say rather better than his chief; but he was, perhaps, a little careless of the diplomatic amenities.

So, at any rate, Monroe and his advisers seem to have thought. Calhoun, having heard the Adams masterpiece in the cabinet meeting of November 25, was even doubtful as to whether it would be proper to deliver *any* such paper to the Russian minister. He thought it would be sufficient to deliver to Tuyll a copy of the President's message.

> Foreign powers might not feel themselves bound to notice what was said in that. It was like a family talking over subjects interesting to them by the fireside among themselves. Many things might be said there without offence, even if a stranger should come among them and overhear the conversation, which would be offensive if they went to his house to say them.[42]

A proposal so prompted by weakness was rejected by the rest of the cabinet. Wirt and Southard came to the aid of Adams.[43] As for the Secretary of State himself, his sturdy American gorge rose, and he expressed himself with such force and eloquence as to reduce Calhoun to silence. But, though he had the satisfaction of seeing his communication approved in principle, he had to listen to much criticism of its details. Wirt, the Attorney General, objected to the first paragraph as "a hornet of a paragraph,"[44] and the President expressed the fear that the republicanism of the dispatch might "indispose the British Government to a cordial concert of operations with us."[45] The objections raised in the cabinet meeting of November 25 were renewed next day, and Calhoun again took up the matter, censuring what he called the "ostentatious display of republican *contrasted* with

[42] Adams, *Memoirs*, vi, 200.    [43] *Ibid.*, pp. 200 f.
[44] *Ibid.*, pp. 201 ff.    [45] *Ibid.*, p. 203.

monarchical principles, always showing the superiority of the former." [46] At all this criticism Adams was deeply perturbed. The first paragraph, which called forth so much comment, he regarded as the cream of his paper. With true New England spirit he clung to such "a distinct avowal of principle" as "absolutely required." [47] The views which he expressed in the cabinet meeting he reiterated to the President in a private interview of November 27. [48]

None the less, the objectionable paragraphs were stricken from the dispatch before it was read to Tuyll. The President treated Adams with the greatest tact with regard to the whole problem. He did not insist on the elimination of the obnoxious sections of the dispatch; he even consented to their inclusion on account of the weight which the Secretary attached to them. [49] But he urged the great importance of unanimity in such a crisis, and reiterated his apprehensions with regard to the language used as "a direct attack" upon the Holy Alliance. [50] Adams took the advice of his chief, and the homily on republican principles was never read to the Russian minister.

The episode is not, perhaps, of the first importance. But it has considerable interest as illustrating the relations between the President and his Secretary of State. John Quincy Adams was by temperament confident of his own judgment, and scornful of that of others. But he accepted and apparently respected the point of view expressed by his chief with regard to the most important diplomatic document of his administration. The notion of a flabby and bewildered chief executive being led by the nose by his stronger-minded associate is a notion which hardly does justice to James Monroe. Not a towering personality in the sense in which we love to think of the figures of history, Monroe played a worthy and not inconspicuous rôle in the grave debates and momentous decisions of the autumn of 1823. His personal influence was very real indeed.

It is interesting to note that the dispatch to Tuyll was not paralleled by a similar communication to any other power. The

---

[46] Adams, *Memoirs*, vi, 206.    [47] *Ibid.*, p. 209.    [48] *Ibid.*, p. 211 f.
[49] *Ibid.*, p. 213.    [50] *Ibid.*

danger, if it existed at all, was likely to be fully as great from France as from Russia. Yet Adams never proposed a curtain lecture for the ministers of Louis XVIII. Indeed, he acted with great restraint. It is a little amusing, after reading the vigorous language of the communication to the Russian minister, to turn to the instructions to Brown, the new envoy to France, and find the following:

> The sentiments expressed in the message of the President of the United States to the Congress at the commencement of the present session will serve as guides to your conduct on this subject [i.e., Spanish America]. It is hoped that the European Continental Alliance will ultimately perceive the inexpediency of their interference in the contest between Spain and South America; but, while manifesting on proper occasions the disposition of this country concerning it, you will avoid any measure by which the Government might be prematurely implicated in it, and observing with vigilant attention the progress of the Allies with regard to their general policy, will report as frequently as may be convenient the result of your observations.[51]

Not even definite instructions to make known the views of the United States! Of course it is true that France had given no direct occasion for such a statement as was addressed to Tuyll. There was nothing to which to tie a diplomatic communication of the same character as that given the Russian minister. And yet, even so, it must be admitted that there is a striking contrast between the cautious sentences just quoted and the militant language addressed to the representative of the Tsar.

But if the note to Tuyll stands alone so far as an American communication to the Holy Allies is concerned, it is not the only important state paper that John Quincy Adams had to frame in those tense November days of 1823. What return was to be made to the overtures of Canning? This was a question that demanded the serious consideration, not only of the Secretary of State, but of the President himself, and all his advisers.

Monroe's first impulse, indeed, was to accept the British overtures unqualifiedly. Shortly after the receipt of the Rush dispatches, and during Adams's absence from Washington, the President sent the correspondence, along with a letter of his own, to the venerable Jefferson. He was, he wrote, "sensible of the

---

[51] Washington. State Department. Instructions to Ministers; Dec. 12, 1823.

extent, and difficulty of the question." He was, of course, well
aware that acceptance might mean entanglement, and of the
arguments against such entanglement. But, he asked,

if a case can exist, in which a sound maxim may, and ought to be departed
from, is not the present instance precisely that case? . . . My own impression
is that we ought to meet the proposal of the British gov^t, and to make it
known, that we would view an interference on the part of the European
powers, and especially an attack on the Colonies, by them, as an attack on
ourselves, presuming that if they succeeded with them, they would extend
it to us.[52]

Mr. Jefferson replied to the President's queries in a well-known
and often quoted letter.

Our first and fundamental maxim [he declared] should be, never to en-
tangle ourselves in the broils of Europe. Our second, never to suffer Europe
to intermeddle with cis-Atlantic affairs. America, North and South, has a
set of interests distinct from those of Europe, and peculiarly her own. She
should therefore have a system of her own, separate and apart from that of
Europe. . . . Great Britain is the nation which can do us the most harm of
any one, or all on earth; and with her on our side we need not fear the whole
world. With her, then we should the most sedulously cherish a cordial
friendship; and nothing would tend more to knit our affections than to be
fighting once more side by side, in the same cause. Not that I would purchase even her amity at the price of taking part in her wars. But the war
in which the present proposition might engage us, should that be its consequence, is not her war, but ours. Its object is to introduce and establish the
American system, of keeping out of our land all foreign powers, of never
permitting those of Europe to interfere with the affairs of our nations. It is
to maintain our principle, not to depart from it.

Thus did Jefferson reconcile coöperation with Canning with the
notion of America for the Americans. One may or may not agree
with his reasoning. It is possible to believe that the acceptance
of Canning's overtures, however successful it might be in clos-
ing the New World to Continental Europe, would only increase
Great Britain's influence and power in South America. But,
wisely or not, the venerable ex-President spoke in favor of close
association with a European power in a matter in which he conceived the interests of the United States might be promoted by
such an association. His only objection to such a course was that
full acquiescence in the Canning proposals would tie the hands

[52] This letter is quoted in full in W. C. Ford's article, *Am. Hist. Rev.* (July, 1902),
vii, 685 f. See also Monroe, *Writings*, vi, 323 ff.

of the United States with regard to the acquisition of Cuba. But this consideration was not sufficiently powerful to alter the character of the advice which he tendered to Monroe.[53]

Madison, too, to whom, as well as to Jefferson, the President sent the Rush correspondence, was wholly in favor of accepting the British overtures.

There ought not to be any backwardness, therefore, I think, in meeting her in the way she has proposed [he wrote]. Our coöperation is due to ourselves & to the world: and whilst it must ensure success in the event of an appeal to force, it doubles the chance of success without that appeal.[54]

With such advice from the oldest, most trusted, and most experienced of his friends, it is not strange that Monroe's first inclination was to meet the advances of the British Foreign Secretary. In the cabinet, Calhoun, from the beginning of the discussions, was in favor of giving to Rush a discretionary power to join in a declaration against the interference of the Holy Allies,[55] and this view commended itself to the President.[56] It was, however, from the beginning, stoutly opposed by Adams, who was not very likely to let matters get out of his own hands, if it could be helped. The Secretary of State, like Rush, strongly distrusted the sincerity of the British overtures.

The object of Canning [he wrote in his diary under date of November 7] appears to have been to obtain some public pledge from the Government of the United States, ostensibly against the forcible interference of the Holy Alliance between Spain and South America, but really or especially against the acquisition by the United States themselves of any part of the Spanish-American possessions.[57]

Throughout the cabinet discussions, he remained the sturdy partisan of a policy which would not commit the American government too deeply, and which would make British recognition of the new states a condition antecedent to common action.[58] And

---

[53] Monroe, *Writings*, vi, 391 f.    [54] *Ibid.*, p. 394.
[55] Adams, *Memoirs*, vi, 177.    [56] *Ibid.*, p. 192.    [57] *Ibid.*, p. 177.
[58] *Ibid.*: "Mr. Calhoun inclined to giving a discretionary power to Mr. Rush, ... even if it should pledge us not to take Cuba or the province of Texas; because the power of Great Britain being greater than ours to *seize* upon them, we should get the advantage of obtaining from her the same declaration we should make ourselves."

"I thought the cases not parallel. We have no intention of seizing either Texas

in the two state papers which he drew up for Rush's guidance in the last days of November, his views were framed in this sense.[59]

But in their final drafting Monroe again played a part. In deference to his Secretary, he abandoned the idea of a discretionary power to Rush, but he modified the language of Adams, in so far as it was a flat refusal of coöperation on any other basis than British recognition of Spanish-American independence. "You will explicitly state that without this basis of Right and coöperation," the American Secretary of State had written, "we can see no foundation upon which the concurrent action of the two Governments can be harmonized."[60] So definite a commitment seemed to Monroe unnecessary. He was not willing to close the door on the possibility of coöperation. He accepted, perhaps with reluctance, the view of his adviser that, for the present, no such coöperation was desirable. But he wished the way left clear for such a course.

> Should an emergency occur in which a *joint* manifestation of opinion by the two Governments, may tend to influence the Councils of the European Allies, either in the aspect of persuasion or of admonition [read the dispatch in its final form] you will make it known to us without delay, and we shall according to the principles of our Government and in the forms prescribed by our Constitution, cheerfully join in any act, by which we may contribute to support the cause of human freedom and the Independence of the South American Nations.[61]

Thus the question of at once accepting the British overtures was virtually decided in the negative. Monroe spoke out frankly in his message to Congress, without waiting for British concur-

---

or Cuba. But the inhabitants of either or both may exercise their primitive rights, and solicit a union with us. They will certainly do no such thing with Great Britain. By joining with her, therefore, in her proposed declaration, we give her a substantial and perhaps inconvenient pledge against ourselves, and obtain nothing in return." On November 20, Adams told the President he was utterly averse to any discretionary power being given to Rush." *Ibid.*, p. 192.

[59] These two papers covered in part the same general ground. But the first was an answer to Canning's five principles stated to Rush on August 20 (see *antea*, p. 64). The second was for Rush alone, and was a franker expression of American policy, and of the American interpretation of the British overture.

[60] See original and revised text in W. C. Ford's article, "John Quincy Adams and the Monroe Doctrine," II, *Am. Hist. Rev.* (Oct., 1902), viii, 33–38.

[61] *Ibid.*, p. 38.

rence; and coöperation was made conditional on the recognition of colonial independence, or on the hypothesis of a new emergency. And yet at the same time it is highly significant to note that the idea of association with a European power was not lightly thrust aside, or entirely repudiated. The President, Jefferson, Madison, Calhoun, and Southard all leaned toward an acceptance of the British overture.[62] Even Adams, whose vigorous mind and will had much to do with the decision that was taken, would have favored coöperation on the basis of Canning's acknowledgment of colonial independence. Where American interests were concerned, the statesmen of 1823 were not averse to common action with a state of the Old World.

But what attitude would the United States assume toward a congress of European powers on the colonial problem? This question, it will be remembered, had come up in 1818, and at that time both Adams and Monroe had played with the idea of American participation. Much water had flowed under the bridge since then, and the tone was not the same in 1823. The opinion of the President and his advisers was, of course, in general against such participation,[63] though Monroe himself does not seem to have been absolutely clear on the point.[64] Yet the instructions to Rush, though taking quite a definite stand on the matter, did not absolutely exclude all possibility of common action, but, instead, made such action dependent upon the reception in the projected congress, of representatives of the new republics on an equal footing with all other powers. If, in a sense, this was the practical equivalent of a refusal, it does at the same time show that there *were* terms on which even an Adams could

[62] Even after the dispatch of the reply to Rush, however, Monroe wrote to Jefferson early in December, "And considering the crisis, it has occurred, that a special mission, of the first consideration from the country, directed to Engld. in the first instance, with power, to attend, any Congress, that may be convened, on the affrs. of So. Am: or Mexico, might have the happiest effect." Monroe, *Writings*, vi, 345.

[63] Adams, *Memoirs*, vi, 178.

[64] In the cabinet meeting of November 7, the President seemed to think that we should attend a congress only if South American independence were the object thereof, but he introduced no such qualification in his letter to Jefferson, written shortly after the publication of the message. See note 62, above.

envisage the possibility of contact with the Holy Allies themselves. Were those terms not met, the attitude of the government of the United States would be clear. There was, of course, to be no truckling to European views.

We would not sanction by our presence [wrote Adams], any meeting of European Potentates to dispose of American Republics. We shall, if such meeting should take place . . . solemnly protest against it, and against all the melancholy and calamitous consequences which may result from it.[65]

In these words the dispatch to Rush supplements the answer to Tuyll and the language of the message itself.

By December, 1823, therefore, the policy of the United States on the colonial question had, in all respects, in public message and private diplomatic correspondence alike, been accurately defined. Before taking leave, however, of this formative period in the history of the Monroe Doctrine, it may be well briefly to survey an historic controversy hitherto omitted from consideration, that is, the controversy as to its authorship. In the literal and verbal sense, of course, there is no doubt that the Doctrine was the President's. Moreover, it is not to be forgotten that it was on his initiative, very clearly, that it was decided to deal with the South American question in the forthcoming message to Congress. But, grant all this, and there remains the broader question of credit for the ideas which the message contained, for the clear line which it drew between the New World and the Old, for its emphasis on the rival political systems of Europe and America, for its militant republicanism and proscription of monarchy from the New World.[66] On this side of the matter, there

---

[65] W. C. Ford, *op. cit.*, p. 48.

[66] With regard to this last point, antagonism to monarchy, it is only fair to say that it has sometimes been maintained that the message was not directed against monarchical government; that, when the President spoke of American hostility to the extension of the European "political system" to this hemisphere, he was thinking, not of monarchy, but of the whole system of alliances, and the dogma of intervention. In support of this view, it has been pointed out that the United States recognized the royalist government of Iturbide in Mexico, and that shortly after the presidential declaration, it extended recognition to the Empire of Brazil.

There is, perhaps, something to be said for such reasoning. Nevertheless, it would be futile to deny that the question of forms of government was not much in the President's mind when he framed the message of 1823. He may not have been hostile to monarchy in the broadest sense, but he was certainly hostile to European

have been many different expressions of opinion.  Charles Sumner once wrote that George Canning was "the inventor, promoter and

monarchy of the type then existing in most of Continental Europe.  He had more than once shown his sympathy with the constitutional movements in the Old World, and had, as has already been seen, wished to condemn their repression.  In the background of the discussions of 1823, behind the fear of intervention for the re-conquest of the colonies, there lurked another idea, the fear of the establishment of monarchical governments in the New World *under European tutelage*.  As early as 1820 there had been an exposure of a French plan to set up a Bourbon prince in La Plata (for this intrigue, see Villanueva, *Bolívar y El General San Martín*[ Paris, 1912], pp. 89–160, also *postea*, pp. 107, 108), and these facts were known to Adams; in 1821, Torres, the Colombian agent in Philadelphia, had warned of a similar project to be attempted in the case of Mexico (*American State Papers, Foreign Relations*, iv, 835); and in 1822, the presence of French agents in the New World seemed to suggest that some monarchical intrigue was still being pressed from the other side of the water.  (See *postea*, p. 108.)  In his instructions to Rodney, the American minister sent out to La Plata in the spring of 1823, Adams had mentioned the project of Bourbon monarchies, to condemn it, not, of course, on theoretical grounds,— theoretical opposition to monarchy was far from the Adams temper,— but as dangerous to the interests of the United States.  (Adams, *Writings*, vii, 426–432.) It is entirely probable that the President, who closely supervised the drafting of the more important dispatches, knew of and approved this stand.

It is true that the word "system," in the parlance of 1823, might be used to describe either a form of government or a general principle of international policy. Monroe uses the word in both senses in his writings.  But that he meant the first and not the second when he used the word in the message seems clear from the whole phraseology.  In one sentence he declares his faith that "our southern brethren" will never adopt the European political system of their own accord. How can such a reference be otherwise construed than as a reference to monarchy? No one would have thought of the principles of the Holy Alliance as likely to be adopted by the new states, nor was there any chance that they would accept the doctrine of intervention, so dear to Metternich and Alexander.  The difference in systems, says the President in another place, "proceeds from that which exists in their respective governments, and to the defense of our own, which has been achieved by the loss of so much blood and treasure and matured by the wisdom of our most enlightened citizens, and under which we have enjoyed unexampled felicity, the whole nation is devoted."  How can such language be taken otherwise than as referring to the antagonism of republican and monarchical forms as the basis of distinction between the Old World and the New?  Consider, moreover, the language of Adams's note to Tuyll.  In this note, drawn up contemporaneously with the message, and intended, in Adams's language, "to correspond exactly" with it (Adams, *Memoirs*, vi, 199), the opposition to monarchical forms is expressed with absolute definiteness.  The note certainly came under the eyes of Monroe.  It was carefully examined by him.  It must have interpreted his own thought with tolerable accuracy.  In the light of it, there can be little doubt that the President did intend to ban monarchy, at least European monarchy, from the New World.  By the term "political system" he may have meant more than this; but that he meant no less may be considered incontestable.

champion" of the American pronouncement.[67]   Mr. C. L. Chandler would have us believe that it was of South American origin.[68] James Schouler would give much of the credit to Jefferson.[69] And the bitterest controversy of all has raged over the respective claims of Adams and Monroe.[70]

So far as George Canning is concerned, the case is pitifully weak. That Canning's interviews with Rush had a very great influence indeed in prompting the message of 1823 no sober historical student would be likely to deny. That both England and the United States were opposed to the reconquest of the colonies is obvious. But further than this it is impossible to go. The British Foreign Secretary suggested no presidential manifesto, and was, as will be seen, by no means overjoyed at its publication. The republican idealism of the message, the dividing line drawn between America and Europe, were bound to be as uncongenial to him as they were to the powers of the Continent. The spirit of Monroe's manifesto has little in common with the temper of Canning, save for a common hostility to the principle of intervention.   Charles Sumner's description of the British minister as "inventor, promoter and champion" of the Doctrine, is more than two thirds false. Even as regards the "promotion" of the message, it expresses only a very partial truth.

It is equally futile to seek to ascribe the message to South American influence. The case for this theory rests upon the proposals made from time to time by South American states to the United States for an alliance in defence of American liberty. Except for the very beginning of the struggle, these proposals came chiefly from Colombia, and the most important are perhaps the Torres note of 1821 [71] and the overtures of Vice-President

[67] Charles Sumner, *Prophetic Voices* (Boston, 1874), pp. 157 f.

[68] C. L. Chandler, *Inter-American Acquaintances*, 2d ed. (Sewanee, Tennessee, 1917), pp. 161–169.

[69] James Schouler, *History of the United States* (Washington, 1880–91, 5 vols.), iii, 291, note. See also the article by J. W. Richardson, "Jefferson and the Monroe Doctrine," in the *New York Evening Post* for April 12, 1923, p. 8.

[70] See W. C. Ford's article, [mentioned above]; also Reddaway, *The Monroe Doctrine*, pp. 66–86, and W. A. McCorkle, *The Personal Genesis of the Monroe Doctrine*.

[71] It is this proposal to which Chandler attaches particular importance in the work cited. *American State Papers, Foreign Relations*, iv, 834.

Santander to the American agent, Todd, in June, some two years later.[72] But no one of these proposals has any direct relationship to the cabinet meetings of the fall of 1823, nor was any of them referred to by either Adams or Monroe. The latter, indeed, may never have heard of them; and what the former thought of alliances with other American states may be gathered from his contemptuous statement confided to his diary in 1821, after an interview with the Abbé Correa, the minister from Portugal: "As to an American system, we have it — we constitute the whole of it." [73] Moreover, the dominant ideas of the message are no more characteristically South American than they are characteristically English. The doctrine of the two spheres was no established principle in the republics to the south. They were as ready to seek aid from Great Britain as from the United States.[74] And it would, of course, be absurd to trace the republican temper of Monroe's message to South America, where republicanism was of so much later growth than in the United States. Monroe certainly did not derive the general principles that dominate the message from any contact with South America. Those principles, whatever else may be said of them, were indigenous to the soil of the United States. They were no importation. That much at least is clear.

But, on the other hand, there was nothing about them that was peculiar to Monroe. Ideas are not copyright; and the most influential of them are all-pervasive. They cannot be deemed the private property of any single individual. They were in the air, and had been absorbed by the President; they had not emanated from him. They are to be found in the utterances of many different figures of the age, and of the age that preceded. Gilman, in his *James Monroe*, has collected numerous examples of the expression of the principle of an American and a European sphere of action, some of them antedating by many years Monroe's famous declaration.[75] It would be possible to make a collection of the

---

[72] See, on this subject, F. J. Urrutia, *Páginas de la historia diplomatica; los Estados Unidos de América y las Repúblicas hispanoamericanas de 1810 hasta 1830* (Bogotá, 1917), especially pp. 285–288.

[73] Adams, *Memoirs*, v, 176.　　　[74] On this point, see *postea*, Chapter VII.

[75] D. C. Gilman, *James Monroe* (Boston and New York, 1900), pp. 162–170.

same kind as regards the enunciation of the other principal doctrine of the message, that of a sturdy and militant republicanism,
and of a sense of republican solidarity. Moreover, long before the
message was penned, the two cardinal doctrines taken together
are to be found in their specific application to South America, in
the utterances of Henry Clay. His ardent faith in, and sympathy
with, South American republicanism were clearly set forth in the
great speech of March, 1818.

> We are their great example [he declared of the states of South America].
> Of us they constantly speak as of brothers having a similar origin. They
> adopt our principles, copy our institutions, and, in many instances, employ
> the very language and sentiments of our revolutionary papers.

Their incapacity for self-government Clay was ready to deny.
"It is the doctrine of thrones, that man is too ignorant to govern
himself. . . . I am strongly inclined to believe that they will, in
most, if not all parts of their country, establish free governments." [76] On the separation of the New World from the Old,
Clay, in 1820, took the loftiest possible tone, asserting the duty
of the United States, not only to exclude European influence
from the American hemisphere, but to assert its leadership over
all the new states of the south. He scorned the "deference" of
the administration to the views of foreign powers. "Let us break
these commercial and political fetters," he cried; "let us no longer
watch the nod of any European politician; let us become real and
true Americans, and place ourselves at the head of the American
system." [77] In a speech delivered at Lexington in the early summer of 1821, Clay sounded the alarm against Europe. "We owed
our exemption from peril," he declared, "to our distance from
Europe, and to the known bravery of our countrymen. But who
can say, that has observed the giddiness and intoxication of
power, how long this exemption will continue? It had seemed to
him desirable, that a sort of counterpoise to the Holy Alliance
should be formed in the two Americas in favor of national independence and liberty." [78] Words such as these clearly foreshadow
the declaration of Monroe.

---

[76] *Life and Speeches of Henry Clay*, compiled by Daniel Mallory, 4th ed. (New York, 1844, 2 vols.), i, 329 f.

[77] *Ibid.*, pp. 429 f.　　　　[78] *Niles' Register*, xx, 301.

But, on the other hand, it is impossible definitely to ascribe to them any direct influence upon the President. That Monroe was nervously aware of Clay's attitude in 1818 and 1820 is certain. That he read Clay's speeches is not unlikely. But that he consciously took over Clay's doctrines in the message is beyond proof, and beyond probability. When it comes to direct connection with the language of the message, there are only two figures of significance, besides the President, and they are Jefferson and Adams. Of the first it is not necessary to say much. As early as 1808, Jefferson had expressed his sympathies with the principle of American solidarity,[79] and the famous letter to William Short, in 1820, sets forth the same view.[80] But more important, in connection with the message, is the fact that Monroe referred the Rush correspondence to the ex-President, and received an answer in which the doctrine of the separation of the New World from the Old was laid down in the clearest terms. Such a letter may have had a part in forming the principles of the message. And yet it is to be noted that Jefferson's letter is dated October 30. It must have been in the President's hands long before the cabinet discussions of the forthcoming communication to Congress. And as late as November 22, as we have seen, Monroe had incorporated into his message a recognition of the Greeks as an independent nation, and a scathing animadversion on the allied intervention in Spain. It was only, then, when added to some other factor that the views of Jefferson affected the temper of the American manifesto.

That other factor was, of course, John Quincy Adams. Bred in diplomacy from his youth, no man had a clearer understanding than he of the American principle of the two spheres. It is to be found again and again in his writings. In the great dispatch to Middleton of July 5, 1820, in which he instructed our minister to

---

[79] "We consider their interests the same as ours, and the object of both must be to exclude all European influence in this hemisphere." *Writings of Thomas Jefferson*, edited by A. A. Lipscomb (Washington, 1903, 20 vols.), xii, 187.

[80] *Ibid.*, xv, 263. "The day is not distant, when we may formally require a meridian of partition through the ocean which separates the two hemispheres, on the hither side of which no European gun shall ever be heard, nor an American on the other; . . . and I hope no American patriot will ever lose sight of the essential policy of interdicting in the seas and territories of both Americas, the ferocious and sanguinary contests of Europe."

Russia as to the attitude of our government toward joining the
Holy Alliance, he had declared that "the European and American
political systems should be kept as separate and distinct from
each other as possible." [81] In the dispatch to Nelson of April 28,
1823, he laid it down as a maxim of the United States "to keep
themselves aloof from the political systems and contentions of
Europe." [82] In the cabinet meetings of November, as we have
seen, he strove earnestly for the sharp differentiation of the South
American question from our more remote interest in the Greeks
or in Spain. His views, if we are to believe the language of his
diary, were decisive in altering the temper of the message in this
regard. They were undoubtedly of great, perhaps one might even
say of profound, importance. It added immensely to the strength
and cogency of Monroe's manifesto that the principle of the two
spheres was introduced into it. Let Europe mind its own affairs,
and we will mind ours, was a maxim the logic of which in 1823
was not without a certain force. The President's reference to the
recognition of the Greeks, or sharp criticism of the intervention
in Spain, would, in a sense, have muddled the issue. Adams was
undoubtedly right when he urged with all his force and eloquence
that we "make an American cause, and adhere inflexibly to that."
The only possible question that can arise as to the value of the
Secretary of State's action springs from the fact that it is he on
whom we depend for the sole account of the matter. It may
be that Monroe's message, as he first drafted it, differed widely
from the copy which he showed to Adams two days later, and
which the latter pronounced quite unexceptionable. But, on the
other hand, is it not possible that Adams may have magnified a
bit his own rôle? There is no way of answering this question.
But it is worth while to suggest it. And yet, in any case, no fair-
minded commentator can deny him credit for the views which
he did express, or fail to admit that he had an important part in
shaping the declaration of 1823.

So much for the doctrine of the two spheres. When it comes to
the republicanism of the message, it must be admitted that in
some respects, at least, sympathy with a republican South

[81] Adams, *Writings*, vii, 50 f.      [82] *Ibid.*, p. 370.

America sits with a better grace upon Monroe than upon Adams. There is nothing in Adams's attitude toward the new states of South America down to 1823 that indicates a burning sympathy with them, or even much confidence in their ability to establish the free institutions of self-governing nations. His tone had consistently been one of pessimism throughout the whole period of the colonial struggle. Monroe, on the other hand, had not scrupled to express again and again in his presidential messages his sympathies with the new states; and there still remained in him something of that theoretical ardor for republican government which had made him such an embarrassing envoy to France in 1794. Sentimental attachment to and faith in republican institutions were far more in accord with his past views than with those of his Secretary of State. And yet it must be remembered that the republicanism of the message was not merely a doctrinaire sentiment. It was connected with the interests of the United States. In asserting it on this basis Monroe and Adams stood on the same ground. Adams had expressed his view, as we have seen, some months before; and the President had made it clear in the language of his message. The former, perhaps, felt this connection the more closely; but the same conception was not absent, as his choice of phrases shows, from the thought of James Monroe.

The net result of this brief examination of the much-mooted question of authorship must be to diminish the importance of the personal element in connection with the enunciation of the Monroe Doctrine. The polemic between the partisans of Adams and the partisans of Monroe is essentially a barren one. A reasonable view of all the circumstances of the message must, I think, incline the balance, which has been so heavily tipped in favor of the New Englander, back toward Monroe. The President it was who determined to treat the South American question in the message; who penned the words in which that question was discussed; who assumed responsibility for the policy enunciated. He had an effective counsellor and co-worker in his Secretary of State; and in the clear line which the message draws between the Old World and the New the President, in large part at least, probably followed Adams's views. But that he played a subordinate rôle, that he was dictated to by a stronger and more dominant personality, it is not necessary to assume. In the last analysis, the highest significance of the message does not turn upon such a question in any case. For the Monroe Doctrine derives its power and authority neither from the name of Monroe, nor from the labors of Adams, nor from the utterances of any other. Its power lies in the fact that it expressed what many men, great and humble, had thought, were thinking then, and were to think in the future. The ideas which it set forth were in the air. True or false, they were views to which the common thought of America might respond. There have been occasions, of course, when the United States has shrunk from following out those views in action, and the message of 1823 was never more flouted in practice than in the years immediately following its enunciation. Nevertheless, the American people have, again and again, found something that appealed to their deepest instincts and traditions in its language, and to this fact the words of 1823 owe their influence. A generation one hundred years removed from the debates of that time may sometimes question the validity of Monroe's principles; but it cannot deny that they expressed a viewpoint which was, and in no small degree is to-day, the viewpoint of the people of the United States themselves.

# CHAPTER IV

## WHAT EUROPE INTENDED

THE statesmen of 1823, in the deliberations which led to the famous presidential declaration, acted, as we have seen, upon the hypothesis that the liberties of South America were in grave and immediate danger from the Holy Alliance. The message was designed to prevent any such intervention by Europe in the affairs of the New World. Because it was *designed* for this purpose, it has often been confidently assumed that it did actually prevent the reconquest of the colonies, and this interpretation of its influence has generally prevailed in historical discussion. It is an interpretation fostered by the not impartial testimony of contemporary American diplomats and statesmen, and by the enthusiastic language of European liberals.[1] It is an interpretation which is gratifying to American national pride. But is it an interpretation wholly in accord with the facts? Were the dangers which threatened the new states in 1823, at the time that Monroe enunciated his famous declaration, as serious as has been generally assumed? What did Europe really intend? How far did she take into account the purpose and point of view of the United States? How far did the trend of affairs in 1823, the actual facts of the matter, justify the solemn warning of the American President? These are all questions of a deep historic interest, and they are questions which can be answered only by an analysis of the policy of the various members of the Holy Alliance. It will be convenient to discuss the standpoint of each of these powers in turn, rather than to consider them collectively, for at no time in 1823 can there be said to have been a general policy, agreed upon by all of them, and bringing into unity and harmony their separate points of view.

[1] See Chapter V, "The Reception of the Message."

The Continental state which had the greatest stake in the colonial question was undoubtedly France.[2] Her policy, broadly stated, was, from a very early period, an attempt to reconcile conflicting interests and conflicting points of view. On the one hand, prevailing political dogmas, and the close association of France with Russia, made it desirable to pursue a course of action entirely favorable to the pretensions of Ferdinand VII. On the other hand, the interests of French commerce, far more important than has generally been realized, created cogent reasons for a line of conduct more sympathetic with the insurgents of the New World, and ultimately leading to the recognition of the independence of the new states.[3] Caught between the political pressure of the merchants and the theoretical devotion of the Ultras, French ministers found it extremely difficult to plot a course of action.

The policy of the Richelieu ministry (1815–18) was, in the main, favorable to the point of view of the traders. A strict neutrality was maintained in the colonial struggle; and at Madrid the efforts of France were directed toward a peaceful settlement of the South American question, rather than toward encouraging Ferdinand in any dreams of reconquest of his dominions. By 1819 the first of a series of agents had been sent out to the New World,[4] while the commander of the French squadron in the Antilles maintained relations with the insurgents which were not without their value in the extension of French commerce. France, as the Duc de Richelieu declared to the Marquis d'Osmond, did not wish to allow Great Britain to possess herself exclusively of the trade of those rich countries.[5]

[2] For an interesting analysis of French policy, not wholly in accord with the views expressed in the text, see the article by Mr. Harold Temperley in *Eng. Hist. Rev.*, xi (1925), 34–53, entitled "French Designs on Spanish America in 1820–5." Mr. Temperley takes the danger from France more seriously than I am inclined to do. For the period prior to the Monroe Doctrine, he brings forward certain data to prove his point, data which receive, for the most part, consideration in the body of this chapter. But he overlooks, in my judgment, most important countervailing considerations. See *postea*, pp. 112–115, 119–120. For French policy in 1824 and 1825, see Chapter VII.

[3] Christian Schefer, *La France moderne et le problème colonial* (Paris, 1907), pp. 229–236.

[4] C. A. Villanueva, *Fernando VII y los Nuevos Estados* (Paris, 1912), p. 180.

[5] Schefer, *op. cit.*, p. 230.

But the interests of the merchants had somehow to be reconciled with the principles of legitimacy, and it is with the Richelieu ministry, too, that there begins the discussion of projects for the foundation of independent Bourbon monarchies in the New World.[6] This idea has a large importance in the development of French policy. It is, indeed, the *ignis fatuus* which France always pursued in the colonial problem. It crops up persistently again and again. It explains and illuminates the whole trend of her diplomatic action. The principle which underlay it was very simple. Princes of the Spanish royal family were to be sent to the New World, and given wide powers of government, amounting almost to independent sovereignty. The rebellious subjects of Ferdinand, it was confidently expected, would willingly accept such an arrangement. The colonial dispute might thus be brought to a happy conclusion, so far as Spain was concerned, while the interests of the trading nations might be secured by opening the commerce of the new states to the ships of all the world.

The idea of independent Bourbon monarchies in the New World is one that was mooted even in the earliest stages of the revolution.[7] But so far as French interest in such a project is concerned, the first mention of the idea is to be found in a note of the French consul at Baltimore, who suggested it to the minister at Washington, Baron Hyde de Neuville.[8] De Neuville found it attractive,[9] and in his turn urged it upon the Duc de Richelieu. The establishment of two constitutional monarchies in Mexico and La Plata would, he thought, suppress insurrection in the other colonies, "stifle the republican spirit," and prevent the domination of Washington and London in the affairs of Spanish America.[10]

The phrase, "stifle the republican spirit," is an interesting one, and suggests one of the aspects of the colonial question which inevitably held a place in the deliberations of Europe. The statesmen of the Old World could hardly fail to view the institutions of

[6] C. A. Villanueva, *Bolívar y el General San Martín*, p. 63.
[7] *Ibid.*, pp. 1–50.
[8] Paris. Aff. Étr., Corr. Pol., États-Unis, vol. 73, Oct. 2, 1816.
[9] *Ibid.*, vol. 74, May 14, 1817.
[10] *Ibid.*

the New with distrust and dread. The antagonism between the rule of the people and the rights of sovereigns was bound to influence their attitude. They regarded the revolutionary movements in America from much the same angle as that from which European conservatives have often regarded recent events in Russia; in the same way they feared the contagion of vicious principles; in the same spirit they sought to undermine the new philosophy. Whether or not there was any danger of intervention in the colonies in 1823, it cannot be denied that a clear hostility to American institutions was a factor in the policy of the Continental powers. The project of Bourbon monarchies was, from the first, an expression of this hostility, as well as of the desire for a compromise between legitimacy and commercial interest.

The Duc de Richelieu seems to have thought well of de Neuville's suggestion, and to have begun very soon to urge it upon Spain.[11] But, at the Congress of Aix, in the fall of 1818, though the project was outlined in detail in the instructions to the French plenipotentiaries,[12] it was not really brought forward for discussion. In the deliberations which took place there, France played second fiddle to Russia, and the views of Alexander I were set on the restoration of Spanish sovereignty. The French ministers seem to have given their cordial support to the Tsar, though they were not, of course, successful in securing action of any kind.[13]

In 1819, however, the project of Bourbon monarchies again appears, indeed approaches nearer to fruition than at any other time. Through a certain Colonel Le Moyne, the Marquis d'Osmond, the French ambassador at London, established relations with the Argentine government, and especially with Pueyrredón, then the Director of the United Provinces.[14] The project of Bourbon monarchies was brought forward, and in the fall of 1818 an Argentine agent, Gomez, was sent to Paris to enter upon negotiations. During the year the project was actively discussed on

---

[11] Paris. Aff. Étr., Méms. et Docs., Amérique, vol. 34, Aug. 6, 1818.

[12] Polovtsov, *Correspondance des ambassadeurs*, ii, 820–830.

[13] See my article, "Russia and the Spanish Colonies, 1817–1818," in *Am. Hist. Rev.* (July, 1923), xxviii, 667 f.

[14] The whole story of this episode is told with a wealth of documentation in Villanueva, *Bolívar y el General San Martín*, pp. 89–160.

both sides of the Atlantic. There were, however, a good many difficulties in the way of its execution. Gomez was instructed to propose as the sovereign of La Plata, not a Spanish Bourbon, but the Duc d'Orléans. The French ministers, on the other hand, though perhaps tempted by such an offer, did not dare accept it. It would surely have met with opposition in England, and the Tsar, when sounded, showed himself entirely hostile to the whole idea. In the Argentine itself, though the congress called together in October accepted the project in principle, it hedged its acceptance about with so many conditions as to make it impracticable. The upshot of long discussions was the collapse of the plan, and its exposure in 1820 through a revolution in Buenos Aires which brought the anti-monarchical party into power. A diplomatic crisis with England followed. Castlereagh demanded and received explanations. France was not only frustrated, but more or less humiliated. That after these events the project of Bourbon monarchies showed a continued vitality is evidence of the strength of the legitimist principle in the formulation of French policy.

But, along with these developments, there is to be noticed a steadily increasing interest in the opening of trade with South America, backed by the pressure of the commercial classes. The first of a series of agents had been sent out, as we have seen, in 1819. In 1821, during the second Richelieu ministry, other agents followed,[15] with instructions to encourage the development of trade. And in 1822, when Jean de Villèle became prime minister, the economic interest found a spokesman and supporter at the very head of the government. Villèle, who was to hold office throughout the crucial days of 1823 and 1824, was of all reactionaries the most practical, and the least given to dogma. Commerce and finance held the first place in his mind. The extension of the trading interests of France was with him no minor or unimportant consideration, but a matter of deep significance. His attitude toward the Spanish colonies was consistently based on the hope of economic advantage, and of the knitting up of trade relations with the provinces of the New World.

[15] Villanueva, *Fernando VII y los Nuevos Estados*, pp. 181 f.

Villèle took office in the winter of 1822, at a time when Spain was in revolution, and when, in France, there was a rising clamor from the Ultras for intervention in the Peninsula, in behalf of Ferdinand. But the Prime Minister himself had other views and ambitions. When the Congress of Verona met in the autumn, he hoped that it might find a way to deal, not with the Spanish, but with the colonial, problem. And the course which, in letter after letter, he urged on the principal French plenipotentiary, the Duc de Montmorency, was, first, an attempt at mediation between the insurgents and the mother country, and, if this failed, the actual recognition of the new states wherever they had made good their claim to independence.[16] At Verona, however, there was very little sympathy among the Continental powers for the viewpoint of the French Prime Minister.[17] Alexander was eager for action in Spain itself, and even talked of marching an army across Europe to the relief of Ferdinand. Montmorency and Chateaubriand, the two French representatives, were themselves far from complete accord with their chief. Both were aware of the interests of French commerce in recognition,[18] and at an earlier date both had been willing to take them into consideration in the formation of French policy. But in the atmosphere of the Congress, both forgot such matters in a common desire to intervene in Spain, and in respect for the views of the Tsar. South American affairs, therefore, figured only at the fag end of the Congress, and then they were brought forward, not by France, but by England. The Duke of Wellington presented a long memorandum setting forth the necessity of a *de facto* recognition of the new governments in the interests of British commerce, and inviting an exchange of views.[19] The duty of answering this com-

[16] Jean, Comte de Villèle, *Mémoires et correspondance* (Paris, 1888–90, 5 vols.)' iii, 69 f., 99, 108, 115, 122.

[17] *Ibid.*, pp. 108, 142 f., 167.

[18] Chateaubriand, when ambassador in London in the spring of 1822, alluding to a rumor of the recognition of Colombia by England, wrote to Villèle as follows: "You will sooner or later be forced to do the same thing, and in that case everything is to be gained by acting quickly" (*Ibid.*, p. 25). Montmorency, just after news of recognition by the United States, wrote in much the same strain to Madrid. (Paris. Aff. Étr., Corr. Pol., Espagne, vol. 714, May 7, 1822).

[19] Wellington, *Despatches*, i, 386 ff.

munication, on behalf of France, fell to the Vicomte de Chateau-briand.

Chateaubriand was, on his return from Verona, soon to be called to the post of foreign minister. During 1823 and early in 1824, or, in other words, during the crucial period in the development of the colonial question, he was the director of the foreign policy of France. As such, his character deserves a word of explanation. In the field of literature he was, no doubt, one of the foremost Frenchmen of his time, the author, in the *Génie du Christianisme*, of one of the great books of the epoch. But the genius of Christianity is not the genius of diplomacy! As a diplomat Chateaubriand was fanciful and irresolute, easily played upon by those around him, prudent and rash by turns. At Verona the part he played was not a happy one. In common with the Duc de Montmorency, he went far to commit France to a policy of intervention in Spain, a venture sure to antagonize Great Britain, and to arouse the suspicions of Canning. And in the field of colonial affairs he was no less maladroit. For in answer to Wellington's memorandum on the South American question he responded only with vague postponements of what was becoming, for England, an increasingly pressing matter, and laid down the unfortunate principle that "a general measure, taken in common by the several cabinets of Europe, would be the most desirable." [20] By the assumption of such a position France was doubly bound to the chariot wheels of the Continental powers, pushed on toward a fruitless enterprise of intervention in Spain, and more or less committed to common action with them in the affairs of the New World.

The trend of events at Verona was, of course, far from agreeable to Jean de Villèle. Largely with the colonial problem in view, he still resisted, for a time, at least, the rising tide of opinion among the Ultras in behalf of interference in the Peninsula. And when, in the spring of 1823, he found himself forced to act, and dispatch the armies of France across the Pyrenees, he still gave much of his thought to the South American question, and strove to de-

[20] This note is published in René de Chateaubriand, *Congrès de Vérone* (Leipzig, 1838, 2 vols.), i, 64 f.

velop a practicable and reasonable policy against the day when the work of restoring Ferdinand should have been accomplished, and France made free to turn her energies to projects more productive of real benefit. The policy to which he turned was the familiar compromise between legitimacy and commerce, the establishment of Bourbon monarchies on the other side of the Atlantic.

The project of Bourbon monarchies, though temporarily discredited in 1819, had by no means lost its charm for French statesmanship. It was brought forward again in 1821;[21] the Duc de Montmorency suggested it with especial emphasis in May, 1822, when the recognition of the colonies of the United States became known;[22] and Villèle mentions it in his correspondence of the fall of the same year.[23] For its revival in 1823, the credit was to be taken at a later date by Villèle's Foreign Minister, Chateaubriand.[24] It may be that it was really he who first brought it forward again. But Chateaubriand is the worst of all witnesses in matters that concerned himself. His monumental egotism blinded him not only to his own deficiencies, but to the ideas and contributions of others. Certainly, if one is to measure interest in the project of Bourbon monarchies by the number and character of the references to it in the summer of 1823, one is likely to come to the conviction that the rôle of the Foreign Secretary was a subordinate one, and that Villèle himself had the principal part in formulating French policy in the colonial question, pressing it on his colleagues, and securing its adoption by the whole cabinet. At any rate, as early as July 5, 1823, important decisions were taken with regard to South America in the French Council of State. These decisions the Prime Minister recalls in his *Mémoires*. After the establishment of Ferdinand upon his throne, Infantes were to be sent out to the New World, one to Mexico, one to La Plata, one to Chile and Peru. The aid of the French fleet and army might be given in consolidating their power. The new monarchies thus founded were to be opened to the commerce of the world, with a preference of 10 per cent in favor of Spain.[25]

---

[21] Paris. Aff. Étr., Corr. Pol., Espagne, vol. 714, Nov. 19, 1821.
[22] *Ibid.*, May 8, 1822.          [23] Villèle, *op. cit.*, iii, 70.
[24] Chateaubriand, *Congrès de Vérone*, i, 65.
[25] Villèle, *op. cit.*, iv, 190 f. See also pp. 188 f., 200.

This plan, which may be taken to represent French policy in the summer of 1823, deserves examination. It involved — and of this there can be little doubt — the granting of armed aid to Spain. Knit up with the project of Bourbon monarchies there had always been the suggestion that France might actively aid in its execution. The suggestion of naval aid had been made several times in the course of discussions between Madrid and Paris on the colonial question. Richelieu,[26] Pasquier,[27] and Montmorency had all mentioned such a possibility.[28] It was, then, no novelty when brought forward in 1823.

But the extent of the aid which Villèle intended to offer must not be exaggerated. The truth is that the French Premier, with an optimism that betrays the happiest ignorance of the facts, believed that, if force were needed at all, it would be needed only in a very minor degree. He would never have committed himself to great expenditures in money or men. He believed that a "few troops and a little money"[29] would suffice. He spoke of "detachments,"[30] not great expeditions.

In all those countries [he wrote to the Duc d'Angoulême] there exist armed partisans of the mother-country; if the Infantes did not find kingdoms already reduced to submission, they would at least find kingdoms easy to conquer with the aid of our marine and our credit.[31]

Very clearly, he underestimated the difficulties in the way of any such enterprise as he proposed. Otherwise he would probably not have proposed it. The man who had only with the utmost reluctance embarked upon intervention in Spain, to put down revolution at the very doors of France, was hardly likely to favor lavish expenditure of men and money across thousands of miles of intervening ocean to restore legitimist principles in the New World. The scheme which he brought forward was no royalist crusade, but a compromise measure, dictated by French commercial interest as much as by a devotion to legitimacy. It was not a proposal for the resubjugation of the colonies. "In vain," wrote the

[26] Seville. Archivo General de las Indias, Estado, América en General, legajo 4 p. 63.
[27] Paris. Aff. Étr., Corr. Pol., Espagne, vol. 714, Nov. 19, 1821.
[28] Seville. Archivo General, Estado, América en General, legajo 4, p. 63.
[29] Villèle, op. cit., iv, 201.    [30] Ibid., p. 188.    [31] Ibid., p. 240.

French Prime Minister, "would be the effort to restore the dominion of the mother country." [32] The wisest step was to "compromise," to find a solution "agreeable to the other cabinets of Europe," [33] satisfying "the reasonable desires of the inhabitants" of the new states,[34] preserving to Spain "commercial advantages which would compensate her for the loss of her sovereignty," [35] and rendering "more tolerable to France, by the new markets which it will furnish to our commerce, the burden of the expenditures we have made and shall have to make in Spain."[36] This is not the language of a man bent on any ambitious enterprise of force. This view of Villèle's policy is supported, moreover, by the language of Chateaubriand. The latter, it is true, did, in the spring of 1823, make a rather obscure statement to the Austrian minister which may be construed as squinting at the use of force in the solution of the colonial problem.[37] But there is no hint of any such design in the *Congrès de Vérone*, nor, more important still, in the instructions sent to Talaru in June, 1823.[38] "Care, reason, and skill" are the Foreign Minister's prescription for

[32] Villèle, *op. cit.* iv, p. 239.    [33] *Ibid.*, p. 201.    [34] *Ibid.*, p. 239.
[35] *Ibid.*, p. 201.    [36] *Ibid. Loc. cit.*

[37] Chateaubriand spoke of "des moyens maritimes . . . mis à la disposition du Roi d'Espagne, appui de l'aider s'il était possible, pour conserver une partie des Colonies qui n'étaient pas entièrement detachés de la métropole." Quoted in Mr. Temperley's article in *Eng. Hist. Rev.*, xi (1925), 40. This phrase may have referred to no more than Cuba and Porto Rico, though it is possible to extend it to Peru, which was still in Spanish hands, and, possibly, even to Mexico, where Spain still held the castle of San Juan de Ulloa. It is a slender basis, however, on which to build up any theory whatsoever.

[38] Paris. Aff. Étr., Corr. Pol., Espagne, vol. 722, fol. 56, June 9, 1823. "Aprés le rétablissement du roi sur son trône, la plus importante affaire qui puisse être traitée sera celle des colonies espagnoles. Si on considère l'état des Colonies Espagnóles dont on peut resulter la séparation on voit qu'il y en a quelquesunes, comme la Havane et Porto-ricco, qui ne demandent qu'à être protegées par la Mère Patrie, en conservant les avantages que les tems et les circonstances leur ont donnés; le Pérou sera facilement ramené et retenu sous la domination du Roi; il n'y a guère que les Villes des Côtes qui se soient declarées indépendantes, l'intérieur du pays est resté fidèle. Le Mexique n'est encore que bien imparfaitement separé de l'Espagne. Avec des soins, de la raison et de l'habileté, il seroit peut-être possible d'établir en Amérique de grandes Monarchies gouvernées par des Princes de la Maison de Bourbon. On combattrait par ce moyen le système croissant des Républiques; l'Espagne conserverait la Souveraineté et d'immenses avantages dans les belles colonies qui sont prêtes à lui échapper."

dealing with the colonial question. These things are not, perhaps, exclusive of the granting of armed aid. But they are certainly not suggestive of intervention on a grand scale.

Furthermore, even the limited aid which was perhaps intended was, in the view of the French ministers, to be made contingent upon a reasonable policy on the part of the restored Ferdinand. It went hand in hand with a project for a limited measure of constitutional rule in the Peninsula. France would give no support to the reëstablishment of absolute government. If Ferdinand, freed from the trammels of the revolutionists, were to revert to despotism, the French government, though it might make some provision for the safety of the royal family, would withdraw the rest of its army from the Peninsula, and refuse to be made the instrument of a blindly reactionary policy.[39] It would also, as a matter of course, refuse to lend its aid to Spain in the carrying out of any project for the establishment of independent monarchies in the New World.

A policy which was dependent upon any indication of reasonableness on the part of his Catholic Majesty, Ferdinand VII, was, as events were later to prove, a policy based upon a very large and an extremely false assumption. The chances that that unenlightened monarch could have been induced to favor the project of Bourbon monarchies were far from promising. The plan had, as we have seen, been frequently brought forward. It had been no less frequently repelled, repelled with as much vigor when connected with a suggestion of armed aid as when unaccompanied by any such suggestion. The policy which the French cabinet formulated in the early summer of 1823 was one easier to formulate than to carry out. This is a fact to be borne in mind in assessing its importance. Indeed, speaking generally, to consider Villèle's suggestion of armed aid to Spain without taking into account the circumstances which surrounded it, the mood and interest which prompted it, the reservations attached to it, and the difficulties in the way of translating it into action, is to give to the proposal a significance far beyond its due. That, in certain contingencies, aid might have been offered to Spain is no doubt true; but that

<hr />
[39] Paris. Aff. Étr., Corr. Pol. Espagne, vol. 722, fol. 56, June 9, 1823.

the French plans seriously menaced the new states would be difficult to prove. And by no stretch of the imagination can those
plans be converted into a scheme of reconquest such as has been
frequently assumed to exist and to have evoked the vigorous language of Monroe.

On the other hand, it cannot be denied that the trend of French
policy was such as could hardly be acceptable to American opinion, and that it ran counter to the known viewpoint of the United
States. The project of Bourbon monarchies was adopted not only
in disregard of, but in antagonism to, the views of the American
government. Gallatin, before his departure from France, had
warned Chateaubriand that the colonial question, from the
American standpoint, could be settled only on the basis of independence, and that Bourbon monarchies in the New World would
not by any means be considered a satisfactory solution.[40] At the
time, as we have seen, he had received assurances that France
would not meddle in the affairs of Spanish America. Yet, as early
as June 9, Chateaubriand mentioned the project of Bourbon
monarchies to Talaru, the new French minister sent to Spain,[41]
and a month later the cabinet as a whole set the seal of its approval upon the project. The views of the United States were
ignored, and previous assurances calmly put aside. And Villèle
spoke with some animus to Stuart, the British ambassador, of
the "agents of the United States" who "labor to counteract our
measures, only for the purpose of establishing a system favorable
to the democratic and calculating principles of their own Government, and attaining the commercial objects of which they never
lose sight."[42]

Antagonism to the republican system had a part, though no
doubt a minor one, in the formulation of French policy. The
dominant motive behind the project of Bourbon monarchies was
the reconciliation of commercial interest with the principle of
legitimacy; the economic factors were highly important; but the
French cabinet, like other Continental cabinets, was naturally

[40] Gallatin, *Writings*, ii, 271.
[41] Paris. Aff. Étr., Corr. Pol., Espagne, vol. 722, fol. 56, June 9, 1823.
[42] London. P. R. O., F. O., France, vol. 291, desp. 285, June 23, 1823.

hostile to the growth of democratic institutions in the New World. From the beginning, it ignored the United States in the formulation of its programme.

Its attitude toward Great Britain, however, was very different. Villèle, at least, was favorable to an understanding with that power. He spoke with frankness to Wellington of the plans of the French government when the Duke was in Paris in the late fall of 1822.[43] He set forth his views with no less candor to Stuart the following June, and added that the French government was "ready to concert with his Majesty's Government an arrangement which may tend to preserve the monarchical form of government in the new states."[44] Despite the bad relations between France and England, due to the intervention in Spain, there was at least a chance of an understanding between the two states on the colonial question in the early summer of 1823.

But Canning never took the hint dropped by Villèle to Stuart. And on his side, the French Foreign Minister, Chateaubriand, was not alive to the necessity of an immediate exchange of views. He instructed the Prince de Polignac, French ambassador at London, to avoid all reference to the colonial question.[45] His confidence to Stuart, in mid-August, 1823, that France would seek to find a solution of the colonial question in a congress of the allied powers,[46] far from quieting the suspicions of Canning, only aroused a deep distrust, which expressed itself in the British minister's negotiations with the United States. An early exchange of views between Paris and London might have altered very considerably the diplomatic history of the period, dispelled

[43] Wellington, *Despatches*, i, 664.
[44] London. P. R. O., F. O., France, vol. 291, desp. 285, June 23, 1823.
[45] Paris. Aff. Étr., Corr. Pol., Angleterre, vol. 617, fol. 18, July 17, 1823. "Le sort des Colonies españoles ne peut manquer d'occuper fortement l'Angleterre. Sur ce point-là nous devons annoncer aussi la volonté de nous entendre avec tous nos alliés et de continuer d'agir de concert avec eux. La politique de la France est de mettre ses soins à ce que l'Espagne tire le meilleur parti possible de ses colonies. C'est le meilleur moyen qu'elle-même en tire quelque utilité. Le gouvernement français n'a pour le moment aucune ouverture à faire au Gouvernement anglais sur ce point. Il doit même éviter d'en paraître occupé d'une manière particulière, de peur d'exciter la jalousie de la Grande Bretagne."
[46] See *antea*, p. 65.

the gathering suspicions of Continental designs on Spanish America, and had a profound effect upon the deliberations of the cabinet at Washington. But it was not until October that such an exchange came. And then it was due, not to the French, but to Canning. Having failed in his overtures to Rush, the British Foreign Secretary turned to a direct understanding with France. In the first days of October, in a series of important conversations with the French ambassador at London, the Prince de Polignac, he set forth the views of Great Britain and asked for those of the French government in return. The result was the famous Polignac memorandum of October 9.

"The British Government were of opinion," run the most significant sentences of this important document, "that any attempt to bring Spanish America again under its ancient submission to Spain must be utterly hopeless; that all negotiation for the purpose would be unsuccessful; and that the prolongation or renewal of war for the same object would be only a waste of human life, and an infliction of calamity on both parties, to no end!"

"The British Government would, however, not only abstain from interposing any obstacle, on their part, to any attempt at negotiation, which Spain might think proper to make, but would aid and countenance such negotiation, provided it were founded upon a basis which appeared to them to be practicable; and that they would, in any case, remain strictly neutral in the War between Spain and the Colonies, if war should unhappily be prolonged."

"But that the junction of any Foreign Power in an enterprize of Spain against the Colonies, would be viewed by them as constituting an entirely new question; and one upon which they must take such decision as the interests of Great Britain might require."

This viewpoint of Canning's was speedily reported to Paris by Polignac. Without the slightest delay Chateaubriand hastened to put British fears to rest. Polignac, acting under instructions, declared:

"That his Government believed it to be utterly hopeless to reduce Spanish America to the State of its former relation to Spain.

"That France disclaimed, on her part, any intention or desire to avail herself of the present state of the Colonies, or of the present situation of France toward Spain, to appropriate to herself any part of the Spanish possessions in America. . . .

"That she abjured, in any case, any design of acting against the Colonies by force of arms." [47]

Thus, two months before the Monroe message, France had given assurances of her pacific intentions in the New World, and Britain had uttered a warning against a policy of coercion — a warning, it is true, directed to France alone, but before many weeks communicated to the other Continental powers by Chateaubriand himself.[48]

By virtue of this episode, British historians have more than once accorded to Canning the credit which Americans have claimed for Monroe — the credit, that is, of checking plans hostile to the liberties of Spanish America. The priority of Canning's warning is undeniable. But, in the light of facts just outlined, we must, I think, conclude that the effects of the Polignac interviews were less important than has commonly been asserted by British commentators. French policy in the colonial question was highly contingent upon a variety of circumstances. The obstacles to its realization, exclusive of the British attitude, were nothing short of formidable. The British Foreign Secretary may have induced the abandonment of a project which involved a measure of armed aid to Spain. But it is more than doubtful whether that project could, in any case, have been carried out. Moreover, it is to be remembered, the French plans were not meant as a challenge to Great Britain, and their abandonment cannot be pictured as a tremendous diplomatic victory wrung from a jealous rival. Villèle had been, as we have seen, somewhat inclined to an understanding with Great Britain. There is little reason to believe that he ever intended, in the formulation of his policy, to adopt a line directly opposed to that of England. On the contrary, he hoped for her support. It is, therefore, difficult to visualize the Polignac

---

[47] *British and Foreign State Papers*, xi (1823–24), 49–54. Reprinted in Monroe's *Writings*, vi, 416–419.

[48] See Paris. Aff. Étr., Corr. Pol., Autriche, Nov. 3, 1823.

conversations as involving a sharp clash of viewpoints, in which the stronger will of Canning prevailed, and hard to imagine that France was about to embark upon a policy directly contrary to that of Britain, and was compelled to desist by the veiled menaces of the British Foreign Secretary.

The Polignac conversations, indeed, far from being conducted in the spirit of an international diplomatic duel, seem actually to have led to an attempted rapprochement. Polignac himself, in reporting his interviews with Canning, strongly emphasized the fact that the British minister seemed to desire an understanding.[49] Indeed, he became rather the advocate than the reporter, and urged such a course upon his chief. Could not France become the spokesman for all the Continental powers on the subject of South America? As such could she not arrange a settlement directly with Great Britain?

At first Chateaubriand rejected any such idea. To his romantic mind it seemed like treason to Spain. He spoke of it as a measure to despoil Spain of her colonies, as "a double game that France is too noble to play." [50] But a little later he thought better of Polignac's suggestion. On November 1, he communicated the Polignac memorandum to the courts of the allied powers, and with it he transmitted certain questions. One of these questions, significantly enough, ran as follows: "The Court of —— having no colony, would it regard itself as disinterested, leaving France and England to take such course as they might deem proper?" [51] Clearly here was an effort to establish French liberty of action in the colonial question, and to pave the way for an understanding with Great Britain.

The other questions in this remarkable communication illuminate still further the drift of French policy.

If England recognizes the independence of the Spanish colonies without the consent of His Catholic Majesty will the Court of —— do the same? . . . If the Spanish government should refuse to come to an understanding with its colonies, and persisted in claiming a *de jure* power over them without

[49] Paris. Aff. Étr., Corr. Pol., Angleterre, vol. 617, fol. 133 ff., Oct. 1, 1823; and *Ibid.*, fol. 137 ff., Oct. 3, 1823.
[50] Chateaubriand, *Congrès de Vérone*, ii, 136.
[51] *Ibid.*, p. 245.

having any means of establishing it in fact, would the Court of —— consider that it was released from any obligation, and free to act according to its particular interests with regard to the Spanish colonies?

Such queries show clearly that France feared British recognition, and that she wished to shape her own policy so as to be able, in such a contingency, to recognize the new states in her turn.

Finally, with regard to the circular of November 1, there is a significant omission which completes the revelation of the trend of French policy. In the original draft of the circular, as found in the *Congrès de Vérone*, a fourth question is put, along with the three just given: "Is the Court of —— determined to make common cause with France, if France is obliged to side with Spain in refusing to recognize the independence of the Spanish colonies recognized by England?" This question was omitted from the draft finally sent to the Continental courts. The French ministers, faced with the choice of action looking toward recognition and coöperation with Great Britain on the one hand, and strong support of Spain in concert with the allied powers on the other hand, clearly desired to make an election in favor of the former.

But they were not really free to do so. France had been pledged at Verona to the principle of common action in the colonial question. Whatever the temptations, Villèle and Chateaubriand did not dare to cut loose from the Continental powers. On the very day on which Chateaubriand communicated the Polignac memorandum to the other courts, he wrote to Talaru at Madrid a dispatch of a very different tenor. In this dispatch he directed the French minister to urge Spain to demand the formal mediation of the allied powers.[52] He was not willing to wait for the answers of the various states to his questionnaire. He wished to hurry the calling of a congress on the colonial question. Such action he believed would prevent Great Britain from taking a separate line of action, and perhaps from recognizing the independence of the colonies.

The months of November and December, 1823, the months when the Monroe message was being debated at Washington, and when it was on its way across the Atlantic, were largely devoted,

[52] Paris. Aff. Étr., Corr. Pol., Espagne, vol. 724, fol. 149, Nov. 1, 1823.

then, to preparations for a congress on the colonial question. They were months of feverish energy on the part of France, but of energy directed toward a very different end from intervention. The dominant note of French policy was fear that England would recognize, and get the upper hand over France in colonial commerce by so doing.

France, despite its good will, must take a stand in the question, of the independence of the colonies, if the cabinet of Madrid refuses a reasonable arrangement [wrote Chateaubriand], for she would injure the interests of her commerce in a vital spot if by her lack of foresight she let the monopoly of colonial trade pass into the hands of the English or the Americans.[53]

To prevent such a contingency there must be a general discussion of the colonial question without delay. It was for Talaru to prepare the way for a meeting of all the powers.

To do this, however, was not precisely an easy task. The Spanish government, as was usual in the South American problem, could think of nothing but some ambitious project of reconquest. And it was not willing to pay any attention to British susceptibilities or to invite Great Britain to the forthcoming congress. The much-plagued Talaru sent dispatch after dispatch explaining his difficulties to the government at home. A first draft of the Spanish invitation to a Congress was sent to France, and rejected as too provocative of dissension, and as squinting at intervention.[54] A second note, following on a change of ministry in Spain, was a little more satisfactory. Talaru worked vigorously to eliminate from it everything that might give umbrage to Great Britain, and did secure some modifications. But he could not persuade the ministers of Ferdinand to address the note directly to Great Britain, and when it was finally sent it was addressed to the Continental courts alone, and a copy given to the British ambassador at Madrid.[55] The course of events with regard to it was anything but satisfactory to Villèle and Chateaubriand.

Still, the project of a congress did go forward. This much, at least, was in accordance with French desires. As to what such a

[53] Paris. Aff. Étr., Corr. Pol., Espagne, vol. 724, fol. 149, Nov. 1, 1823.
[54] Paris. Aff Étr., Corr. Pol., Espagne, vol. 724, Dec. 6, 1823.
[55] Ibid., Dec. 19, 1823.

congress should do if it met, the French ministers were not quite so clear. Chateaubriand still clung to the project of Bourbon monarchies. He urged Talaru to bring it forward, in his dispatch of November 1,[56] and again on November 12.[57] Villèle, too, still played with this idea,[58] though to Stuart he spoke of it a little disparagingly and hinted at the possibility of a settlement based on the recognition of colonial independence with certain concessions to Spain.[59] What no one thought of, what no one had the temerity to suggest, was an active policy of reconquest. There can be little question of this fact. The assurance that had been given in October was sincerely intended. The French squadron in the West Indies had been weakened, not strengthened;[60] Sheldon[61] and Stuart[62] both reported that the French navy was in no shape for operations in the New World; and the language of Chateaubriand shows not only indifference, but repugnance, to an active policy. "From whom," wrote the French Foreign Minister to Talaru, "can Spain expect aid to reconquer her colonies? Surely she cannot think that France would furnish her money, vessels, or troops for such an enterprise."[63] Whatever France intended, she certainly did not intend intervention on a grand scale.

She desired, on the contrary, to be on good terms with the

[56] Paris. Aff. Étr., Corr. Pol., Espagne, vol. 724, Nov. 1, 1823.

[57] Ibid., Nov. 12, 1823.          [58] Villèle, *op. cit.*, iv, 489.

[59] London. P. R. O., F. O., France, vol. 291, desp. 562, Nov. 3, 1823. "He admitted that he had listened to visionary schemes for sending the Younger Branch of the Spanish Royal Family to South America, and had persevered in that opinion until his conviction of the utter incompetence of all the persons placed about them had compelled him to place all his reliance upon the efforts of a Congress to settle the mode of establishing the independence of those countries."

[60] Paris. Aff. Étr., Corr. Pol., Angleterre, vol. 617, fol. 145, Oct. 5, 1823. "Nous avons rappellé le seul vaisseau de guerre, le *Jean Bart*, que nous eussions dans les Antilles."

[61] Washington. State Dept. Dispatches, France, vol. 22, no. 16, Nov. 29, 1823. "The French government is putting out of commission several of their ships of war, and have already discharged and are discharging numbers of their seamen."

[62] London. P. R. O., F. O., France, vol. 305, desp. 33, Jan. 15, 1924. "They have with difficulty been enabled to collect the Seamen necessary to man the Vessels which are to be sent from that Port [Brest] to relieve their different Foreign Stations."

[63] Paris. Aff. Étr., Corr. Pol., Espagne, vol. 724, fol. 147, Oct. 30, 1823.

new states, and to remove the painful impression created by the invasion of the Peninsula. As early as May, 1823, the governor of Martinique, Donzelot, had brought to the attention of the Minister of the Marine, Clermont-Tonnerre, the unfavorable position in which French commerce with the new states was placed by the intervention in Spain, and suggested the sending of a secret mission to Colombia. Clermont-Tonnerre in July communicated this information to Chateaubriand, and at the very moment when Monroe was warning against the nefarious designs of the Alliance the French cabinet was preparing to send agents to the New World who should reassure the new states as to the views of France.[64] Instructions for two of these agents were drawn up on November 29 [65] and December 1, 1823,[66] for the naval lieutenant Samouel, who was to proceed to Mexico, and for Chassérieu, who had served two years before on a similar mission, and who was to go to Colombia. The agents are adjured to do their utmost to remove the impression that France ever promised military or naval aid to Spain for the reconquest of the colonies. They are urged to press upon the Colombian and Mexican governments the desirability of opening negotiations with the mother country, in which France, through her special relationship to Spain, may serve as the most convenient and useful intermediary. The suggested bases of a settlement are independence, with commercial privileges for Spain, in the case of Colombia, and with wider concessions, perhaps even the reception of a viceroy who would set up a purely Mexican administration, in the case of Mexico. The interests of French commerce are emphasized again and again, and the agents informed that Spain will be told that France cannot wait indefinitely on the good pleasure of Ferdinand before recognizing the new states.

In the latter months of 1823, at the moment when Monroe was formulating his famous warning against intervention, it may confidently be said that French policy, though rather indeterminate,

[64] Paris. Aff. Étr., Corr. Pol., Espagne, vol. 722, July 23, 1823.
[65] Paris. Aff. Étr., Méms. et Docs., Amérique, vol. 39.
[66] Paris. Archives Nationales, Minist. de la Marine, BB⁴ 405 bis. These instructions are published almost in full in C. A. Villaneuva, *La Santa Alianza* (Paris, 1912), pp. 44–50.

was drifting toward recognition rather than reconquest, and was certainly dictated by no violent hostility to the new states of South America. The danger from France was, at the moment, at least, much less real than the President and his advisers supposed.

At the same time, it must be admitted, the French attitude toward the new republics took little account of the position of the United States. We have already seen how the United States was ignored in the formulation of the plans of the court of the Tuileries in the summer of 1823. The same fact stands out in the discussions over the possible participation of the United States in the projected congress on the South American question.

In the earlier period, in 1817 and 1818, France had been by no means disregardful of the American point of view. The initial stages of the discussions, it is true, passed without any attention being paid to the government at Washington. But in August, 1818, when the inquiries of Gallatin had to be answered, Richelieu declared it to be his opinion that nothing could be done in the Spanish American question without the coöperation of the American government.[67] Two months later, at Aix, in concert with the Russians, he formally suggested the participation of the United States in whatever discussions should take place on colonial affairs.[68]  No doubt the chief object of this proposal was to prevent independent action on the part of the government at Washington; the agitation for recognition and the propaganda of Clay had their part in forming the French decision. But, whatever the motives of the French ministers, the views of the United States were at least accorded some consideration.

In 1822 and 1823, however, the attitude was very different. The recognition of the republics of the New World by this country had apparently affected the French attitude to a considerable degree. "The United States recognized the independence of certain of the Spanish colonies last year by act of Congress," wrote Chateaubriand to Polignac; "they are consequently disinterested, and entirely out of the picture."[69] "The United

[67] Washington. State Dept. Despatches, France, Aug. 10, 1818.
[68] See my article, cited above, in *Am. Hist. Rev.* (July, 1923), xxviii, 667 f.
[69] Chateaubriand, *Congrès de Vérone*, ii, 245.

States, it is true," read the instructions to the French agent, Chassérieu, "have proceeded in a more explicit manner, but this power is entirely outside the political system of Europe, and its determination can have no influence on that of the great powers." [70]

Chateaubriand, it is clear from these quotations, was determined to pay very little attention to the American government. He never offered any explanation of French policy to the American minister at Paris, and on the only occasion when the colonial question was discussed, in the spring of 1823, he seems, as we have seen, to have responded soothingly but disingenuously to the representations of Albert Gallatin. His attitude was pretty nearly that of ignoring the United States.

Accordingly, Canning's proposal of American participation in a congress,[71] should one be held to discuss South American affairs, the French Foreign Minister rejected entirely. The British minister's suggestion seemed to him "malevolent" and "short-sighted"; [72] and the exclusion of the United States from European gatherings "might serve in case of need as a supplementary article of the public law of Europe." [73] Nothing could have been much more positive than this.

Chateaubriand's views, moreover, were shared by Polignac and by Villèle. The mere mention of the idea of America's participation seemed to irritate the French premier. He told Stuart that it would be better to have no congress at all than to consent to such a step.[74] "He certainly did not think it expedient to admit a Government into our deliberations upon this subject whose political principles are directly at variance with those of every other Power, and which, however much they might agree upon the principal points under consideration, would for the sake of trifling local advantage always be disposed to overset the ar-

---

[70] Paris. Aff. Étr., Méms. et Docs., Amérique, vol. 39, fol. 81, Dec. 1, 1823.

[71] Canning stated at the time of the Polignac interviews that "he could not understand how a European Congress could discuss Spanish American affairs without calling to their councils a power so eminently interested in the result as the United States of America."

[72] St. Petersburg. F. O., Reçus, no. 21, 224 (Encl.), Dec. 25, 1823.   [73] *Ibid.*

[74] London. P. R. O., F. O., France, vol. 295, desp. 557, Oct. 31, 1823.

rangements upon which their Plenipotentiaries may agree." [75]
Not a flattering view of the United States, it must be admitted!
but none the less revealing as to the respect in which the American
government was held in 1823. The French attitude at this time
is an interesting presage of the reaction to Monroe's message
itself.

## RUSSIA

If it was France which, of all the Continental powers, had the
greatest interest in the colonial question, it is Russia, on the
other hand, that seems to have been most feared. At least this
was true of the administration at Washington. Canning had his
eyes pretty steadily fixed on Paris, but Calhoun and Adams and
Monroe, with a different set of facts on which to go, were chiefly
afraid of Alexander. Were these suspicions justified in the fall of
1823? Had the Russian autocrat formed a sinister design against
the liberties of the states of the New World?

The interest of the Tsar in the question of Spanish America is a
matter that admits of no doubt. Alexander seems to have had
a peculiar tenderness for Spain and for Ferdinand, a tenderness
which most European statesmen were far from feeling, and Ferdinand certainly far from deserving. In 1816, when Portuguese
troops invaded the Banda Oriental, still theoretically Spanish,
Alexander showed strong indignation at such aggression, and
even talked of putting the collective power of Europe behind the
Spanish cause. [76] The next year, when the Spanish government
requested permission to construct some vessels of war in Russian
shipyards, the Tsar obligingly offered the sale of the Russian
fleet. [77] And, in the course of 1818, acting on the suggestion of
Spain, he urged the admission of a Spanish plenipotentiary to
the projected congress at Aix-la-Chapelle, in the hope that the
result might be favorable to a discussion of the South American
problem before that body. [78]

[75] London. P. R. O., F. O., France, vol. 296, desp. 568, Nov. 4, 1823.

[76] Polovtsov, *Correspondance des ambassadeurs*, ii, 732 f.

[77] Hermann Baumgarten, *Geschichte Spaniens vom Ausbruch der französischen
Revolution bis auf unsere Tage* (Leipzig, 1865–71, 3 vols.), ii, 196. See also C. K.
Webster, *Foreign Policy of Castlereagh*, pp. 94, 412.

[78] See my article, cited above, in *Am. Hist. Rev.*, xxviii (July, 1923), 666.

Even more positive, moreover, were the views of Pozzo di Borgo, the vigorous and influential Corsican diplomat who was so long the Tsar's representative at Paris. On Pozzo the question of Spanish America seemed to exercise a singular fascination. Throughout the years 1817 and 1818, he was busily engaged in seeking to secure some kind of international action which would bring about a reconciliation between Spain and her revolted subjects. Frequently going beyond his instructions, frequently pressing his views on the Tsar himself, he worked with might and main to accomplish his object.[79] Frustrated in the earlier period, he was, as we shall see, to play an equally active rôle in 1823 and 1824.

Of the zeal of both the minister and the sovereign for the cause of Ferdinand there need, therefore, be very little doubt. But this does not necessarily imply a policy of stark reconquest, and certainly the antecedents of Russian policy, down to the critical year 1823, do not indicate that anything of the kind was in the wind. Even Pozzo, in his scheming, had not proposed anything so sweeping. He advocated compromise and concession as the basis of a settlement, with force as a possible measure in the background.[80] The Tsar never went even so far as this. He was aware, from the beginning of the international discussions of 1817, that intervention would mean a clash with Great Britain. Castlereagh's memorandum of August 28 had made that perfectly clear. In his cautious statement of his policy, in November of the same year, Alexander

[79] *Am. Hist. Rev.*, xxviii (July, 1923), especially pp. 666 ff.

[80] Polovtsov, *Correspondance des ambassadeurs*, ii, 230, 393, 231. "To assume to subjugate and govern America by force of arms," Pozzo wrote, "without having recourse to any moral or political expedient, is like attempting to impose silence on the tempests and hurricanes of those regions. Instead of obstinately persisting in fruitless military ventures, Spain ought to present to Europe a plan of pacification with the colonies, whose basis should be a better local administration, provincial privileges, and a considerable freedom of commerce." As to the use of force, "my intention would not be, lightly to promise or to grant any armed assistance, but only not explicitly to base the mediation on a contrary policy, since such a declaration would certainly deprive our efforts, in the eyes of the American insurgents, and of the rest of the world, of that imposing uncertainty which reveals force in the background behind the just counsels of monarchs." In the event of Spain's accepting a reasonable program, the Allies might combine persuasion with "whatever force might be available, and advice with the means of making it effective."

went no further than to suggest that Spain should grant a constitutional charter to the colonies; that the dispute between Spain and Portugal should be settled, thus leading to a discussion of the "policy which the two courts propose to follow in concert toward the insurgent peoples"; and, finally, that economic pressure might be employed against the colonies if they refused to accept reasonable terms.[81] He was, he wrote, "disposed to accept the views of the majority," [82] and not "to anticipate the decisions of his august allies." [83] He certainly at this time meditated no breach with Great Britain. At Aix, indeed, when the colonial question came up for discussion, and when the Tsar was made aware, through a long interview with Castlereagh, of the strength of British opposition to any project of coercion, he willingly dropped even the idea of economic pressure, and consented to a mild and innocuous proposal to intrust the Duke of Wellington with preparing the way for a mediation at Madrid.[84]

All this, of course, proves nothing whatsoever as to Russian purposes in 1823 and 1824. Alexander at Aix-la-Chapelle was still in his liberal phase. He was to view the colonial question a little differently five years later. But there are, none the less, elements in the Russian policy of 1817 and 1818 that may fairly be described as continuous. Coöperative, not isolated, action was the Tsar's whole notion of European policy. The fear of British hostility could hardly fail to be a powerful element at all times in forming Alexander's decisions. And the necessity of some concessions on the part of Spain, as a mere matter of practical statesmanship, would form a permanent element in the solution of the colonial question. If, in the discussions which we are later to analyze, there appears from time to time a more reactionary, a more militant, note than in the debates of 1817 and 1818, it must not, on that account, be concluded that the Tsar was ever

---

[81] Polovtsov, *op. cit.*, ii, 474–482. "De la négociation relative à la question du Rio de La Plata et, en général, de la pacification des colonies. Mémoire à communiquer aux puissances intéressées, ainsi qu'aux cabinets des puissances médiatrices." Also in Wellington, *Supplementary Despatches*, xii, 125–131.

[82] Polovtsov, *Correspondance des ambassadeurs*, ii, 658.

[83] *Ibid.*, p. 478.

[84] See my article, cited above, in *Am. Hist. Rev.*, xxviii (July, 1923), 669 f.

ready for intervention by force in the New World. The considerations which governed his policy in 1817 and 1818 were to have their influence in the later period.

Steadfastly loyal to 'legitimacy,' to the cause of Spain, so far as legal right was concerned, Alexander always, of course, remained. In 1819, when the French government sounded him on the plan for Bourbon monarchies, he rejected the whole project vigorously, on the ground that it was distasteful to Ferdinand.[85] No doubt he watched with sympathy the King of Spain's preparations in 1819 and 1820 to equip a fleet for the conquest of the colonies. And in the troubled years of revolution in the Peninsula, he very naturally stood firmly by the principle that Spain must herself decide the question as to her attitude toward the new states, and that Russia would not under any circumstances anticipate her decisions.[86] In 1823, he reiterated his point of view in this regard, as we have seen, in a communication to the government of the United States, in which he announced that he would not receive any agent from any of the states of the New World.[87] At the time when Monroe penned his famous message, the Tsar still based his policy on the rights of Spain over her former dominions.

But what was Alexander's notion of the way in which those rights should be protected or made secure? What were Russia's positive intentions in the fall of 1823? The answer to these questions is obscure. For the truth of the matter is that the Russian court had hardly begun to face the colonial problem when the President issued his famous challenge. It had not as yet decided definitely upon anything more than a general deliberation on the question of South America. The language of the Russian diplomats at the various courts of Europe was contradictory in the extreme. At London, Prince Lieven was urging that the wisest course would be to invoke the mediation of Great Britain as the mandatory of all the powers; [88] Pozzo di Borgo was reported by

[85] Polovtsov, *Correspondance des ambassadeurs*, iii, 131 f.
[86] See W. S. Robertson, "The United States and Spain in 1822," *Am. Hist. Rev.*, xx (July, 1915), 781–800, especially p. 796.
[87] See *antea*, p. 70.
[88] St. Petersburg. F. O., Reçus, no. 9032, Nov. 18, 1823.

Stuart to favor a conditional acknowledgment of colonial independence,[89] and by Talaru to be urging Spain to an effort of armed
reconquest;[90] and Bulgari, the Russian minister at Madrid, seems
actually to have advocated the giving of armed aid to Spain,
conditional on the surrender by the mother country of her trade
monopoly in the New World.[91] In the meantime, all that had
clearly been decided upon at St. Petersburg was that there ought
to be a general congress on the colonial question. Alexander was
still formulating his views when Monroe published his manifesto.
Events moved more rapidly than the mind of the Tsar. Just as,
in 1817, he had replied to Pozzo's homily on colonial affairs only
after a five months' interval, so in 1823 he was to formulate a
policy only very slowly and cautiously, and after the other powers
had expressed themselves. There was no note of vigorous leadership in his handling of the colonial problem. And, in all fairness,
it must be confessed that there was, before the American pronouncement, little time in which to determine upon a definite line
of action. The intervention in Spain reached its final goal with
the liberation of the King only in the last days of October. The
Polignac interview, which was bound to precipitate a discussion
of affairs in the New World, was not known to the other Continental courts till the beginning of November. And it required
virtually a month for Pozzo to transmit the news of that famous
interview to St. Petersburg, and another month to secure from
that court instructions as to the course to be pursued. All things
considered, then, it is not strange that Monroe's manifesto found
the Russian government without any matured policy whatsoever.
"Everything is in confusion in America," remarked the Tsar to
La Ferronays, the French ambassador, "let us leave this chaos
for a while to reduce itself to order."[92]

There are, however, certain observations that may be made
with regard to the approximate orientation, if not the precise intentions, of Russian policy. The principle of a general deliberation on the colonial question was, as we have seen, willingly

[89] London. P. R. O., F. O., France, vol. 296, desp. 568, Nov. 4, 1823.
[90] Paris. Aff. Étr., Corr. Pol., Espagne, vol. 724, fol. 252, Nov. 21, 1823.
[91] Ibid., fol. 367, Dec. 19, 1823.
[92] Paris. Aff. Étr., Corr. Pol., Russie, vol. 165, fol. 281, Nov. 28, 1823.

accepted by Alexander. He had spoken in this sense at Verona,[93] and to Chateaubriand's effort to exclude the other Continental powers from a voice in the colonial question he had answered with becoming dignity that Russia had colonies of her own, and that in any case the colonial question had reference to all Europe, and that glorious precedents did not permit a policy of indifference.

A general interest has led to the reëstablishment of legitimacy in France. It has led to the downfall of revolution in the Two Sicilies. It has led to its exile from Piedmont. It has led to its defeat in its last entrenchments in Spain. How could this same interest, after all this, after the ten years struggle of the powers against revolution, after a triumph over it in the Old World, permit the recognition of revolution in the New? The contradiction would be manifest, and the continental alliance undermined to its foundation. Too many examples demonstrate that the contagion of revolutionary principles is arrested by neither distance nor physical obstacles. It crosses the seas, and often appears with all the symptoms of destruction which characterize it, in places where not even any direct contact, any relation of proximity might give ground for apprehension. France knows with what facility and promptitude a revolution can be carried from America to Europe. No bond united Naples to Spain, and the Spanish constitution, suddenly proclaimed in the Two Sicilies, was hardly known there. To these great lessons from recent experience, must be added a circumstance which the Allied Courts ought not to forget. The affairs of the colonies have already been the subject of common deliberations, and when these deliberations took place, it resulted from the very fact of their existence that the Allied Courts recognized reciprocally the right to intervene in the matter. How could some have retained and others lost this right? They would then have taken part in the discussions without any justification, or would give up participating without any reason. The second contradiction would be no less evident than the first. The Emperor therefore shares completely the opinion pronounced on this point by the foreign minister of His Most Christian Majesty to the cabinet of London, that the future state of Spanish America concerns the interests of all the Allies, and that it is between them and with the King of Spain that this important question ought to be treated and decided by common accord.[94]

Such an accord, however, might, in the view of the Tsar, be reached in a congress of sovereigns. But the preparation for such a congress ought to be reached by preliminary conferences [95] in which Great Britain ought to be included.[96] In this reference to

---

[93] Paris. Aff. Étr. Corr. Pol., Méms. et Docs., Paris, France, vol. 699, fol. 233.
[94] St. Petersburg. F. O., Expédiés, no. 8829, Nov. 25, 1823.
[95] Ibid.
[96] Ibid., no. 9044, Jan. 9, 1824.

preliminary conferences and to British participation we have the clearest indication of the caution with which Alexander wished to move in the colonial question.

But if the Tsar was by no means disposed to hasty action, the same cannot be said of Pozzo di Borgo. Just as he had precipitated a discussion of the colonial question in 1817, so in 1823 he was to take matters pretty much in his own hands, and go blithely ahead without waiting for the instructions of his august master. Pozzo, like Chateaubriand, seems to have been thrown into a panic by the Polignac conversations. He seems to have thought, with the French minister, that it was necessary to act promptly if Great Britain were to be immobilized in the colonial question and prevented from recognizing the independence of the colonies. In October, 1823, he set forth for Madrid.[97] There were many matters afoot there in the solution of which he wished to exert his influence. He was anxious to take a hand in the internal affairs of Spain, and, apparently, to prevent too violent and bloody a reaction as a consequence of Ferdinand's restoration. But he was also anxious to bring about, and to accelerate, an appeal from Spain to the allied powers for their mediation in the colonial question. In the drawing up of the Spanish note asking for such mediation the Russian minister undoubtedly played an active part — so active a part, indeed, that Talaru, the French ambassador, actually complained that the note was edited in the Russian embassy.[98] There seems every reason to believe, moreover, that, despite the very different language he had used to Stuart, Pozzo rather encouraged than discouraged the pretensions of the Spanish court. The first draft of a note to the allied powers was drawn up in the last days of November, by the King's confessor and prime minister, Saez.[99] The whole tenor of this document was distinctly that of an application for positive aid to Spain in her conflict with her former colonies. And it apparently met with only mild objection so far as the Russian minister is concerned.[100] He was, if we are to believe Talaru, urging

[97] See Adrien Maggiolo, *Pozzo di Borgo* (Paris, 1890), p. 273.
[98] Paris. Aff. Étr., Corr. Pol., Espagne, vol. 724, Dec. 6, 1823.
[99] Ibid.                         [100] Ibid.

Spain to dispatch a fleet to the New World, and stiffening Spanish resistance to any reasonable policy of concession.[101] Perhaps, too, he encouraged the Spanish court in its desire to exclude Great Britain from the congress on the colonial question. He may even, as the sequel will show, have been thinking of the giving of actual aid to Spain.

But, in all this, it is perfectly clear that he was acting without the slightest authorization from St. Petersburg. The first instructions from his court which deal with the colonial question are dated November 26, 1823, and reached Paris a full month later. In these instructions, as we have said, the Tsar advocated the notion of a general congress. Just what a congress would do he does not venture to say. But he declares that Spain ought not to be presumed to be unwilling to make equitable arrangements with her former subjects, and, in particular, to leave them open to the commerce of the world. He speaks of negotiations — negotiations which, like the preceding ones, will have as their object the aiding of Spain to reëstablish her power on bases as useful to the people of America as to the mother country. He envisages the possibility that such efforts might be fruitless. The possibility of the use of force is not distinctly disclaimed. But there is, on the other hand, nothing that suggests that the Tsar had in mind any interventionist enterprise.

Russian policy, to repeat the point already made, was still unformed. That is the essence of the matter.

With regard to the attitude of the Tsar toward the United States, a few special words should be said. Despite the fear of Russian designs at Washington, there was really no European power more kindly disposed toward the United States than the great empire of the Slavs. This had been true at every stage in the development of the colonial question, and true not only with regard to South America, but with regard to almost every problem. The American government in 1817 had been invited — one might almost say pressed — to join the charmed circle of the Holy Alliance; and in the discussions with regard to the colonies in 1818 the Tsar had recognized the right of the United States to

[101] Paris. Aff. Étr., Corr. Pol., Espagne, vol. 724, Nov. 29, 1823.

be consulted, and had pressed his view upon the other powers. No doubt his motives, like those of the French at the same time, were somewhat mixed; no doubt in both cases one motive was a desire to stave off recognition of the new states; and yet it is to be noticed that there was a very friendly attitude toward the United States in general. Much the same thing can be said in 1823. Alexander, unlike the other Continental powers, did honor the United States with an occasional explanation of his policy. Grotesquely enough, the communications which he put forward in a spirit of amicable condescension were the reason why he was regarded with suspicion. The note of August 30 and the note of October 16, 1823, were, there seems little reason to doubt, dictated not by hostility, but by a very contrary feeling. They were, of course, a bit superior in tone, like many Alexandrian pronouncements. But that they concealed any deep-dyed hostility is not the case. As a matter of fact, Alexander was willing to recognize the interest of the United States in the colonial question. He did not, as five years earlier, propose the admission of the American government to the councils of the allied powers. Even before he had an opportunity to do it, Metternich, as we shall see, had majestically pronounced the banishment of this country from the deliberations of the Old World. But the Tsar did suggest the expedient of simultaneous declarations to be made to Washington, declarations which would reassure the American government as to the purposes of the Continental powers, making it clear that "in any case the interests of commerce would be respected, and that there will be no question of reëstablishing the old monopolies," and that "the intervening powers of Spain wish only to maintain with them relations of complete sympathy, and that furthermore no one of them seeks as the price of its good offices either exclusive advantages or even an influence which might alarm other governments."[102] This is a far more generous view of the position of the United States than was taken by any other power. In view of the fact that the American government had recognized the independence of the colonies, it was perhaps as generous as could fairly be expected.

[102] St. Petersburg. F. O., Expédiés, Jan. 9, 1824.

Alexander might, perhaps, fairly complain that he had a right to expect something better than a homily on the virtues of republicanism from the administration at Washington in the last months of 1823.

## AUSTRIA

The policy of Austria in the colonial question might seem, at first sight, to be of secondary importance. But it has, none the less, a very real interest. The close relations of the Russian and Austrian courts in 1823 and 1824 make it highly desirable to understand the Austrian viewpoint, which could hardly fail to have its influence with the Tsar. And the whole story of the Austrian attitude toward the South American problem sheds much light upon the ideas and statesmanship of one of the dominating personalities of the time, the powerful and influential Chancellor, Prince Metternich.

Metternich has frequently been regarded as the most doctrinaire and extreme of reactionaries. He has served to typify the spirit of resistance to change, and a militant spirit of resistance to change, at that. But the more one examines his character, the more one reads his diplomatic dispatches, the less of an ideologue he appears. He was primarily *Austrian* in his aims and point of view. Austria needed tranquillity, and Austrian interests required that revolutionary movements in Germany and Italy should be promptly suppressed; how, then, could an Austrian minister be other than reactionary, and interventionist? But Metternich never cared much for the generalization of his principles of action; he was by no means enthusiastic about the French intervention in Spain, and his formula, when the Greeks revolted against the Turk, was hardly that of an ardent champion of legitimacy. The Austrian Chancellor was no theorist, no idealist, but a very practical statesman, and the question of South America he viewed, as he viewed most others, with a sober judgment far removed from the vagaries of the doctrinaire.

Despite Austria's relatively secondary interest in the Spanish colonies, it is a curious and interesting fact that nowhere was there better or fuller information on the actual state of affairs in the New World than in the Austrian archives, nowhere a less biased interpretation of the events taking place across the Atlantic. This may have been due, in part, to the intimate contact between the Austrian and British governments, at least during the foreign ministry of Castlereagh. But it was due, too, no doubt, to Metternich's principal adviser, his "alter ego," as he has often been called, Freiherr Friedrich von Gentz.[103] Gentz in his youth had written a remarkable essay on "The Effect of the Discovery of America on Europe." He had written a pamphlet comparing the French and American Revolutions. He had shown a keen interest in the affairs of the New World. He had studied with care the revolutionary movement in the Spanish colonies. His opinions undoubtedly guided Metternich on the whole problem.

What those opinions were may be seen from a letter which Gentz wrote to the Russian Chancellor, Nesselrode, in January, 1818. His tone was one of profound pessimism as to the chances either of inducing a reconciliation between King Ferdinand and his revolted subjects, or of reconquering the former dominions of Spain. "I see no truly conciliatory disposition on either side," he wrote, "and the Spanish government has for three years followed a system too false and disastrous for its overtures to produce any effect." Then follows an analysis of the situation in South America, remarkable for its clarity and good sense.

It may still be possible to save Mexico and Peru, by adopting an enlightened and liberal system, and that without losing an instant; but Buenos Aires, the provinces of La Plata, Venezuela, New Grenada are too far advanced, not only in success, but also in hatred of the Spanish government, to listen to proposals of conciliation. It will perhaps be possible some day to reëstablish the royal authority, taking advantage of the civil dissensions which will arise in those unhappy countries; but I do not think that either a continuation of the war or direct negotiations will restore them to Spain.[104]

This extremely practical and cold-blooded view of the colonial question was the view which guided Austrian policy at every stage. It was given an added force by the exigencies of Continental politics. For Prince Metternich made it one of the

[103] For Gentz's views see his "Ungedruckte Denkschriften, Tagebücher, und Briefe," in his *Schriften*, edited by Gustav Schlesier (Mannheim, 1838–40, 5 vols.), vol. v, especially pp. 102–112.

[104] *Lettres et Papiers du Chancelier Comte de Nesselrode* (Paris, 1904–12, 11 vols.), vol. v, p. 294.

principal maxims of his policy to keep on good terms with Great Britain. He admired and found it easy to coöperate with Lord Castlereagh. And even when George Canning, the "malevolent meteor hurled in the face of Europe," succeeded to the control of British foreign relations, the Austrian Chancellor was loath to embark upon any course of action that would antagonize the government at London. A policy of active intervention in Spanish America could hardly have failed to produce such a result. This was obvious after the British memorandum of August 28, 1817. No wonder, therefore, that in the colonial question the Austrian policy was a policy of restraint.

In the negotiations of 1817 and 1818, indeed, Austria showed only the mildest interest in the whole problem. The Russian memorandum of November 27, 1817, was apparently never given an official answer. At the Congress of Aix-la-Chapelle, the Austrian Chancellor took but little part in the colonial discussions, intervening, whenever he did so, to sustain the British in their opposition to any policy of force.[105] He lent not the slightest encouragement to the ambitious designs of Ferdinand.

But, on the other hand, Austria was at all times willing to uphold Spain's claims "in principle." She had, of course, no interests which impelled her toward the recognition of the colonies. In the absence of such interests, she was ready, as a matter of course, to uphold those legitimist dogmas which were the prevailing philosophy of the period. When the Spanish government, following on Monroe's message of March 8, 1822, entered into discussions with the various European courts on the South American question, Metternich was entirely willing to give assurances that he disapproved of the revolts in the New World, and of all steps which looked toward the acknowledgment of the revolutionary governments which had been formed there.[106] And, some eight months later, at the Congress of Verona, in answer to the memorandum presented by the Duke of Wellington, the Austrian

[105] C. K. Webster, "Castlereagh and the Spanish Colonies," I, *Eng. Hist. Rev.*, xxvii (1912), 78–95, especially p. 89.

[106] Carrero to Martinez de la Rosa, June 8, 1822. Seville. Archivo General de las Indias, Estado, América en General, legajo 5.

Chancellor declared that Austria would never recognize the independence of the new states until that independence had been recognized by Spain herself.[107] From this view the government at Vienna never deviated in the whole course of the colonial question.

As time went on, moreover, Metternich seems to have been increasingly disposed to treat the problem of Spanish America as a problem of general European interest. The growing friendship with the Tsar Alexander, particularly after Troppau and Laybach, may have strengthened him in such a course. And the trend of British policy, which looked more and more toward recognition, may also have lent force to the belief that, if a shock to legitimist principles were to be avoided, it was highly desirable to arrive at a common accord on the colonial question. At any rate, when in November, 1823, Chateaubriand sought to free the hands of France by dissociating the other Continental powers from the solution of the American problem, Metternich repudiated the notion that Austria might stand aside. The fate of the New World, he declared, was "too intimately bound up with the tranquillity and welfare of the whole of Europe" for such a course to be possible.[108]

Metternich's conception of common action was not, however, that of Pozzo di Borgo or of Chateaubriand. He wished merely preliminary conferences, not a solemn appeal to a congress.[109] He

---

[107] Paris, Aff. Étr., Méms. et Docs., France, vol. 699, fol. 221. "Relative to the question of the *de facto* recognition of the new Governments established in the different parts of the Spanish territory in America, the Austrian minister is commanded to declare in the name of the Emperor, his master, That his Imperial Majesty, invariably faithful to the great principles on which the social order and the maintenance of legitimate governments depend, will never recognize the independence of the Spanish American provinces, so long as His Catholic Majesty has not freely and formally renounced the sovereign rights that he has heretofore exercised over those provinces."

[108] St. Petersburg, F. O., Reçus, no. 20,616 (Encl. 1), Nov. 26, 1823.

[109] Vienna. Staats-Archiv. Spanien, Varia, Metternich to Brunetti, Dec. 26, 1823. "The idea of a Congress put forward by Monsieur Pozzo is an indigent one. Things have not come to that point yet. Before talking about Congresses, it is necessary to come to an accord on many matters, and the way to do this is through simple conferences. As England views matters to-day, such conferences are feasible, I flatter myself. I call to your attention the difference between a *Congress* and

would have liked to have those conferences held in London,[110] in order to avoid antagonizing Great Britain. He would have proceeded with the utmost caution, and certainly with no notions of reconquest in view.

Indeed, he was entirely convinced that reconquest was an impossibility. In July he told Wellesley, the British ambassador at Vienna, that in his opinion all projects of the kind were hopeless, and that Spain would do well to confine her efforts to retaining Cuba.[111] Somewhat later he declared to the Russian ambassador that Spain should limit her policy to the retention of those colonies which still remained faithful, and decide frankly to compromise with those which, on terms of mutual advantage, might consent again to become subject to her.[112]

Far more important than these passing statements, however, in assessing Austrian policy in the fall of 1823, is a memorandum of Metternich's, addressed to the Austrian minister at Madrid, but communicated to all the allied powers, and dated December 26. This memorandum is the most authentic statement of the Austrian Chancellor's point of view. The colonies are divided into three classes:

> There are some wholly under the authority of the King. There are some in which the struggle between the legitimate power, and the pretensions of factions, is not yet over. There are some which have constituted themselves independent states, and in which the struggle between the *de jure* and the *de facto* authorities have ceased. The first preoccupation of Spain should be to assure as completely and as permanently as possible the possession of the important island of Cuba, not only by measures suitable to defend it against unjust aggression, which, happily, it is not necessary to predict, but also by a régime conformable to its present condition, and based above all on the protection and prosperity of its inhabitants. . . . The contemplation of the present and future welfare of the faithful colony cannot fail to strengthen the legitimist party where that party is still *condemned* to struggle against the partisans of independence; it will serve perhaps to revive the courage of friends of the ancient order in other colonies, where attachment to the mother country is repressed rather than destroyed.

---

*conferences*. I admit that in Spain, where in general diplomacy is a bit barbarous, this distinction is not easy to understand. But everything has to have a beginning."

[110] London. P. R. O., F. O., Austria, vol. 179, Dec. 12, 1823.

[111] Ibid., vol. 178, desp. 5, July 23, 1823.

[112] St. Petersburg. F. O., Reçus, no. 20,516, Nov. 25, 1823.

This is all that the Austrian Chancellor has to say with regard to those colonies where the struggle was not yet over. As to those where the revolution had completely succeeded, he declared:

It appears to us that all that wisdom should dictate at this time is to keep open the question of legal right. It is *certainly* not over this *immense part* of the American continent which Spain formerly possessed as colonies that the efforts of the mother country can now be directed with any chance of success whatsoever. In deeming it possible to regain all, she would be practically sure to lose all.[113]

It is clear from this memorandum that Austria had no interest whatever in the reconquest of the colonies for Spain. Metternich was, of course, willing to confer with the rest of the powers on the South American question; and he obviously sought to prevent, and was indeed anxious to prevent, isolated action on the part of Great Britain. But his influence, in the formulation of a positive program, was sure to be cast on the side of moderation. This fact will become more clear when we turn to the discussions of 1824. But it stands out in every line of the important document just quoted, and in every utterance of the Austrian minister on the subject of the colonies.

## PRUSSIA

Of the last of the great Continental powers, Prussia, it is necessary to say only a word. Prussia had no important commercial interests in South America; her rulers, no such passion for regulating the affairs of the universe as Alexander, and no such dominant influence upon the European continent as Metternich. In the affairs of Spanish America, as in many other questions, the Prussian government was at this time little more than a satellite of Austria. In the deliberations of 1817 and 1818, Hardenberg, the Prussian Chancellor, followed in the footsteps of his Austrian colleague, in opposition to any enterprise of force, and in coöperation with Great Britain; and at Aix-la-Chapelle he supported the views of Metternich and Castlereagh.[114] In the course of the ensuing years Prussia, like Austria, supported the principle of

113 St. Petersburg. F. O., Reçus, no. 21,221 (Encl.). Italics mine.
114 Castlereagh, *Correspondence*, xi, 385.

legitimacy, assuring Spain of her loyalty in 1822,[115] and assenting to the principles of the rest of the allied powers at the Congress of Verona.[116] Her attitude was, no doubt, the same in the fall of 1823. But as to any measures of reconquest, these were certainly not contemplated with favor by the government of Berlin. In the instructions to Baron Werther, the Prussian ambassador at London, dated October 30, 1823, it is clearly indicated that Spain has no resources for the task, save "the débris of revolutionary forces," which would themselves be revolutionized.[117] As for the allied powers, says another dispatch, they "lack arms to reach America, or even a voice to make themselves heard there." [118] The colonial question must be faced without illusion, with regard to the distances and forces involved,[119] and in recognition of the fact that any action taken without Great Britain offers "chances as uncertain as unfavorable." [120] As for a positive policy, Prussia had none at the end of 1823. Nowhere more than in the archives at Berlin does the fact stand out that the discussion of the colonial question had only begun when Monroe penned his famous manifesto.

When we examine the Prussian attitude toward the United States, it is interesting to note that in 1817 Prussia took the lead in suggesting American participation in the councils of the allied powers, anticipating both Alexander and the Duc de Richelieu.[121] But in 1823 Berlin associated itself without reserve with the more exclusive views expressed by Metternich and Chateaubriand. There was a suggestion that jealousy of the United States might be used to persuade England to common action.[122] But of regard for American interests, there is not a whit.

How sum up the conclusions of this chapter? Speaking generally, it may be said that no immediate danger to the new states

---

[115] See W. S. Robertson's article, "The United States and Spain in 1822," *Am. Hist. Rev.* (July, 1915), xx, 794.

[116] *Ibid.*, p. 799.　　　　[117] Berlin. Staats-Archiv, England, 69.

[118] Ibid., Russland, Rep. I, 82, Dec. 19, 1823.　　　　[119] Ibid.

[120] Ibid., Oesterreich I, 96 II, Dec. 23, 1823.

[121] London. P. R. O., F. O., France, Dec. 18, 1817.

[122] Berlin. Staats-Archiv, Oesterreich I, 96, Dec. 9, 1823.

of South America existed at the time when Monroe framed his message. That the Continental powers projected a congress on the colonial question was, of course, true; but there is every reason for believing that from such a congress no very active policy could possibly have resulted. The attitude of Russia was, no doubt, problematical; and if the Tsar remained noncommittal, it must be admitted that the intrigues of Pozzo were of sinister omen. But Russia, had she been so inclined, could hardly act alone; and the rest of the powers were certainly far from desiring intervention by force in the New World. Not only had France pledged herself against such intervention, but the interests of her commerce actually inclined her toward recognition rather than toward a contrary policy; and at the very time when there was most suspicion of her purposes, French agents were dispatched to the South American states to carry reassuring messages as to the intentions and point of view of the ministers of Louis XVIII. Oscillating between the desire to be on good terms with Great Britain and the necessity of standing by the principles of legiti- macy and European coöperation, the French government was really incapable of a vigorous decision, and could certainly not be counted on to favor the resubjugation of Ferdinand's dominions. As for Austria and Prussia, there was as little to be hoped from them. Metternich saw, perhaps more clearly than any other European statesman, the actual situation of the New World; and no romantic dream of restoring Spanish sovereignty possessed his clear and practical mind. Prussia was a negligible factor. The materials for an aggressive policy on the part of the Holy Alliance were not impressive.

Indeed, a positive policy scarcely existed. Of all the na- tions of the Continent, France alone had a definite solution to suggest. That solution was the foundation of Bourbon monar- chies in the New World. The scheme was of long standing, and a continuous element in French policy. Fundamentally, it was in- tended to reconcile the interests of French commerce with the principle of legitimacy. The menace of the republican dogma, the danger of American solidarity based on similarity of political institutions, was felt by many European statesmen, and found frequent expression in the diplomatic correspondence of the time. The best way to deal with that menace, in the eyes of a long line of French ministers, was to set up independent kingdoms in the new states that had sprung from the dominions of Spain. In the execution of this idea, there was, on occasion, some suggestion of the use of force; but the aid contemplated was never very extensive, and we hear no more of aid at all after the discussions of Canning with Polignac in October, 1823.

The project of Bourbon monarchies was, of course, in part directed against the United States. The attitude of Europe toward the American government was, in general, one of mild hostility at the time of Monroe's pronouncement. At an earlier period, virtually all the Continental powers had been willing to consider the admission of the United States to the councils of the allied powers; but by 1823, the situation had changed, no doubt owing to the recognition of the new republics by the United States, and Metternich and Chateaubriand were surer of nothing than of the utter undesirability of admitting the American government to the European council table. Chateaubriand never even offered any explanations to the American minister as to the French policy; and his assurances to Gallatin in June of 1823 that France would not interfere in any manner in the American question were proved false by the subsequent course of events. Only Russia showed some measure of kindliness toward the young republic of the West. There was condescension in Alexander's tone, it is true; but he did at least recognize the existence of an American interest in the fate of the Spanish colonies. The rest of Europe was ready to treat the views of Washington as of no importance whatever. It could have had no more unpleasant shock than the vigorous and decisive language in which President Monroe dealt with the question in his message to Congress, all the more, no doubt, because the imputations of the message were so far from justified on the basis of existing facts. Of the emotions of European statesmen in this regard, however, it is not necessary here to speak; for the reception of the message may properly form the subject of a chapter by itself.

# CHAPTER V

## THE RECEPTION OF THE MESSAGE

THE message of President Monroe was published in the United States on December 2, 1823, and was naturally, before many weeks had gone by, republished in the newspapers of Europe and of Spanish America. It will be interesting to examine the impression which it produced in all these instances, the reception which was accorded it in the press and among public men, and the interpretation which was put upon its resounding phrases.

As to the message in the United States, it is hardly necessary to say that in the majority of instances it was received with great cordiality, not to say enthusiasm. The American people, notwithstanding their frequently manifested devotion to peace, have never been any more averse to a "strong" foreign policy than the rest of the world. For months, for years, one might say, the press had been pouring scorn on the institutions and policies of Europe. The President's declaration, with its eulogy of American principles and its solemn warning to the autocrats of the Old World, could hardly fail to be a popular document.

The message [wrote Addington to Canning] seems to have been received with acclamation throughout the United States. . . . The explicit and manly tone, especially, with which the President has treated the subject of European interference in the affairs of this Hemisphere with a view to the subjugation of those territories which have emancipated themselves from European domination, has evidently found in every bosom a chord which vibrates in strict unison with the sentiments so conveyed. They have been echoed from one end of the union to the other. It would indeed be difficult, in a country composed of elements so various, and liable on all subjects to opinions so conflicting, to find more perfect unanimity than has been displayed on every side on this particular point.[1]

The language of Addington seems in the main to be borne out by the general tone of newspaper comment on the message. Almost without exception the press of the country rallied behind the

---

[1] London. P. R. O., F. O., America, vol. 185, no. 1, Jan. 5, 1824.

President, and praised the sentiments which he had promulgated to the world. Almost without exception, too, they took the portentous language of the President's declaration at its face value. Only one newspaper out of a score which I have examined was really sceptical of the grave danger which menaced the United States.[2] The rest seem to have taken the peril for granted. They took for granted, too, the ability of the country to repel any threat which might be offered. The self-confident nationalism of the "era of good feeling" is nowhere better illustrated than in the reaction to Monroe's manifesto. The idea that there could be any doubt about the capacity of the government to make good its words in action was hardly suggested. Barring an occasional appeal for increased military preparation,[3] there was, in the public press, no hint of any kind that the United States was not ready to meet the Holy Alliance in its designs, and successfully oppose them.

Here and there the suggestion of coöperation with Great Britain was put forward. Some intimation of the conversations between Rush and Canning penetrated into the newspapers. But no such idea was widely diffused, and in general the possibility of British aid in the protection of colonial liberty was ignored. The Albany *Argus* cynically argued that the British government would, in all probability, maintain a circumspect neutrality.[4] But it seemed not a whit cast down on this account.

Now and again, there was some deviation from this self-confident and exulting tone in which most of the journals of the country treated the message. Most significant, perhaps, is the reserved tone of the Richmond *Enquirer*, a paper of high standing, and by no means hostile to Monroe. The *Enquirer* did not condemn the message out of hand. But it obviously was not wholly content.

The President takes bold ground [it observed]. We are solicitous to know what attacks are meditated; and we presume that Congress will call for such information as may be in the power of the Executive to give, and which it might be expedient to submit, calculated to shed any light upon this interesting subject.[5]

[2] The New York *Spectator*, Dec. 5.
[3] The *National Gazette and Literary Register*, Dec. 11.    [4] Dec. 6.
[5] Quoted in the *New England Palladium*, Dec. 9.

This attitude of mild mystification is outdone by the frank condemnation of several Federalist papers in the North. The New York *Advertiser* found that the President had made use of language "too broad and comprehensive for the occasion," and added, "We much doubt whether our country will be satisfied to go to war with France and Spain on this account" (that is, to prevent the reconquest of the colonies).[6] The Salem *Gazette* could not see how it would be dangerous to our peace and safety if the Patagonians or the Eskimos adopted despotic government;[7] and a writer in the Boston *Advertiser* demanded:

> Is there anything in the Constitution which makes our Government the Guarantors of the Liberties of the World? of the Wahabees? the Peruvians? the Chilese? the Mexicans or Colombians? . . . In short, to reduce it to the actual case, though we acknowledged the disturbed and unsettled Governments of South America as being de facto independent, did we mean to make that act equivalent to treaties offensive and defensive? I hope not.[8]

This critical tone, extremely rare in the newspaper press, was perhaps a little more general in the halls of Congress. Or, to put it more cautiously, the national legislature showed no unrestrained enthusiasm for the Presidential declaration, and was, apparently, loath to commit itself to the doctrines which that declaration contained. At the moment that the message was sent to Congress, James Barbour, a senator from Virginia, and later a member of the Adams cabinet, seems to have thought of proposing a resolution calling for coöperation by treaty with Great Britain to repel the danger in which the New World stood.[9] But no such resolution was actually introduced, despite the favoring comment which Madison, to whom Barbour wrote, gave to the proposal.[10] On January 20, Henry Clay, who had told Adams that the section on foreign policy was "the best part of the message," [11] brought forward a resolution of his own. It read as follows:

[6] December 6.
[7] December 9.
[8] Quoted in the Salem *Gazette*, Dec. 16.
[9] *Writings* of James Madison, edited by Gaillard Hunt (New York, 1900–10, 9 vols.), ix, p. 171.
[10] *Ibid.*, pp. 171 ff.
[11] Adams, *Memoirs*, vi, p. 224.

*Resolved, by the Senate and House of Representatives of the United States
of America in Congress assembled,* That the people of these States would
not see, without serious inquietude, any forcible interposition by the Allied
Powers of Europe in behalf of Spain, to reduce to their former subjection
those parts of the continent of America which have proclaimed and established for themselves, respectively, independent Governments, and which
have been solemnly recognized by the United States.[12]

This, of course, was a proposal to commit Congress directly and
explicitly to the support of the Monroe declaration. But it never
came to a vote in the House of Representatives, and some months
later Clay himself withdrew it, declaring that the circumstances
had so changed as to render it no longer necessary.[13]

The truth of the matter seems to be that, under the surface,
there was at least a measure of opposition to the decisive tone
taken by Monroe. John Randolph of Roanoke condemned the
stand taken in the South American question as quixotic,[14] and
declared that, if the governments of South America, having
achieved their independence, had not valor to maintain it, he
would not "commit the safety and independence" of the United
States in such a cause.[15] Floyd of Virginia denounced the message, so he tells us at a later date, as

assuming an unwarrantable power; violating the spirit of the Constitution;
assuming grounds and an attitude toward European Powers, calculated to
involve us in the strife which there existed, and in which we had no interest;
and indirectly leading to war, which Congress alone had the right to declare.[16]

There was, also, perhaps, a reluctance to believe that the situation was as perilous as Monroe's words implied. It is a significant and interesting fact, illustrating the attitude of Congress
toward the message, that, in the debate on a bill for the construction of additional sloops of war, the danger of a struggle over
South America was not once mentioned;[17] and the bill itself never
came to a vote in the House. There were, of course, members of

---

[12] *Annals of Congress,* Eighteenth Congress, First Session (Washington, 1856), i,
col. 1104.

[13] *Ibid.,* ii, col. 2763.  [14] *Ibid.,* i, col. 1112.

[15] *Ibid.,* col. 1188.

[16] *Register of Debates in Congress,* Nineteenth Congress, First Session (Washington, 1826), ii, col. 2446.

[17] *Annals of Congress,* Eighteenth Congress, First Session, i, cols. 210–232.

Congress who took the danger of intervention seriously. This appears clearly enough from the debate on Webster's resolution for the recognition of the Greeks in the first weeks of 1824.[18] But nothing in the *Annals of Congress* makes it seem likely that the majority of the legislators responded very militantly to the militant mood of Monroe, or were much afraid of European intervention. In the House the only action taken was a request for further information on the whole South American question;[19] and when this was answered by the President with a statement that he possessed "no information on that subject, not known to Congress, which" could "be disclosed without injury to the public good,"[20] the result was, to all appearances, to discourage any further consideration of the problem. In the Senate there was, so far as the *Annals* reveal, no discussion at all of the foreign policy sketched out in the message. In the increasingly cautious attitude of the administration in the later months of 1824 (an attitude subjected to analysis in a later chapter), there may be traced, perhaps, something of the reluctance of the legislative body to approve the vigorous language of the Chief Executive.

As to the attitude of public men, outside the national legislature, it is difficult to judge. Only a few isolated examples of comment seem to have been preserved to us. Madison declared that the message could "do nothing but good."[21] John Marshall gave more cautious adhesion in the declaration that we "cannot look on the present state of the world with indifference."[22] At least two state legislatures passed resolutions commendatory of the President's stand.

To judge from these meagre examples, the favorable reaction of the press found its counterpart in the reaction of those individual politicians or statesmen who had no direct responsibility to make Monroe's words good. It was only in Congress that a salutary reserve tempered the enthusiasm which the President's declaration might have been expected to arouse. In the rest of

[18] *Annals of Congress*, Eighteenth Congress, First Session, i, cols. 1110, 1137, 1169, 1211. Several members advanced the argument that it was not wise to antagonize Europe on a European question at a time when the liberties of the New World were in danger.    [19] *Ibid.*, col. 868. By Mallary.
[20] *Ibid.*, col. 986.    [21] Monroe, *Writings*, vi, 408.    [22] *Ibid.*

the country, the general impression of the message appears to have been wholly an agreeable one.

So much for the reaction to Monroe's message in the United States. How was it received in those countries in whose interest it was promulgated? In order to answer this question, it is desirable to understand the circumstances, looked at from the Spanish American point of view, which prevailed at the moment of the President's manifesto.[23]

In the first place, it is worth observing that the directors of the policy of the new states had none of the sources of information which made such a deep impression upon Monroe and his advisers. The communications of Baron Tuyll, which were of such importance in the evolution of the Doctrine, and which did so much to confirm the suspicions of the American cabinet, were probably entirely unknown in the states to the South. They certainly do not figure in the instructions of the American Secretary of State to any of the American ministers to the new republics; and, indeed, the latter of the Russian notes was so nearly contemporaneous with the message as to make it extremely unlikely that it could have been known prior to the publication of that document itself. In the pages of Adams's diary, an unusually full record for the period from November 7 to December 2, 1823, there is not the slightest hint of any conversation with any one of the South American diplomats at Washington in which the Tuyll correspondence might have been mentioned. Nor, conversely, in the reports of the representatives of the American government at the various capitals of the new republics is there any evidence that the attitude of Russia furnished the subject of any exchange of views. It is impossible to assume finality on the basis of these negative indications; but this cumulative evidence must be regarded as of very considerable importance.

Moreover, it is not likely that the confidences of George Canning to Richard Rush, the British minister's warning of a projected

---

[23] The subject has been discussed in Lockey, chap. vi, pp. 223–262, and in an article by W. S. Robertson on "South America and the Monroe Doctrine, 1824–1828," *Pol. Sci. Quart.*, xxx (1915), pp. 82–105.

congress on the South American question, which played so large
a part in the debates of the cabinet at Washington, had any
counterpart in the relations of the representatives of the new
republics with the British or American government. In the voluminous correspondence of Santander and Bolívar, in the collection of diplomatic dispatches known as the *Diplomacia Mexicana,*
there is no hint of any such confidence. There is no allusion to it
in the diplomatic dispatches of our ministers. The Polignac interview, directly affecting in the most positive manner the fate of
the new states, and vitally related to British policy, was made
known to no South American government, as we have seen, before
the end of 1823. If Canning chose so long to withhold information on a matter of such importance, it is entirely unlikely that
he had talked with the South American agents in London as to
the plans of the Continental allies. Nor was there any sound reason why, so long as British policy remained in its formative stage,
he should have done so.

In view of these circumstances, it is unlikely that anywhere in
South America was there so definite a conviction of impending
danger as there was in the mind of Monroe. And in certain instances, at any rate, there was a very distinct tendency to minimize the peril with which the new states were threatened. Perhaps
the most striking example of this temper is to be found in the
attitude of Don Bernadino Rivadavia, the Minister of Foreign
Affairs for Buenos Aires. In July, 1823, Rivadavia had signed a
treaty with the commissioners sent out by the constitutional government of Spain, and throughout the fall of 1823 he was working
through commissioners sent to the other South American states
to bring the whole colonial struggle to a conclusion. The collapse
of the liberal cause in the Spanish Peninsula forced him to surrender these hopes, but he was not on that account perturbed as
to the possibility of European intervention. In the middle of
December, he declared improbable any interference on the part
of the Holy Allies.[24] A fuller expression of his views is to be found

[24] *Documentos para la historia argentina,* edited by Emilio Ravignani, vol. xiv
("Correspondencias generales de la provincia de Buenos Aires relativas á relaciones
exteriores," Buenos Aires, 1921), p. 389.

in the important circular sent on February 5, 1824, before the arrival of the message, to the representatives of Buenos Aires in the other republics of South America. In this circular, it is true, Rivadavia speaks of the necessity of solidarity, and gives assurances of the support of Buenos Aires, in case of European action, but at the same time he distinctly discounts the danger. The impotence of Spain, he writes, has always made it unlikely that the Holy Allies would seek to restore her authority in a campaign 2,000 leagues removed from Europe; there would be no assurance of success, and still less that Ferdinand VII could retain his ancient dominions were he once put in possession of them. The chances were that the European powers would seek rather to make their political views prevail by negotiation than to interpose by force of arms.[25]

The views of Rivadavia are in a measure reproduced by another Spanish American Foreign Minister, Don Lucas Alamán, of Mexico, one of the most conspicuous figures in the revolutionary history of that republic. In his report to Congress of November 1, 1823, Alamán, though admitting the possibility of intervention, indicated that such intervention was not likely to be attempted.[26]

In Chile, on the other hand, there was more apprehension. As early as December 4, 1823, the Chilean legislative body proposed the sending of a joint Chilean, Colombian, and Peruvian mission to England and the United States, to urge recognition and seek to persuade the two Anglo-Saxon governments to protest against the attitude of the Holy Alliance, "which was casting its eyes" on South America.[27] It recommended such action on December 4 to the Supreme Director, and again on January 7 and Febru-

---

[25] *Documentos para la historia argentina*, xiv, pp. 434–439, "Circular á los estados independientes de América, exponiendo las vistas del gobierno con motivo de la tendencia de las naciones de Europa á ingerirse en los negocios del Nuevo Mundo y restaurar el dominio de España," Feb. 5, 1824.

[26] *British and Foreign State Papers* x, (1822–23), p. 1074. "It [i. e., Mexico] may have reason to apprehend that the Allied Monarchs who have interfered in the internal affairs of Spain, may extend their views to the possessions formerly belonging to that kingdom on this Continent; but the sentiments manifested by England have, in some degree, relieved this suspicion."

[27] *Sesiones de los cuerpos lejislativos de la república de Chile*, 1811–45, edited by Valentin Letelier (Santiago, 1887–1906, 29 vols.), viii, p. 499 f.

ary 9.[28] A few days later instructions were drawn up for the Chilean member of this mission.[29] The envoy was never sent, and the deliberation with which the whole matter was treated may serve to indicate that, though there was apprehension, there was no very serious fear of immediate intervention; but the danger at any rate was one which justified the taking of countervailing measures.

In the case of Colombia, there are evidences of a considerable degree of anxiety. The historian Restrepo, himself a witness of the events of 1823 and 1824, declares that there was great excitement along the littoral, and a genuine fear that France would intervene in favor of Spain. Martial law was proclaimed in some of the coast provinces.[30] The Vice-President, Santander, in direction of Colombian affairs during Bolívar's absence in Peru, had proposed to the American agent, Todd, as early as June, 1823,[31] an alliance to ward off the threatened danger, and in November he wrote to the Liberator about the designs of France in terms of apprehension.[32] At the end of December the Colombian Foreign Minister, Gual, approached the newly arrived American minister, Anderson, with new suggestions of a more intimate connection between the two states.[33] All these facts taken together suggest that the Colombian government was quite fearful of European action.

The attitude of Bolívar, who, in the period with which this chapter deals, was engaged in the liberation of Peru, is less easily defined. The tone of his correspondence is rather contradictory, depending perhaps in part upon the moods of his extremely volatile nature. Writing to Heres, the Peruvian Foreign Minister, at the end of December, he asserted flatly that France would do nothing as to South America.[34] To Santander, on March 10,

[28] Chile, *Sesiones*, viii, p. 499; ix, pp. 40, 81 f.    [29] *Ibid.*, ix, p. 90 f.

[30] J. M. Restrepo, *Historia de la revolución de la república de Colombia*, 2d. ed. (Besançon, 1858, 3 vols.), iii, p. 403.

[31] Washington. State Dept., Despatches, Colombia, vol. 2, no. 55, June 16, 1823.

[32] *Archivo Santander*, edited by Ernesto Restrepo Tirado (Bogota, 1913–26, 22 vols. to date), xi, 327. Santander's letter itself is on pp. 133 ff.

[33] Washington. State Dept., Despatches, Colombia, vol. 3, no. 5, Dec. 29, 1823.

[34] *Cartas de Bolívar, 1823–1824–1825*, edited by R. de Blanco Fombona (Madrid, 1921), p. 95.

while still apparently without the reassurance of Monroe's message or encouraging tidings from the Old World, he expressed himself in the same strain. "This fear [of yours]" he declared, "does not appear to me to be justified; since no situation can persuade me that France will enter upon plans hostile to the New World, after respecting our neutrality in days of calamity." [35] Finally, on March 21, the Liberator wrote to Sucre, "I do not believe at all in the League between France and Spain. We have documents that prove the contrary." [36] But on the other hand there are two letters of a very different tenor in January. In neither of these does he flatly predict intervention; but the temper of both is distinctly one of alarm.[37] Balancing these contrary

[35] *Archivo Santander*, xi, p. 327.

[36] *Cartas de Bolívar*, p. 190. What these documents are it is difficult to surmise. The Polignac correspondence was brought to Bogotá by the British commissioners, who arrived there the second day of March. This is far too late for its transmission to the Liberator on the date of the letter to Sucre. But could it have been dispatched by some other route?

[37] *Ibid.*, pp. 139 f., and note on pp. 143 f. These letters deserve quotation. That to Santander runs as follows: "The interest of the world political drama, and in particular that of America, increases proportionately as the dénouement approaches. Yesterday we learned the terrible news of the catastrophe of the liberal cause in Spain, and the complete and sudden triumph of the reactionaries. This event rapidly increases the speed of the wheels which conduct the chariot of our revolution; but at the same time that it hastens it, it opposes bumps and jars, which will not fail to give us terrible shocks. The reunion of Ferdinand to the reactionaries and the Allied victory over the constitutionalists disturbed me, since it must cause some reaction on American affairs; from now on, the Spaniards will be free from a part of their European preoccupations. For the rest, the royalists of America will not fail to hope for the continuation of the war and for Spanish aid, as is already known from the news of neutral foreigners who brought the news of the triumph of the reactionaries and of Ferdinand. The royalists of Peru have boldly declared up to now that they would not recognize the independence of America, even if Spain recognized it; all this before their victories. They will know now, what we took care to publish, the proclamation of the Duc d'Angoulême with regard to the submission of America; and they will deduce from this political profession of France that the war against us is to continue with more vigor. Consequently, we must expect more than blood and fire from the followers of Canterac, La Serna, and Valdés; consequently we can hope for liberty only from the 12,000 Colombians whom I have asked to be sent to Peru."

The essential sections of the letter to Gual run as follows: "The Holy Alliance has carried its arms to the walls of Cadiz; the Old World is already gravitating toward the New; the balance between the two hemispheres has been destroyed; and

views, it is perhaps to be indicated that Bolívar, while not free from doubts, was by no means as apprehensive as the government at Bogotá.

So much for the attitude of the leading figures of Spanish American politics toward the danger of intervention at the time when Monroe penned his declaration. But in order to understand the reception accorded to that document there is another consideration which deserves to be emphasized, the consideration that in virtually every case Spanish American statesmen, in so far as they believed in the danger at all, were inclined to look toward Great Britain rather than toward the United States to avert it. There were exceptions to this rule. The Chilean Foreign Minister, while declaring that Great Britain and the United States might both be useful in warding off threatened danger, was ready to contract an alliance with the United States, as compared with the mere extension of commercial privilege to the British.[38] Santander was more ready to cement Colombian relations with this country than with England, as the proposal to Todd in June of 1823 serves to illustrate. But on the other hand, in writing to Bolívar he attached more significance to British than to American policy in so far as its effect upon the Holy Allies was concerned.[39]  At Buenos Aires, Rivadavia declared as early as December 16 that the sending of British consuls, a measure announced in October, would operate as a check upon the designs of the Continental powers,[40] and he reiterated this viewpoint in the second circular

only England, mistress of the seas, can protect us against the united force of European reaction.

"Already fears are expressed that King Ferdinand will try to get rid of an army which has not been able to be faithful to him, and which ought not have been so. He will therefore send it to America, that is to say, where it will be easiest to transport it, and where it can triumph with more safety. France can give him whatever maritime aid he needs; this measure must enter into the calculations of the Spaniards; it will give France a decided preponderance over England."

From these extracts it will be seen that Bolívar feared the encouragement of the reactionaries, and possible maritime aid from France, rather than intervention on a large scale.          [38] Chile, Sesiones, ix, p. 90 f.

[39] Archivo Santander (Jan. 6, 1824), xi, p. 234. "I am convinced that Spain will try to get France to help her, and that when by the intervention of England French aid does not succeed, she will continue to make war alone."

[40] Documentos para la historia argentina, xiv, p. 389.

of February 5.[41] Alamán took the same stand in the report of November 1, and at the same time his agent in London was strongly pressing for an alliance.[42] Gual, the Colombian Foreign Minister, was confident that Great Britain would oppose intervention if it were attempted.[43] Bolívar wrote to Santander in his letter of January 23, 1824, that only England could change the course of the present policy of the Allies,[44] and urged Gual, in his letter of January 24, to invite the British government to recognize Colombian independence, and insistently to demand of Spain recognition "of all the parts of America." [45] The gaze of all these statesmen was fixed far more on Great Britain than on the United States. Nor is the fact in the slightest degree to be wondered at. Great Britain's opposition to the allied intervention in Spain had been made clear to the world. Her material power was incomparably greater than that of this country. Her commercial relations with the new states were very much more important. More was to be hoped from her citizens in financial aid. The services which Englishmen had performed in the War of Independence were incalculably more important than any performed by citizens of the United States. From whatever point of view the matter is regarded, it is easy to understand the Spanish American interest in the attitude of England.

Facts such as these must have qualified the enthusiasm with which Monroe's famous declaration was received in the lands to the south. They did not prevent it from being noticed, and from being favorably regarded; but they must very much have diminished the ardent gratitude that might otherwise have been felt at its enunciation.

Even so, it will be interesting to observe the circumstances under which the President's manifesto was made known in America, and the impression which it produced. The materials for the

[41] The second circular was directed to the ministers to Chile, Peru, and Colombia. *Documentos para la historia argentina*, xiv, pp. 439 f.

[42] *Diplomacia Mexicana*, edited by Enrique Santibáñez (Mexico, 1910–13, 3 vols.), ii, p. 171.

[43] Washington. State Dept., Despatches, Colombia, Dec. 22, 1823.

[44] *Cartas de Bolívar*, p. 140.

[45] *Ibid.*, p. 144, note.

study of this question are, it must be confessed, rather scanty; none the less they are worth recording.

In the case of Mexico, the first allusion to the message is to be found in the *Aguila Mexicana* for February 12, 1824. This, however, is a mere report from "a person who left New Orleans on the fifteenth of last month," to the effect that Monroe had taken his stand against the reconquest of the colonies. The language of the President was not published till February 26, and then only a short extract, by a writer who was obviously much more interested in the prospects of British recognition than he was in the attitude of the United States. Of the impression which it produced, in the immediate sense, we have virtually no knowledge. There was no American minister at Mexico City to describe, as did Rush from London, its enthusiastic reception; nor is the declaration mentioned in the reports of the British agent, or in the papers of the French agent, Samouel, who was in Mexico in the early summer of 1824. What Mexican officialdom thought of it, it is difficult to say. There are, however, several facts that deserve to be indicated with regard to it. Early in December, Migoni, the Mexican agent in London, wrote definitely that Great Britain would prevent intervention;[46] and only a little later a Mexican named Thomas Murphy transmitted to his government the account of an interview with Villèle in which the friendly feelings of the French government were made clear.[47] It was therefore not long after the arrival of the message before other facts were presented to the directors of Mexican policy which must sensibly have diminished its effect. This conclusion seems, in a measure, to be borne out by the circumstance that Alamán in his *Historia de México*, no less than in his report of January 11, 1825, to the Mexican Congress, gave a very subsidiary place to the Monroe Doctrine in describing the international situation of 1823 and 1824, and that other Mexican historians of the epoch took the same view.[48] It is noteworthy, too, that the message finds

[46] *Diplomacia Mexicana*, ii, p. 183.    [47] *Ibid.*, pp. 247–251.

[48] Lockey, pp. 227–232. The historians cited are J. M. Tornel, *Breve reseña histórica de los acontecimientos más notables de la nación mexicana* (Mexico, 1852), J. M. Bocanegra, *Memorias para la historia de Mexico independiente* (Mexico, 1892–

no place in the public manifestoes and speeches of the Mexican President, Victoria.[49]

On the other hand, too much should not be made of such facts. Jealousy of the United States, rather than indifference to the message, may have prompted all the silences as to Monroe's declaration, and it would be unfair to deduce from them that the message was speedily relegated to oblivion. As will appear in a later chapter, Mexican statesmen, in common with many others, were sufficiently interested in the President's pronouncement to make appeal to it in the years immediately following its enunciation.

In the case of Colombia, Monroe's manifesto was known at least as early as February 1, 1824. It was, if we are to believe the American minister at Bogotá, received with "great and unaffected joy." [50] Santander, the Vice-President, who had always been sympathetic toward the United States, hailed it with enthusiasm. In his inspired sheet, *La Gaceta de Colombia*, appeared a long eulogy of the message,[51] and in his communication of April 6, 1824, to the Colombian Congress, he declared Monroe's declaration to be "an Act eminently just, and worthy of the Classic Land of Liberty . . . a policy consolatory to human nature," and assigned to it an importance much greater than he did to the attitude of Great Britain,[52] though the latter was by this time certainly known to him.[53] On the other hand, Bolívar, who, as has been seen, put his faith in Canning from the beginning, never seems to have been very strongly impressed with the pronouncement of Monroe. There is no specific allusion to the message in all his

97, 2 vols.), and Lorenzo de Zavala, *Ensayo histórico de las revoluciones de Méjico* (vol. i, Paris, 1831; vol. ii, New York, 1832).

[49] Lockey, pp. 232 ff.

[50] Washington. State Dept., Despatches, Colombia, vol. 3, no. 8, Feb. 7, 1824.

[51] Given in full in Lockey, pp. 241 ff.

[52] *British and Foreign State Papers*, xi (1823–24), p. 810.

[53] As early as February 6 Santander wrote to Bolívar, "It appears that England opposes intervention in South America." *Archivo Santander*, xi, 285. The British commissioners sent out by Canning arrived in Bogotá in early March. On March 8 they were presented to the Vice-President by Gual, the Colombian Foreign Minister, and gave assurances that Great Britain would not permit any other power to aid Spain in the reconquest of the colonies.

correspondence. There are, of course, references to the attitude of the United States in discussions of the international situation, such, for example, as the letter to Sucre of April 9, 1824, and two later letters, one to Admiral Guise, the commander of the Peruvian navy, on April 28, and one to Olañeta, the Spanish general, on May 21.[54] But in all of these the position taken by the government of the United States is subordinated to that assumed by Great Britain. There cannot be the slightest question as to the relative significance which the Liberator assigned to the policy of the two Anglo-Saxon powers. His attitude, it may be added, was distinctly more usual than that of Santander. Colombian press comment on the international situation in 1824 uniformly lays the emphasis on Great Britain. And this is the more readily understood since the Polignac correspondence was surely known in Colombia shortly after the arrival of the British commissioners in the middle of March,[55] as was also Canning's refusal to enter a congress on the colonial question.[56] The message occupied the field alone for only a short time. Moreover, there was no general confidence that it would prevent intervention. While some were ready to believe this to be the case, "others," wrote the American minister, "less sanguine in their opinion of its preventive tend-

[54] *Cartas de Bolívar*, pp. 196, 213, 222. These references deserve to be cited. To Sucre Bolívar wrote: "The English envoys who have arrived at Santa Marta have assured us that we shall be promptly recognized and aided against France in case of a rupture with us. The Americans offer the same. Spain can do nothing, because she has neither ships, army or money, and everything she does will be attributed to France, and will be fought as a foreign usurpation and as opposed to England and liberty. Anything the Holy Alliance does will be contested by England and North America." This is the first reference to the message.

To Guise, commander of the Peruvian navy, setting forth the hopeful elements in the situation, he wrote: "England is decided to recognize the independence of the republics of South America, and regard as a hostile act any intervention by European powers in the affair. . . . In the United States of the North they have solemnly declared that they will regard as a hostile act any measure taken by the Continental powers and in favor of Spain."

To Olañeta, the Spanish general, urging him to come over to the patriot cause, and giving reasons for doing so, he wrote: "England and America protect us, and you know that they are the only two maritime nations today, and that the Spaniards can only come by sea."

[55] *Cartas de Bolívar*, p. 235.

[56] *Archivo Santander*, xi, p. 338.

encies, seemed to derive their joy from the contemplation of the actual aid which the course indicated might give in the expected emergency." [57] The notion cherished by Rush and Middleton, that Europe would meekly alter its policy if Monroe declared his views on South America, was apparently not accepted on all sides by the politicians at Bogotá.

In Argentina, the first public notice of the message was its citation in *La Gaceta Mercantil* on February 9. On February 18 *El Argos* reproduced it, calling special attention to the non-colonization and non-intervention clauses. Rivadavia, put in possession of it, seems to have transmitted it immediately to the other South American republics, to Chile, Colombia, and Peru, as a document of considerable importance.[58] In the message of May 3, 1824, to the legislative assembly,[59] and again at the close of 1824,[60] reference was made to Monroe's declaration. But in the case of Argentina, as in the case of Colombia and Mexico, too much emphasis should not be laid upon the impression which it produced. Rivadavia looked far more toward England than toward the United States.[61] The disappointment at the reception of Monroe's pronouncement is only partially concealed by the language of Rodney, the American minister, who, while declaring the message to have been "productive of happy effects," declared that he looked "not so much to its temporary influence, as to its permanent opera-

---

[57] Washington. State Dept., Despatches, Colombia, no. 8, Feb., 1824.

[58] *Documentos para la historia Argentina*, xiv, p. 448.

[59] *British and Foreign State Papers*, xi (1823–24), p. 805. Allusion is made to the two principles of "the Abolition of Piratical Warfare, and that of Non-European Colonization of American Territory," and it is added that the Argentine minister to the United States has been instructed to suggest a third principle, to the effect that "none of the new Governments of this Continent shall alter by force their respective Boundaries as recognized at the time of their emancipation." In the instructions to Alvear, as later noted in the text, this comparison with the message is not made.

[60] *Ibid.*, xii (1824–25), p. 860. "That Republic, which, from its origin, presides over the civilization of the New World, has solemnly acknowledged our Independence. It has, at the same time, made an appeal to our national honour, by supposing us capable of contending single-handed with Spain; but it has constituted itself guardian of the field of battle, in order to prevent any foreign assistance from being introduced to the aid of our Rival."

[61] Washington. State Dept., Despatches, Buenos Aires, no. 37, June 17 to 22, 1826. Forbes says, "He [Nuñez] returned, as did Mr. Rivadavia, quite cured of his previous strong predilection in favor of Great Britain."

tion." [62] In the instructions to Alvear, commissioned minister to Washington, Rivadavia seems to have paid little attention to the American manifesto, and certainly did not direct that any particular gratitude should be expressed for the American stand.[63]

In Chile, the message was better received than in any other part of Spanish America, if any generalization at all can be erected upon the small number of facts that appear with regard to it. It was published in the Santiago papers in April, 1824, and here again, as in the other states, the views of the United States were linked with those of Great Britain. But the cordiality with which Monroe's declaration was welcomed is well attested by the American minister, who was received by the Chilean government on April 22, offered a guard and a house at public expense, and complimented profusely by the Minister of State, who declared that Chile uniformly recognized in the United States its best and most powerful friend, and that it was grateful for the recognition of the independence of the new states, and for the recent pronouncement which placed it beyond the reach of European monarchs.[64] The American attitude "cheered all hearts," wrote Allen, and there was apparently a confidence in the efficacy of American protection that was not always present elsewhere. On such scanty facts it is difficult to erect any general theory, but the cordial views of the Chilean government seem borne out by the offer of alliance which we have already noticed. That offer was not the offer of the Foreign Minister alone, but of the whole legislative body.[65] It may have reflected a general sentiment, and a general point of view. On the other hand, as to the standpoint of Freire, the Supreme Director, we know nothing.

How summarize the South American attitude toward the Doctrine? The temptation, on the basis of the facts just analyzed, might well be unduly to minimize the rôle of Monroe's message. From the exaggerated view of its significance common to the conventional historical narrative, it is easy to fall into a contrary error. That the attitude of the United States was regarded as of

---

[62] Washington. State Dept., Despatches, Buenos Aires, no. 5, May 22, 1824.
[63] Documentos para la historia argentina, xiv, pp. 453–458.
[64] Washington. State Dept., Despatches, Chile, vol. 1, no. 1, Apr. 29, 1824.
[65] Chile, Sesiones, ix, p. 81 f.

less importance than that of Great Britain must be frankly recognized. That the circumstances under which the President's manifesto was made known operated to diminish its effects is probable. That there was far less apprehension in most Spanish American capitals than in Washington, and therefore a cooler estimate of the importance of the United States attitude, is tolerably clear. But all these things taken together must not be pressed too far. Monroe's declaration was by no means disregarded. Nor was it, once observed, relegated to oblivion. It was almost everywhere assumed by South American statesmen that Monroe meant what he said, and that the ægis of North American protection had been extended over the new republics. And in the years following its enunciation, as will be seen later, more than one appeal was made to the message of 1823 by the rising nations of the New World.

Having thus considered the reception of the message in North and South America, it is necessary to turn back to the Old World, and seek to discover what effect Monroe's declaration produced in the capitals of Europe. The President's pronouncement arrived in London on December 27, and in Paris on December 30, and was duly noted in most of the newspapers. In the former capital the paragraphs on the Spanish colonial question met with pretty general approbation. Papers like the *Courier*, the *Times*, *Bell's Weekly Messenger*, the *Morning Chronicle*, and the Liverpool *Advertiser* pronounced Monroe's language to be of high significance, and contrasted its "manly plainness" with "the Macchiavellianism and hypocrisy" of the courts of Continental Europe.[66] The danger of intervention in the New World might, in the opinion of most of these sheets, be considered as at an end.

After so clear and explicit a warning [wrote the editor of the *Courier*], there is not one of the Continental powers, we suppose, that will risk a war with the United States, a war in which they could not expect to have either the aid or the good wishes of Great Britain, but a war in which the good wishes of Great Britain, if she did not choose to give more efficient succor, would be all on the side of the United States.[67]

After this explicit declaration [declared the *Chronicle*], the Allies will in all probability deem it expedient to leave America to itself. They are aware that

---

[66] The *Morning Chronicle*, Dec. 27, 1823.  [67] Dec. 27, 1823.

no force which it is possible for them to convey across the Atlantic could make the slightest impression on the United States, and that it would not be difficult to predict the fate of any armament which any of them might send in defiance of the latter.[68]

Rejoicing in the firm and decided language of "Colonel Monroe," the British press found it easy to believe that that language would put an end to the dangers which threatened the new states.

Of the commercial rivalry between Great Britain and the United States for the trade of South America — a rivalry which, as we shall see, was to be clearly demonstrated in the later policy of George Canning — there is hardly a hint in the comment of the most important of the British newspapers. Only the *British Monitor* drew the melancholy conclusion that the American government had "been beforehand" and had secured by treaty special advantages with regard to the new republics. And the very jealousy which led it to this conclusion led it also to suggest a doubt as to the willingness of Monroe to make good his words by deeds, and to call attention to the cautious policy of the administration in the years 1818 to 1822, as a justification of its scepticism.[69]

If, almost without exception, the London press hailed the message with delight, the Paris papers displayed a very different attitude. In more than one instance the language of the President's declaration was garbled in publication, and in some cases the most striking passages were entirely omitted.[70] In still others, the American manifesto came in for the roundest condemnation.

What is this power [wrote the ministerial sheet, *L'Étoile*] which haughtily avows maxims so contrary to the right of sovereignty and to the indepen-

---

[68] December 27, 1823.          [69] December 28, 1823.

[70] The *Étoile*, the *Moniteur*, the *Drapeau Blanc*, and the *Gazette de France* avoided all citation of the paragraphs of the message which related to Spanish America. The *Quotidienne*, another reactionary sheet, published, on December 31, the following extraordinarily perverted condensation of those paragraphs of Monroe's declaration which related to the colonial question: "The United States desire the happiness of those people from whom they are separated by the ocean. But they have never taken part in the wars of European powers among themselves; such a participation does not enter into our policy. We take up arms only when we are attacked, menaced, or insulted, only in our own defense. We are necessarily more clearly and more intimately connected with the political movements of this hemisphere than with those of Europe."

dence of every crown? What is this power which pretends to fix the limits of subjects' obedience? What is this power, above all, which does not fear to compromise the existence of the entire social order, declaring in the face of Heaven that it refuses to recognize any distinction between the de jure and the de facto governments? . . . Surveying at once all these assertions, all the doctrines included in the message, it is comforting to think that it has not yet received the sanction of the country in which it originated, and that, in a word, Mr. Monroe's opinions are still those of a private citizen.[71]

On the other hand, the opposition papers made the most of the American manifesto. They were, as we have seen, particularly enthusiastic about the non-colonization principle. But they were ready also to applaud the attitude of the President with regard to South America, and to declare, in the language of *Le Constitutionnel,* for example, that Monroe had "with calm, but with strength, set limits to the retrograde movement which men wish to impress upon the age in which we live." [72]

By both reactionaries and liberals, it may fairly be said, the American manifesto was at least dignified by comment, rather than passed by in silence.

The message had its reaction, too, upon the stock exchanges. In London its effects were immediately visible in a rise in the price of Spanish American securities, in increased trading, and in a corresponding fall in the value of the bonds of Spain.[73] In Paris the Spanish American issues were not quoted on the Bourse, but Spanish issues slumped badly in the week following the reception of the message, and purchases of them sharply declined.[74] Com-

[71] January 4, 1824.
[72] January 2, 1824.
[73] See the London *Times* for quotations. In London, Chilean and Colombian bonds stood at 69¼ and 59 respectively on Saturday, December 27, the day of the reception of the President's message. On Monday, Chileans went to 70¼, and continued to rise throughout the week, standing at 74¼ by January 5. Colombians did not respond so promptly, being quoted at 59 again on the twenty-ninth, but they rose to 60⅜ by January 5. The trend continued upward after this date. The stimulus to the American bonds may be contrasted with the reaction on the Spanish. The latter fell off a half-point on the day following the news of Monroe's pronouncement, and continued to decline thereafter.
[74] See the Paris *Étoile* for quotations. In Paris, the South American issues were not quoted on the Bourse. But the Spanish securities slumped steadily in the week following word of the message, falling more than three points between December 31 and January 8.

mercial opinion evidently found something in Monroe's pronouncement worth the noting.

If we turn from press and market to examine the reception of the President's declaration by individuals, we shall find, naturally enough, that the sympathizers with the new states were extremely enthusiastic in its praise, and, like the liberal newspapers, entirely confident of its effects. Rush and Middleton seemed to think that it settled the whole South American problem.[75] In the British House of Commons, members of the opposition, like Brougham, eulogized the courageous stand of the American government,[76] and in the House of Lords Lord Lansdowne held similar language.[77] In France such friends of the United States

[75] Washington. State Dept., Despatches, Great Britain, vol. 30, Dec. 27, 1823. "The most decisive blow to all despotick interference with the new states is that which it has received in the President's message at the opening of Congress. On its publicity in London which followed as soon afterwards as possible, the credit of all the Spanish American securities immediately rose, and the question of the final and complete safety of the new States from all European coercion, is now considered as at rest."

See also ibid., Great Britain, Jan. 6, 1824. "The timely and explicit assurance of the cause of South American independence," added Rush a little later, "has met with approbation from all classes of the community, as far as has come to my knowledge."

Ibid., Russia, vol. 10, Feb. 5, 1824. "The decided tone of the President's message," wrote Middleton, "is considered generally as having gone far toward deciding the question against interference."

[76] Hansard, *Parliamentary Debates*, New Series, x, col. 68, Feb. 3, 1824. "The question with regard to South America," declared Brougham, "was now disposed of, or nearly so; for an event had recently happened, than which no event had ever dispersed greater joy, exultation, and gratitude over all the freemen in Europe — an event in which he, as an Englishman, connected by ties of blood and language with America, took peculiar pride and satisfaction — an event, he repeated, had happened, which was decisive on the subject; and that event was the speech and the message of the President of the United States to Congress. The line of policy which that speech disclosed became a great, a free, and an independent nation; and he hoped that His Majesty's ministers would be prevented by no mean pride, no paltry jealousy from following so noble and illustrious an example." These observations were made in the debate on the King's speech at the opening of the session.

[77] *Ibid.*, col. 20, Feb. 3, 1824. "But if we had been tardy," observed the noble lord, "it was a satisfaction to find that America had, on this occasion, taken that decisive step which so well became its character and its interest. As that important decision was of the utmost consequence to every portion of the world where freedom was valued, he could not grudge to the United States the glory of having thus early thrown her shield over those struggles for freedom, which were so important, not

as Lafayette [78] and Barbé-Marbois [79] warmly praised the President's stand. And in Prussia, where liberals were scarce, Varnhagen von Ense attributed to it the most salutary and decisive influence.[80]

But what is more important than the reaction of such men as these is the effect that Monroe's declaration produced upon the diplomats and statesmen who were directly concerned with the problems which it raised.

In this connection it is important, first of all, to remember that

merely to America herself, but to the whole world." See also *ibid.*, col. 982, Mar. 15, 1824. With regard to republican government, the noble lord said, "Can it have escaped the attention of those who wish to indulge their predilection for particular forms of government on this occasion — that there exists in that part of the globe, a great and mighty power — and I am glad that it is a great and mighty power — I mean, the United States of North America — a power which has a right (and as far as propinquity is concerned) a better right, to act upon a similar predilection, though in favour of different principles. And, if any attempt should be made by any European power, to bring back the Spanish colonies to a monarchical or aristocratical government, is there not reason to apprehend, that the United States, seeing the foundation of their own institutions attacked, may think it necessary to lend the whole force of their union, to direct these neighbouring states toward a republican form of government?" Lord Landsdowne was speaking to his own resolution for the recognition of the colonies.

[78] Monroe, *Writings*, vii, 14. "I am delighted with your message, and so will be every liberal mind in Europe," wrote Lafayette to Monroe. Cf. Lafayette's remark to McRae, an American agent sent out by Monroe at the end of 1823, that the message was "the best little bit of paper that God had ever permitted any man to give to the World." Washington. State Dept., Special Agents' Series, McRae Papers, Nov. 3, 1824.

[79] Monroe, *Writings*, vi, 435. "M. de Marbois expressed in strong terms his approbation of your message," wrote Brown, the American minister at Paris, to Monroe, "which he said was not only the *best* but the *best-timed* state paper which he had ever read, and he hoped that Europe would be benefited by the check it might give to a career contrary to her own true policy and interests."

[80] *Briefwechsel* of Varnhagen von Ense and Oelsner (Stuttgart, 1865, 3 vols.), iii, pp. 177, 184 f. "The speech of the President of the United States," wrote Varnhagen to his friend, Oelsner, on January 10, 1824, "has made a strong impression upon public opinion, and upon the cabinet." And at a later date, speaking of possible plans for the conquest of Mexico, he declared, "But such proposals become insignificant, when the picture of the United States presents itself. The American government cannot possibly permit any Franco-Spanish conquests. They have the justification and the means for maintaining their favored commerce, which they carry on with the South American insurgents. The subjection of the Spanish colonies would have to be accomplished in the twinkling of an eye, like a conjurer's trick, or discord would be unavoidable."

to the chancelleries of Europe the President's message came like lightning from a clear sky. In a sense, American repugnance to a policy of intervention was, of course, known. Gallatin had made clear the opposition of the United States to the reconquest of the colonies in 1818, in conversations with the Duc de Richelieu and Pozzo di Borgo, and again to Chateaubriand in the spring of 1823. Adams had expressed to Tuyll, in answering the memorandum of October 16, the hope that Russia would continue to maintain absolute neutrality in the colonial struggle. But none of these things can be taken as presaging any such vigorous declaration as that to which the President gave utterance on December 2. Monroe and Adams had not waited for any exchange of views with the Continental powers; they had made no effort to establish the facts as to European policy, to discover what was in actuality intended, or to prepare the way for a definite declaration; they had, in what purported to be a document of exclusively American character, a mere communication to the national legislature, laid down in the most sweeping language the principles on which they expected the policy of the Old World to be governed in relation to the New. Those principles were principles which the Continental powers regarded with detestation; they embodied a challenge on the part of republican America to monarchical Europe; and the language of the message itself must have worn much the same aspect to a Metternich or a Chateaubriand that the manifestoes of Moscow wore to the conservative statesmen of 1919 or 1920.

There could be, then, no very pleasant reception in official circles for Monroe's declaration; and in all the Continental courts, and from most European statesmen, it met with profound condemnation. "Blustering," [81] "monstrous," [82] "arrogant," [83] "haughty," [84] "peremptory," [85] "unmeasured in its ambition," [86] "consecrating the principles of disruption" [87] — these are some

[81] Galabert, a French agent at Madrid, in Paris. Aff. Étr., Corr. Pol., Espagne, vol. 726, fol. 121, Jan. 8, 1824.

[82] Lebzeltern, in Vienna. Staats-Archiv, Berichte Russland, no. 64, Litt. B.

[83] Tuyll, in St. Petersburg. F. O., Reçus, no. 21,341, Feb. 2, 1824.

[84] Lieven, in ibid., no. 21,304, Jan. 2, 1824.

[85] Pozzo, in ibid., no. 20,298, Jan. 30, 1824.

[86] Tuyll, in ibid., no. 21,341, Feb. 2, 1824.       [87] Ibid.

of the terms applied to it. Perhaps the most crushing criticism came from the pen of the great Metternich.

These United States of America [wrote the Austrian Chancellor], which we have seen arise and grow, and which during their too short youth already meditated projects which they dared not then avow, have suddenly left a sphere too narrow for their ambition, and have astonished Europe by a new act of revolt, more unprovoked, fully as audacious, and no less dangerous than the former. They have distinctly and clearly announced their intention to set not only power against power, but, to express it more exactly, altar against altar. In their indecent declarations they have cast blame and scorn on the institutions of Europe most worthy of respect, on the principles of its greatest sovereigns, on the whole of those measures which a sacred duty no less than an evident necessity has forced our governments to adopt to frustrate plans most criminal. In permitting themselves these unprovoked [*sic*] attacks, in fostering revolutions wherever they show themselves, in regretting those which have failed, in extending a helping hand to those which seem to prosper, they lend new strength to the apostles of sedition, and reanimate the courage of every conspirator. If this flood of evil doctrines and pernicious examples should extend over the whole of America, what would become of our religious and political institutions, of the moral force of our governments, and of that conservative system which has saved Europe from complete dissolution? [88]

Such language betrays obvious resentment at the President's declaration. And yet the Austrian Chancellor, despite his indignation, seems never to have thought of a formal protest to the American government against the incendiary principles which it proclaimed, and on which it sought to base the future fate of South America. There was, it is true, no direct diplomatic intercourse between Austria and the United States at this time. But it would have been entirely possible for Metternich to propose common representations on the part of all the allied powers. His ill temper might, reasonably enough, have been expected to lead to some such suggestion. It did not do so. It never extended to action. [89]

[88] St. Petersburg. F. O., Reçus, no. 21,224, Jan. 19, 1824.

[89] Metternich's discontent with the paragraphs of the message which dealt with South America apparently made him feel equally ill-tempered about the rest of it. In another part of the document Monroe spoke of American proposals to declare the slave trade piracy, and to abolish privateering. This is what the Austrian Chancellor has to say on these subjects: "I do not wish to judge with too much severity the proposition to declare a capital crime all participation in the slave trade, however evident it is that in more than one State such a measure of legisla-

In his failure to remonstrate with the government at Washington, however, the Austrian Chancellor was wholly typical. The extraordinary language of Monroe called forth no formal representations from any European court.

One might particularly have expected some such representations from Madrid or St. Petersburg. Spain might reasonably have been affronted at the prohibition laid down by the United States on her seeking aid from any other power for the reconquest of the colonies, especially in view of her long-cherished hopes of such aid. But Ferdinand, it appears, never bothered to read the message,⁰ and the Foreign Minister, the Conde de Ofalia, never gave Nelson the slightest intimation of his displeasure.[91] The Tsar and his ministers, also, might have been especially indignant. Monroe's declaration was flatly opposed to their dogmas. But when Tuyll, from Washington, suggested a formal protest with regard to the American pronouncement, he was answered:

> The document in question enunciates views and pretensions so exaggerated, it establishes principles so contrary to the rights of the European powers, that it merits only the most profound contempt. His Majesty therefore invites you to preserve the passive attitude which you have deemed proper to adopt, and to continue to maintain the silence which you have imposed upon yourself.[92]

---

tion would meet with insurmountable obstacles. But it is entirely otherwise with the project so improperly brought forward to abolish privateering in maritime war, a project which involves the thorniest questions of the law of nations, which half a century of serious discussion has not brought to a successful conclusion, and which England, in particular, will never admit so long as there remains to her a vestige of her maritime power. Proposals of this kind, addressed much less to the Cabinets than to the 100,000 organs of liberalism in every part of the world, bear, it must be agreed, a character of presumptuous temerity on the part of a new Government which is in no way authorized to reform the old public law of Europe."

[90] Berlin. Staats-Archiv, Spanien, vol. 54, Jan. 16, 1824.

[91] Washington. State Dept., Despatches from Ministers, Spain, vol. 23, Jan. 16, 1824.

[92] St. Petersburg. F. O., Expédiés, no. 9241, Mar. 5, 1824. The original text read, in place of "that it merits only the most profound contempt," "that it would hardly be possible to mention it to the Government of the United States without haughtily reproving language so strange. However, such action not being for the moment within the pretensions of His Majesty, he invites you to preserve," etc., as above.

Alexander evidently believed that further discussion would serve only to dignify the American manifesto.

As for Prussia and France, neither power seems to have thought seriously of protest. The message, Varnhagen von Ense wrote, had proved highly displeasing; [93] but there was no disposition to take formal action of any kind. And in Paris, though Chateaubriand, as we have seen, seems to have meditated a protest against the non-colonization clause of the message, and perhaps an even broader rebuke, the idea, like many others of Chateaubriand's, was speedily abandoned.

Not only was there no formal protest against the doctrines of the President, but, with one exception, there seems not even to have been the gentlest intimation to any American diplomatic representative that they could be distasteful to the Old World. The exception is to be found in the language of the Prince de Polignac to Richard Rush. In the midst of a most friendly conversation on the relations between France and America, in March, 1824, in which the two men frankly discussed the possibilities of diplomatic coöperation against the power of Great Britain, the French ambassador interpolated a moderate warning, obviously based on Monroe's declaration. He told the American minister

that it would be prudent for them [that is, the United States] to content themselves with the privileges resulting from their special position, and not to demand in principle what, up to a certain point, they were justified in practising; that France, just issuing from the bloody convulsions of revolution, could easily become alarmed at the promulgation of those very doctrines which, for her, had been the source of evils too recent to be forgotten; and that consequently it was desirable to avoid any action which would tend to render one of the two governments ill-disposed toward the other. [94]

It is much to be doubted whether these mild-mannered observations had a very chastening effect upon the man who listened to them! There is, in fact, no evidence that he ever bothered to report them to Washington.

The silence of the European courts, however, was not wholly complimentary to the United States. It may have proceeded, in part at least, from the slight regard that they had, in many in-

---

[93] *Briefwechsel* of Varnhagen von Ense and Oelsner, iii, p. 188.
[94] Paris. Aff. Étr., Corr. Pol., Angleterre, vol. 618, Mar., 1824.

stances, for the power and resources of the American govern-ment. Only Gentz, the Austrian publicist, among European re-actionaries, hailed the message as more or less decisive, declaring that "if the reconquest of the colonies on the Continent . . . had not already become impossible, this opposition of the North American people, which had so long been developed, and which has now been openly declared, would alone be sufficient to banish all thought of it." [95] In general the tone of comment was dis-tinctly depreciatory, even contemptuous. Most conservative European diplomats do not seem to have reckoned very seriously with the President's declaration as a factor in European policy. They were inclined, on the contrary, to discount the message, and the material force of the United States which lay behind it.

In the first place, there was a strong tendency to ascribe the American manifesto to the exigencies of domestic politics. Menou, the French chargé at Washington, declared that it was, in part at least, a mere electoral manœuvre. With the presidential cam-paign of 1824 approaching, the various members of the cabinet, he wrote, were all seeking popularity, the Secretary of State among the rest.[96] What better way to prove one's generous principles, one's sound republicanism, one's fearless courage, than by a vigorous challenge to the monarchies of the Old World? and perhaps to mount on the wave of popular applause to the high office of the presidency itself?

These observations might have made John Quincy Adams writhe, if he had been privileged to read them, and they were, as a matter of fact, egregiously unfair. Whoever follows the cabinet debates of 1823 must, I think, arrive at the conclusion that some-thing far more important than political advantage was the main-spring of the action that was taken; that Monroe and his advisers, Adams included, acted under a sense of solemn responsibility in what they deemed a perilous situation. The vigorous American-ism of the Secretary of State does not need to be attributed to any self-seeking. Nor does such an interpretation accord at all well with the character of the man whom Menou thus tried to asperse.

[95] Friedrich von Gentz, *Schriften*, v, p. 103.
[96] Paris. Aff. Étr., Corr. Pol., États-Unis, vol. 80, Dec. 11, 1823.

But the fact that the message was thus set down to political machinations is, none the less, an interesting and important one.

There were, moreover, in the opinion of Menou, other political motives at work besides the ambition of Adams. The tendency of those in authority was to increase the powers of the federal government! What better way to secure more power for their leaders at Washington, than by conjuring up real or imaginary dangers? [97]

Here again, the interpretation put upon the message does not seem an entirely happy one. Monroe has certainly not been generally regarded as a president with strong centralizing tendencies. The man who wrote the almost interminable message to Congress in which he sought to demonstrate that the federal government had no right to make internal improvements was hardly the man to grasp at the foreign situation to enlarge the boundaries of national power. But, once more, the fact that such motives were attributed to him is in itself of interest.

Stoughton, the Spanish chargé, had, like Menou, a political explanation of the President's declaration. It was made necessary, he declared, by the decay of the popularity of the President, and of his party, which had almost disappeared. Four new "parties" had made their appearance to disturb the tranquillity of American politics, and to challenge the rule by which the President transmitted the presidential office to his Secretary of State. It was necessary, therefore, to flatter the vanity of the American people by a strong foreign policy, and thus prepare the way for Mr. Adams's election, which at that precise moment seemed most improbable.[98]

Both the French and the Spanish representatives testify to the fact already mentioned, that the message had not received a very cordial reception in Congress. Menou declared that it had fallen absolutely flat, and that the legislative branch, far from reënforcing the pretensions of the President, was disposed, if it acted at all, to moderate the views of the Executive. The United States

[97] Paris. Aff. Étr., Corr. Pol., États-Unis, vol. 80, Dec. 11, 1823.

[98] Seville. Archivo General de las Indias. Estado, América en General, legajo 5, Jan. 2, 1824.

would certainly draw back if it were a question of war. "The Federal government would discover that it was easier to talk than to act." [99]

Taking into consideration [wrote Stoughton] the national character of this people, devoted as it is to commercial success, and considering its extreme repugnance to every kind of expense, and even the niggardliness with which it provides the most indispensable resources for the administration of the government, everything leads to the conclusion that the American Congress would never carry into effect the measures proposed in the President's Message; measures which could have no other result than the complete sacrifice of all those interests.

Many educated and sensible people are of the opinion [declared the Spanish chargé] that it is supremely ridiculous for the President to identify the security and integrity of the United States with all the Continents of the New World.[100]

Perhaps the most complete analysis of the viewpoint of the United States, the most interesting speculation as to its ability to make good the language of the President's declaration, comes from the pen of Baron Tuyll. In a long dispatch to his government he analyzed the state of affairs with much care. If Great Britain should oppose the reconquest of the colonies, the United States, he declared, would probably make common cause with her, confining its support, however, to words rather than deeds, declaiming much, picking up rich prizes with its privateers, and possibly strengthening the squadron of Commodore Porter in the West Indies. "In this manner the American government would risk nothing, would spend little, and would finish in case of success by attributing to itself a great part of the glory of having assured the independence of its allies," thus enabling it "to gratify a national vanity which knows no limits, and to attain an influence to which this government aspires with so much ardor."

But should Great Britain remain quiescent, the United States was hardly to be feared at all.

The American government [wrote the Russian minister] is far from finding in its treasury the pecuniary means indispensable to equip a considerable armament. It appears extremely doubtful whether it would succeed in ob-

---

[99] Paris. Aff. Étr., Corr. Pol., États-Unis, vol. 80, Dec. 11, 1823.

[100] Seville. Archivo General de las Indias. Estado, América en General, legajo 5, Jan. 2, 1824.

taining the authority to impose sufficient taxes for such a purpose unless it was a question of defending from menacing attack the principal states of the Union, and even in such a case it would, to all appearances, find itself a prey to considerable embarrassment. It is also doubtful whether it enjoys either at home or abroad sufficient credit to float loans sufficient to defray the expenses which such an enterprise would entail.

It would probably succeed in sending out a squadron, and it would ruin the commerce of its enemy by means of its numerous, bold, and indefatigable privateers. On the other hand, it is difficult to imagine that it would succeed in raising forces sufficiently imposing to paralyze the efforts of a powerful expedition, directed against New Spain, or against Colombia, and basing itself in every case at Havana. It would succeed only with difficulty in sending aid of any kind, maritime aid excepted, in money, for the reasons explained above; in troops, because they are few in number, and because, in such circumstances, it would have to guard its own coasts. . . .

But will the American government wish to wage a war of this nature? The lofty tone in which it has just expressed itself seems to make such a war a necessity. After having put itself forward with so much arrogance, it would compromise itself in the eyes of its own people, it would lose all its prestige with foreign governments, if it consented to remain the spectator of an expedition directed against the Spanish colonies, of which it has so loftily proclaimed itself the defender. However, the sluggishness inherent in the forms of a federal republic, the scanty powers and means of which this government disposes, the lack of inclination of the inhabitants of this country to make pecuniary sacrifices which offer them no bait of considerable and direct gain, the irritation which would be aroused among the merchants by the cessation of their commercial relation with France, Spain, and the North, the serious damage which the privateers of Havana and Porto Rico would do to the merchant marine of the United States might in some measure calm the warlike ardor of this government. But what is still more probable is that these facts will tend to make such a war, if the federal government should decide upon it, rather a demonstration which circumstances have rendered indispensable, and which is entered upon reluctantly with the secret desire of seeing it ended as soon as possible, than one of those truly national enterprises sustained by every means, and with every bit of energy, which might make it a very embarrassing obstacle.

The attitude which the government of the United States has assumed is undoubtedly of such a nature as to demand in an American expedition undertaken by Spain and her Allies a considerable development of means and of military force. But once the decision is taken to attempt it, I should not think that the course taken by the United States, unsupported by Great Britain, would be of a nature to change such a decision. [101]

Such were the views of one well qualified to judge of the effective power that lay behind the President's declaration. And the view herein expressed was held by many Europeans. In France

[101] St. Petersburg. F. O., Reçus, no. 21,341, Feb. 2, 1824.

there was, in government circles at least, very little respect indeed for the power of the United States. Chateaubriand declared it to be absurd to speak of the United States as a great naval power, and spoke jeeringly of the small forces of which the government disposed.[102] The American agent, Erving, reported to Monroe that the statesmen of France were of the opinion that there was nothing to be feared from the young republic of the West, even in its own hemisphere, and that America's opinion of its own power was at least ten years in advance of what its real circumstances would authorize.[103] In the Parisian press there is reflected much the same standpoint. The *Étoile*, the leading ministerial paper, depreciated the influence and the naval force of the United States; [104] and a pamphleteer of reactionary tendencies, writing a little later, spoke scornfully of the menacing tone of a feeble republic which in 1812 had not even been able to defend its own capital, of a land without military knowledge, corroded by foreign vices since the days of Washington and Franklin, and crippled financially by the alarming atrophy of its commerce.[105]

Behind all such descriptions, of course, there may well have been a considerable element of prejudice and a wish distinctly father to the thought. European reactionaries, in the face of the "delirious ambition" of the United States, as one commentator phrases it, could hardly be expected to judge with entire detachment either the motives that prompted the message or the power of the nation which had, through its President, thrown down so definite a challenge to the Old World.

---

[102] Chateaubriand, *Congrès de Vérone*, ii, p. 281. "It is ridiculous," wrote the French Foreign Minister, "to say that they [the United States] are the second, or one of the first, maritime powers of the world; they have four ships of the line, and a dozen brigs and frigates."

[103] Monroe, *Writings*, vi, p. 432 f.

[104] "The English journals still speak affectedly of the message of the President of the United States. We can answer in a few words the boasting of all the radicals of Europe, supposing they make common cause with the United States. To support them the United States have nine ships of the line, thirteen frigates, and twenty-five hundred soldiers." (Jan. 13.) "There has been a general shocked surprise at the arrogant tone assumed by the temporary chief of a federal republic, which still has only a very feeble navy, and not a single complete division of soldiers." (Jan. 21.)

[105] *Considerations sur l'état moral et physique de l'Amérique espagnole, et sur son indépendance*, by M. de Guillermin (Paris, 1824), pp. 51 f.

And yet, at the same time, such views corresponded in some measure with the actual facts of the situation. On paper the disparity of strength between the United States, on the one hand, and France and Russia, on the other, was very great. The naval force at the disposal of the American government in 1823 consisted of 44 vessels and 4000 men; [106] while that of France, in theory at least, was composed of 183 vessels [107] and 19,000 men,[108] and that of Russia of over 300 vessels and over 40,000 men. Of ships of the line, the United States had 7, France 11, and Russia at least 47.[109] In frigates and corvettes the figures stand respectively 10, 42, and 36. In smaller craft the American navy was still more greatly outnumbered. The significance of these figures, it is true, must be subjected to severe questioning. The official statement of Russian naval strength for 1823 discloses the fact that in the Baltic fleet, actually in active service, Russia possessed only 2 ships of the line and 7 frigates, a striking variation from the paper strength of 30 and 27. For France it is not probable that the gap between theoretical and actual strength was as great, for the French navy under Louis XVIII was much better kept up than that of the Tsar after the end of the Napoleonic struggle; but, on the other hand, it would be unwise to take the figures cited above at their face value. Furthermore, outside of the question of numbers, there are certain facts that would have militated strongly in favor of the United States in a war with the powers of the Holy Alliance. As Tuyll himself had pointed out, the possibility of the American privateers had to be taken into account. More important still, it is clear that neither France nor Russia would be able to concentrate anything like its whole naval force in the New World, and that, though Havana and the French stations in the Antilles might be used as bases, there would be a very considerable difficulty in conducting a naval war in American waters. Yet, making all these allowances, it may still safely

[106] Official statement, furnished by the Navy Department on request.

[107] Paris. Archives Nationales, Minist. de la Marine, BB⁵19.

[108] *Annales Maritimes et Coloniales*, 1823, 2d pt., i, p. 542.

[109] The official Russian figures, furnished me by the Central Archives at Moscow, give a total of 321 vessels. The *Annales Maritimes et Coloniales*, 1826, 2d pt., i, p. 142, and *Niles' Register*, xxvi, p. 333, give 464 vessels and 45,000 men.

be said that a combined French and Russian intervention in American affairs would have constituted a considerable menace, and that the forces of the allied powers would considerably have outnumbered the United States. While it may be that European statesmen were unduly contemptuous of the material power of the American government, there was at least some justification for the depreciatory tone in which they spoke of its resources, and for their refusal, therefore, to take the menaces of Monroe extremely seriously.

But, whatever the judgment of these men on the physical force which lay behind the President's declaration, they were fully alive to the moral implications of Monroe's pronouncement. Very many of them saw in the language of the message the ominous signs of separation of the New World from the Old. The idea of such a separation was, of course, no new one. In an often-quoted memorandum presented by the French and Russian plenipotentiaries to the Congress of Aix-la-Chapelle it had had a prominent place.[110] The project of Bourbon monarchies had from its first inception been in part designed to prevent such a catastrophe. But the message of 1823 brought home the danger in a striking form.

> The European Continent [wrote Pozzo di Borgo] must consider itself warned. Events succeed one another with an incalculable rapidity. What seemed impossible at the Congress of Aix is today a fact, and perhaps what we now regard as a feeble conjecture will soon become a reality. The Christian World tends to divide into two parts, distinct from, and I fear, hostile to, one another; we must work to prevent or defer this terrible revolution, and above all to save and fortify the portion which may escape the contagion and the invasion of vicious principles.[111]

Gentz saw Europe virtually banished from the American hemisphere, and, in course of time, threatened in its own institutions by the trend of events across the seas.

> May this view of the affair which has been revealed to us [he wrote] early incite great statesmen to consider carefully what must be done with that new transatlantic colossus which was formed from such dangerous, hostile elements — not so much because of the material safety of Europe (for this

---

[110] See my article, cited above, in *Am. Hist. Rev.*, xxviii (July, 1923), p. 667.

[111] St. Petersburg. F. O., Reçus, no. 21,298, Jan. 30, 1824.

cannot be menaced from that quarter for the next fifty or one hundred years) as for the moral and political preservation of the Old World upon its present basis.[112]

Such quotations are merely typical of a widespread, nay, almost general, viewpoint. Metternich,[113] Lieven,[114] Chateaubriand,[115] were all more fearful than ever before of the dangers which might emanate from a republican America. Tuyll [116] and Menou [117] both emphasized the possibility of a coalition of the states of the New World. Whatever might be the material power of the United States, its moral influence was a fact to be taken into account; and the statesmen of Europe, many of whom, as we have seen, had already despaired of the physical reconquest of the colonies, fully recognized the support which the President's message in-

[112] Friedrich von Gentz, *Schriften*, v, p. 103.

[113] London, P. R. O., F. O., Austria, vol. 182, no. 10, Jan. 21, 1824. "The Speech, he said, had confirmed him in an opinion he had before entertained that great calamities would be brought upon Europe by the establishment of these vast Republics in the New World in addition to the power of the United States, of whose views no man could entertain a doubt, after reading the Speech in Question. He did not say that the present race would witness these calamities, but it was one of the first duties of a Government to direct its views to the welfare of Posterity, and however remote the danger which he apprehended might be, it was still the duty of every European Statesman to give it due consideration in forming his judgment upon this important question." (Wellesley to Canning.)

[114] St. Petersburg. F. O., Reçus, no. 21,304, Jan. 2, 1824. "The imperious and arrogant tone in which it [the message] is conceived, the open pretention announced in it to oppose all European influence in America under whatever form, the blame affectedly cast on the conduct of the Alliance, the false principle of the law of nations in virtue of which every de facto government is declared legitimate, and finally the specious and perfidious art with which this document contrasts the reciprocal results of the monarchical and republican systems, all seem to unite, Monsieur le Comte, to give this declaration the character of a manifesto, by which the administration at Washington, condemning the principles which have triumphed in Europe, and aiming, so to speak, at the cutting of the bonds which unite the two hemispheres, constitutes itself the champion of democratic doctrines and the sovereign arbiter of the destinies of the whole world."

[115] *Revue politique et littéraire*, Nov. 2, 1912 "Supplément au Congrès de Vérone," p. 548.

[116] St. Petersburg. F. O., Reçus, no. 2,341, Feb. 2, 1824. "Here, then, is the Government of the United States making common cause with the insurgents of America; loftily announcing itself their protector, and constituting itself the head of a democratic league of the New World, in declared opposition to the alliance of the sovereigns of the Continent of Europe."

[117] Paris. Aff. Étr., Corr. Pol., États-Unis, vol. 80, Dec. 11, 1823. "Bolívar has attained his end. Republican America is united against monarchical Europe."

evitably afforded to the pernicious doctrines of republicanism and popular self-rule. On this score there were no illusions, and no depreciation of the significance of Monroe's manifesto.

There was another danger, from the Continental viewpoint, implicit in the President's message — the danger that there existed an entente between the United States and Great Britain in the affairs of the New World. Varnhagen von Ense, who was of course sympathetic with the tone of the American pronouncement, was sure that there had come about a new diplomatic alignment comparable in importance to the reversal of alliances in 1756.[118] The statesmen of the reaction had also to take account of such a possibility, and in many cases expressed suspicions, more or less profound, of a sinister accord between the two Anglo-Saxon powers. They had, of course, no positive information on which to base these suspicions; for the secret of the interviews between Rush and Canning appears to have been well kept — so well kept, indeed, that in the months following the message there is not, in the diplomatic correspondence of the Continental powers, the slightest intimation that it ever became known at all. But it was easy enough to argue from the general circumstances of the case. On the basis of these circumstances, Menou wrote that he would not be surprised to find that the message was due to the diplomatic suggestion of Great Britain.[119] Tuyll found it difficult to believe that the United States would have taken up

[118] *Briefwechsel* of Varnhagen von Ense and Oelsner, iii, pp. 177 f. "The speech of the President of the United States has made a powerful impression here upon the public opinion and upon the cabinet. There seems almost no doubt that England is allied with the great Federation. Thus Spain will prove the culminating point of the Holy Alliance. If England and North America remain united, who in the world can still delude himself with the idea of disturbing the independence of South America with advantage or without positive loss? When in the fifth decade of the previous century, Kaunitz conceived the idea that the two hereditary enemies, France and Austria, should become allies, he astonished the world. What Kaunitz did was, in effect, nothing more than to use common sense to destroy a prejudice. There suddenly arose an immense and hitherto unseen power. The like happens when England renounces the old grudge against North America. The liberated colonies, if they see themselves no longer threatened or despised by their former mother country, are inclined and ready to attach themselves to her by preference. English blood flows in the veins of the North Americans."

[119] Paris. Aff. Étr., Corr. Pol., États-Unis, vol. 80, Dec. 11, 1823.

a position so threatening without the assurance of support from England, though it was possible to explain the President's language as a mere bluff to make the rest of the world believe that an accord existed.[120] Pozzo di Borgo found in the destructive language of Canning a direct incitement to Monroe, and British avidity and American democratic fury almost equally menacing.[121] Count von Bernstorff thought the message in part instigated by the attitude of the court of London.[122] Finally, Chateaubriand, deeply disturbed by the President's declaration, actually undertook to tax Great Britain with responsibility for so melancholy an occurrence, and to intimate that there was a definite understanding between the government at Washington and the government at London.[123]

And yet, curiously enough, despite these suspicions, the general belief in Europe, it may fairly be said, was that the attitude assumed by Monroe would, in all probability, bring Great Britain to a closer coöperation with the Continental powers. If there was one thing clearer than another to the diplomats, it was that jealousy of the United States would inevitably play a part in shaping British policy. They were right, as will be seen in the sequel. But they were a little too confident of the effects of that jealousy. Assuming, in instance after instance, that the result of Monroe's declaration would be to bring Canning into closer association with the Holy Alliance, they showed a faith that was speedily to be refuted by events. And yet the logic on which they based their theory was appealing enough. Pozzo pointed out that the un-

---

[120] St. Petersburg. F. O., Reçus, no. 21,341, Feb. 2, 1824.

[121] Ibid., no. 21,298, Jan. 30, 1824.

[122] Paris. Aff. Étr., Corr. Pol., Prusse, vol. 265, Jan. 15, 1824.

[123] London. P. R. O., F. O., France, vol. 305, no. 8, Jan. 2, 1824. Stuart reported as follows with regard to Chateaubriand: "He began by saying that he could not conceal from me that the striking coincidence of the language of the Message to Congress with the Communication between his Majesty's Government and the Prince de Polignac respecting the affairs of the colonies almost justified in his mind the supposition that these doctrines were now set forth for the first time by the President in virtue of an understanding between the British and American Governments." Chateaubriand expressed the same suspicions in his dispatches to Rayneval (see Paris. Aff. Étr., Corr. Pol., Prusse, vol. 265, Jan. 1, 1824), to Caraman, the French ambassador at Vienna (ibid., Autriche, vol. 166, Jan. 13, 1824), and to Polignac (ibid., Grande Bretagne, vol. 618, Jan. 5, 1824).

measured and unbridled ambition of the United States would never be satisfied with a mere division of influence in the New World, but only with a complete domination, and that Britain had every interest in seeing the colonies under the rule of feeble and far-away princes like those of Spain and Portugal. Bernstorff [124] and Metternich [125] thought that the message must have "a most beneficial effect" in persuading Great Britain to act in concert against "the spirit of insurrection and independence, which threatens to wrest from her her own colonies." Chateaubriand declared that Great Britain had a visible interest in a policy which, while preserving her commercial advantages, would not strike at the political principles on which her government was founded.[126] Even at Madrid the general opinion was that the message would exercise a restraining influence on the policy of Canning, arousing his jealousy of the United States, and cooling his ardor for the establishment of republics in the New World.[127] The diplomats of the Continent, in very many instances, believed that the President's declaration would lead the British Foreign Secretary to accept the invitation to a congress on the colonial question, and to enter into coöperation with the other powers.

The real effect of Monroe's declaration on British policy, as indeed on European policy in general, must be left for consideration in a subsequent chapter. But our analysis of the reception which the message received in the Old World would not be com-

[124] Paris. Aff. Étr., Corr. Pol., Prusse, vol. 265, Jan. 15, 1824, and Jan. 20, 1824. "It is believed here," wrote Rayneval on the latter date, "that it [i. e., the message] will produce an effect contrary to that which the gentlemen of the New World had calculated. The indiscretion with which they put themselves at the head of a revolutionary league, which today wishes no new colonies, and tomorrow will seek to destroy those which exist, is calculated to open the eyes of the possessors of Canada and of Jamaica."

[125] Ibid., Autriche, vol. 405, Jan. 19, 1824.

[126] "Supplément au Congrès de Vérone," Revue politique et littéraire, Nov. 2, 1912, pp. 545–551, containing letters of Chateaubriand. The one referred to in the text is that of Jan. 4, 1824, p. 547.

[127] Paris. Aff. Étr., Corr. Pol., Espagne, vol. 726, Jan. 11, 1824. See also ibid., fol. 121. "The Count of Ofalia," wrote the French agent, Galabert, "appeared to me somewhat reassured as to the outcome of the negotiation, and not too much alarmed at the rather arrogant message of the President of the United States."

plete without some discussion of the reaction which it produced upon the European statesman who had most to do with its utterance—upon George Canning himself.

In a degree, the message undoubtedly pleased the British Foreign Secretary. "The Congress," he wrote joyfully to A'Court, "was broken in all its limbs before, but the President's speech gives it the *coup de grace*." [128] Such a statement was, no doubt, something of an exaggeration. Continental statesmen really remained as confident of the practicability of a congress as ever. Nor were they much impressed with the material power of the United States or its right to be consulted on South American affairs. Canning's estimate of the effects of the message was a deal too optimistic to be an exact one, and was, indeed, in accord with his buoyant temperament rather than with the facts of the situation. But the very fact that he uttered such a judgment shows that, whatever was the truth of the matter, in a measure he welcomed the President's declaration as a step that would strengthen his own hand in his opposition to a congress on the colonial question, and to Continental intervention of any kind in the affairs of the New World. [129]

But the pleasure which he derived from the American pronouncement was certainly a good deal mixed, to put it mildly. Leaving entirely out of account his distaste for the non-colonization principle, already discussed, Monroe's action was very far from gratifying to British pride or British interest. The United States, after all, had scored on Great Britain. Secure (so at least Canning might have said) in the support of the most powerful of European states, the President had struck an heroic attitude in relation to the new republics, and had, without any real risk, successfully posed as the intrepid defender of South American liberties. There could be nothing about such a situation particularly pleasing to the British Foreign Secretary. He was, beyond a doubt, a good deal piqued. His reference to the repeated over-

[128] A. G. Stapleton, *George Canning and his Times* (London, 1859), p. 395.

[129] Compare Canning's statement to Bagot, "The effect of the ultra-liberalism of our Yankee co-operators, or the ultra-despotism of our Aix-la-Chapelle Allies, gives me just the balance that I wanted." *George Canning and his Friends*, edited by Josceline Bagot (London, 1909, 2 vols.), ii, pp. 217 f.

tures to Rush as a "sounding" [130] is a revelation of the wounded self-esteem which lay behind his pleasure at the language of Monroe. And to add to the bitterness of the occasion, at the moment when Canning was reflecting ruefully on the clever diplomatic manœuvre of the American government, he had to put up with the reproaches of Chateaubriand for having instigated that manœuvre. No wonder that he made every effort to demonstrate to the French minister that such was not the case.

It can hardly have escaped Mr. Chateaubriand's attention [he wrote to Stuart] that though there is a general agreement between the sentiments of the two Governments, that agreement is qualified by most important differences. The first and the most essential difference is that the Government of the United States have actually acknowledged the independence of the late Spanish colonies, while his Majesty's Government continue to withhold such recognition. — Again, the two Governments agree in protesting against the forcible interference of any Foreign Power in the dispute between Spain and Spanish America, but if the Message of the President is to be considered as objecting to an Attempt to reconquer the Dominion on the part of Spain, herself, there is again as important a difference between his views and ours, as perhaps it is possible to conceive.

As for the suggestion of American representation at the projected congress, a suggestion which had aroused Chateaubriand's suspicions, Canning declared that so far was it "from being a matter of concert with the United States that, if such a Congress had been held, and if the United States had been invited to it, they would have declined the invitation." [131] At the same time he instructed Bagot to hold the same language at St. Petersburg.[132] Britain might at least be spared the reproach of having arrived at an understanding with the United States, when, as a matter of fact, her often repeated efforts to attain such an understanding had been unsuccessful.

The British Foreign Secretary's effort to allay Continental suspicion had a certain clever plausibility. But in one respect it was based on an entirely false assumption. The allegation, or suggestion, that the United States differed from Great Britain in denying to Spain the right to proceed against the colonies on her

---

[130] See the letter just quoted.

[131] London. P. R. O., F. O., France, vol. 303, desp. 2, Jan. 9, 1824.

[132] Paris. Aff. Étr., Corr. Pol., Russie, vol. 166, fol. 45 f.

own account, though it found some justification in the language of Addington's dispatches,[133] was hardly borne out by the terms of the message itself.

> In the war between the new Governments and Spain [Monroe had written] we declared our neutrality at the time of their recognition, and to this we have adhered, and shall continue to adhere, provided no change shall occur, which in the judgment of the competent authorities of this Government, shall make a corresponding change on the part of the United States indispensable to their security.

On the basis of this language Canning's attempt to make it seem a point of divergence between the British and American views seems either a little labored, or more than a little disingenuous. As for the other two points, though true enough, they of course proved nothing at all. But they were, apparently, sufficiently specious arguments to put to rest Continental suspicions. The notion of a concert of views between the United States and Great Britain disappears from the dispatches after the sending of the British Foreign Secretary's attempted refutation.

The difficulties of Canning were not, however, at an end. He had to justify Great Britain at home, in the face of the enthusiastic eulogies of the attitude of Monroe by opposition spokesmen like Brougham. In Parliament, as in his diplomatic correspondence, he sought to distinguish between the position of the President and his own point of view. And on March 4 the Polignac memorandum was communicated to the House, with the obvious purpose of justifying Great Britain's own position on the colonial question;[134] and in the House of Lords, on the fifteenth, Lord Liverpool, the head of the government, pointed out that England had acted in the South American problem almost two months before the issuance of the American declaration.[135]

Finally, it was necessary to take account of the new republics themselves. It is, again, an interesting commentary on the attitude of the British Foreign Secretary that, in his first instruc-

---

[133] London. P. R. O., F. O., United States, vol. 177, desp. 20, Nov. 20, 1823. "The United States," says Mr. Adams, "deny the right not only of Foreign Powers, but even that of Spain herself, to interfere in the affairs of Spanish America."

[134] Hansard, *Parliamentary Debates*, New Series, x, col. 708.

[135] *Ibid.*, col. 997.

tions to British agents in the New World, following hard upon the message, he communicated the Polignac correspondence, and here, as before the House of Commons, labored to show that Great Britain had been beforehand in assuming the protection of the new states.[136] The Monroe Doctrine may have been, in some sense, acceptable to George Canning, and a buttress to his own policy; but, on the other hand, it is incontestable that it caused him to do a good deal of explaining, and to do it in several different places. Matters certainly had not fallen out precisely as he might have desired.

As for the attitude of other British diplomats or statesmen, representative of the government in power, we know almost nothing. Wellington, in his voluminous correspondence, seems never to have mentioned the message. The British representatives at the various Continental courts sometimes reported the views of the governments to which they were accredited, but gave no hint of their own attitude. Always excepting Canning, we know less of the British official opinion than of any other.

But it is, of course, Canning's views that are most essential. And they illustrate the interesting fact that even in Great Britain, the country most sympathetic with the cause of the colonies, the eloquence of James Monroe awakened no unqualified enthusiasm. One might even go further. Far from uniting the two English-speaking peoples in a common cause, the President's pronouncement was to sharpen the antagonism which divided them, and to stimulate their rivalry for the favor and the commerce of the South Americans. This fact will clearly appear when we analyze, from the European standpoint, the aftermath of the message itself.

[136] London. P. R. O., F. O., Buenos Aires and Mexico, Confidential, Dec. 30, 1823, and Feb. 6, 1824, respectively.

# CHAPTER VI

## THE AFTERMATH OF THE MESSAGE IN
## THE NEW WORLD

WE have examined the reception of the message, and the immediate impression which it produced upon the statesmen of the Old World and the New. It is now necessary to study its actual influence upon policy in the years immediately following its enunciation. Its most important practical effects, it may be said at the outset, are to be found in the attitude of the new republics of South America, and in the attitude of the Congress of the United States. In the years from 1824 to 1826 the principles laid down by Monroe were to be in more than one instance tested and applied.

The first of these tests has to do with the relations of the United States with Colombia. In that country, as has been seen, there had been some fear of the intervention of the Holy Allies, and the President's message had been hailed by Vice-President Santander with considerable enthusiasm. A favorable opinion toward a closer association with the United States had been expressed by both Santander and Gual, the Colombian Foreign Minister; and in March, 1824, doubtless encouraged by the language of the message, the latter renewed his advances to R. C. Anderson, the American minister, and actually proposed a defensive alliance between Colombia and the United States to ward off the possible danger of attack by the Allies.[1] He even went further, and attempted to argue that, in view of the "imbecility" of the mother country, an expedition fitted out by Spain ought to be considered as coming within the scope of the presidential declaration. A month later Santander, in his message to the Colombian legislative body, declared that his government was actually engaged in determining the scope and intent of the policy of the United

[1] Washington. State Dept., Despatches, Colombia, vol. 3.

States,[2] and it seems entirely likely, therefore, that by this time the Colombian minister at Washington, José Salazar, had been urged to discuss the whole question of European intervention with the American Secretary of State.

It is, however, the news of the French mission of Chassérieu to the New World that seems to have led to a definite effort on the part of the Colombian government to ascertain the attitude of the United States. Nothing in the instructions or in the report of the French agent leads to the view that he was charged with any intrigue dangerous to the safety of the Colombian republic, or to the integrity of its institutions.[3]  On the contrary, as we have seen, the stated object of his mission was to allay suspicions of French hostility, and to encourage trade relationships with the new state. But it may be that he had been given verbal orders to seek to promote the establishment of monarchy; and it seems wholly probable that, on his arrival at Caracas, he broadly intimated that such a step would facilitate the recognition of the Colombian government by France.  At any rate, the rumor that France intended to use her influence to establish monarchical institutions was spread throughout the country in the spring of 1824,[4] and transmitted by Gual to Salazar at Washington. The latter, therefore, on July 1, 1824, had a conversation with Adams, in which he pictured Chassérieu as on his way to Bogotá, and declared that France was ready to offer recognition if a monarchy should be established, even a monarchy under the sway of the Liberator himself. The American Secretary of State seems to have remained noncommittal with regard to these observations of the Colombian, and asked him to put them in writing. The result was the very important note of July 2, 1824, in which the professions of the Monroe Doctrine were for the first time put to the test. This document, first given due importance by the fruitful researches of Professor Robertson, deserves quotation in full.

[2] *Archivo Santander,* xi, p. 350.

[3] Paris. Aff. Étr., Corr. Pol., Colombie, vol. 2, fols. 125 ff., Dec. 1, 1823. For Chassérieu's reports, see the same volume, *passim.*

[4] Ibid., fol. 174, Jan. 3, 1825. The English circulated the Polignac memorandum, and emphasized the French prejudice, expressed therein, in favor of monarchical institutions.

*Don José Maria Salazar to the Secretary of State.*

Sir, Washington, *2 July 1824.*

After having had the honour of giving you an informal verbal account of the present political state of the Republic of Colombia, I am about to lay before you, agreeably to your desire, in this confidential Note, the explanations which my Government wishes to be given to that of the United States.

I said in our conference that the Republic has gone on ameliorating in all the branches of its administration, and for this I refer to the Message of the Executive of which I enclose you a copy: everything has revived under the influence of free institutions, and if peace shall perfect the benefit which they produce, the progress of the public prosperity would be very rapid.

Colombia, however, does not flatter herself with this hope, in the present state of affairs of the Governments of Europe, and her fears are founded on the obstinacy of Spain in not recognizing her independence, on the language of the ministerial papers of France, particularly the Journal of Debates of Paris of the months of October and November last in which the antient colonial system is warmly advocated, or to substitute another in a different form; and on the well known views of the Holy Alliance: nothing induces the opinion that she has renounced the direful principle of interference in the domestic concerns of other states, a principle derogatory to its sovereignty and contrary to international law.

There does not appear to be so great an objection on the part of the Holy Alliance to the independence of the new American states as to the principles which they profess, and to the republican form; the attempt to place a Bourbon Prince over Buenos Ayres is well known; the French emmissaries made a similar suggestion in Mexico, and ultimately a gentleman named Chaserieux is just arrived at Caracas who calls himself the envoy of His Christian Majesty near the Government of Colombia, who has used the same language as I have read in the public papers of that city; he says that his Government is disposed to recognize Colombia but on rational terms, and by them he understands, leaving the being a Republic.

Colombia is resolved to defend at every hazard its independence and liberty against every foreign influence and power; for this purpose it augments its army and its marine, it puts in a good state its forts and its internal fortifications, and reposes on the —— devotion of its sons and on the justice of its cause. It has likewise concluded Treaties of Alliance with the other States of America formerly Spanish to insure the issue of their present contest, and the Government is striving to convene an assembly of Plenipotentiaries to represent it and to agree upon its defence.

My Government has seen with the greatest pleasure the Message of the President of the United States, a work very worthy of its author, and which expresses the public sentiments of the people over whom he presides; it cannot be doubted, in virtue of this document, that the Government of the United States endeavours to oppose the policy and ultimate views of the Holy Alliance, and such appears to be the decision of Great Britain from the sense of the nation, some acts of the Ministry, and the language of her Commissioners in Bogotá.

In such circumstances the Government of Colombia is desirous to know in what manner the Government of the United States intends to resist on its part any interference of the Holy Alliance for the purpose of subjugating the new Republics or interfering in their political forms: if it will enter into a Treaty of Alliance with the Republic of Colombia to save America in general from the calamities of a despotic system; and finally if the Government of Washington understands by foreign interference the employment of Spanish forces against America at the time when Spain is occupied by a French Army, and its Government under the influence of France and her Allies.

It appears that it is already in the situation intended by this declaration, since it [sic] generally asserted that an expedition has sailed from Cadiz destined for the coasts of Peru composed of the ship Asia and of some frigates and brigs; there is no doubt that Spain does not furnish this force by herself alone in her present state of despotism and anarchy, without an army, without a marine and without money. This nation notwithstanding its spirit of domination would have ere now decided for peace had it not been assisted for war.

In the name of my Government therefore, and reposing on the sympathy of the United States, I request the said explanations which may serve for its government in its policy and its system of defence.

I pray you, Sir, to accept the sentiments of my most distinguished consideration and respect.

(*Signed*) JOSÉ MARIA ŞALAZAR.[5]

This note of Salazar's, it will be observed, asked two separate questions, the one, whether the United States would enter into alliance with Colombia, the other, whether it would consider an expedition setting forth from Spain as in reality an expedition of the Holy Allies, and therefore coming within the language of the Monroe Doctrine. It took the government of the United States a month to answer these questions, and when it did so it used a language very different indeed from the vigorous sentences of the message of December 2.

It is to be regretted that the deliberations in which the answer to Salazar was formulated are not recorded with the same fullness in the Adams diary as is the case with the discussions on the President's declaration. From this source, indeed, we have simply a curt reference to a cabinet meeting of July 7, attended only by Monroe, Adams, and Calhoun, in which the Colombian note was discussed, and in which it was decided that Adams should draft an answer. "The Colombian Republic to maintain its own inde-

5 Washington. State Dept. (translation), Notes from Ministers, Colombia, vol. 1.

pendence. Hope that France and the Holy Allies will not resort
to force against it. If they should, the power to determine our
resistance is in Congress. The movements of the Executive will
be as heretofore expressed." [6] These are the cautious sentences
in which Adams describes the tenor of the meeting.

As for the President, the little that we know of his attitude is to
be found in two letters written respectively to Madison and to
Jefferson. In these, Monroe's tone is hardly militant. "The attitude which we have to maintain, in this great crisis," he wrote to
Jefferson, "is in the highest degree important to the whole civilized world, since *we stand alone*, with every power beyond the
Atlantic, against us, & with those on this side yielding us a very
feeble, if any, support." [7] With a similar caution the President
declared to Madison, "The Executive has no right to compromit
the nation in any question of war, nor ought we to presume that
the people of Columbia will hesitate as to the answer to be given
to any proposition which touches so vitally their liberties." [8]

Confronted with the troublesome question as to American
willingness to make the words of the message good, and to pledge
resistance to European aggression, Monroe and his advisers manifested the normal diplomatic desire to avoid transforming high-
sounding phrases into binding obligations. The Adams note of
August 6 bears a striking contrast to the reply to Tuyll of the
previous November. Like the communication that it was designed to answer, it is important enough to be given in full.

Don José Maria Salazar,
    *Minister Plenipotentiary from
    the Republic of Colombia.*

Department of State,
Washington, *6 August 1824.*

Sir,
    I have laid before the President of the United States your confidential
Note of the 2nd ultimo, and it has received his deliberate and full consideration.
    He is disposed to hope, that some misunderstanding may have been
occasioned by the language attributed to Mr. Chaserieux at Caracas. Being
unwilling to believe that France or any other European Power, will make its

---

[6] Adams, *Memoirs*, vi, p. 399.
[7] Monroe, *Writings*, vii, p. 30. Italics are mine.       [8] *Ibid.*, p. 31.

acknowledgment of the political Independence of the Republic of Colombia, dependent in any manner upon the form of Government, which the people of Colombia, are alone competent to determine for themselves, and which they have accordingly determined. Were it possible to believe that France should found upon such a principle her conduct towards the Republic of Colombia, the President learns with satisfaction from your Note, that which his respect for your Nation would not otherwise permit him to doubt, that they will maintain at every hazard their real Independence and accept no recognition of it upon conditions incompatible with it. Such a recognition, carrying self-contradiction and absurdity upon its face.

From various recent Acts and Declarations of the French Government, and of Officers acting under it, France appears explicitly to disclaim any design of aiding Spain by any application of Force, for the recovery of her antient dominion in this Hemisphere. — The absurdity of such an attempt becoming from day to day more manifest, leads to the conclusion that France having already assumed this principle, will by the course of time and events be constantly more confirmed in her adhesion to it. Should even the proposals of her Agents, in the first instance present the establishment of a Monarchical or Aristocratic Government, as the price of her recognition, and should such proposals be met, by a firm and unequivocal refusal, the only consequence to be expected will be the postponement of the recognition, and that, as may be readily foreseen only for a short time. With regard to the language of certain political journals, at Paris, in the months of October and November last, it has been since amply ascertained, that the sentiments avowed by them were not such as the French Government has since been willing to support.

With respect to the question "in what manner the Government of the United States intends to resist on its part any interference of the Holy Alliance for the purpose of subjugating the new Republic or interfering in their political forms." You understand that by the constitution of the United States, the ultimate decision of this question belongs to the Legislative Department of the Government. The probability of such interference of the Holy Alliance, having in a great measure disappeared, the occasion for recurring to the dispositions of the Legislature did not occur during the late Session of Congress.

The sentiments of the President remain as they were expressed in his last annual message to Congress. Should the crisis which appeared then to be approaching, and which gave rise to the remarks then made, hereafter recur, he will be ready to give them effect by recommending to the Legislature the adoption of the measures exclusively of their resort, and by which the principles asserted by him, would with the concurrence if given, be on the part of the United States, efficaciously maintained.

As however the occasion for this resort could arise only by a deliberate and concerted system of the allied Powers to exercise force against the freedom and Independence of your Republic; so it is obvious that the United States could not undertake resistance to them by force of arms, without a previous understanding with those European Powers, whose interests and whose principles would secure from them an active and efficient coöperation in the cause. This there is no reason to doubt, could be obtained, but it could only be effected by a negotiation preliminary to that of any alliance between the United States and the Colombian Republic, or in any event coeval with it.

The employment of Spanish force in America, while Spain is occupied by a French army and its Government under the influence of France and her allies, does not constitute a case upon which the United States would feel themselves justified in departing from the neutrality which they have hitherto observed. The force itself being necessarily small; and in no wise changing the nature of the contest in the American Hemisphere.

I pray you, Sir, to accept the assurance of my distinguished consideration.

*(Signed)* JOHN QUINCY ADAMS.[9]

The tone of this interesting communication, it will be observed, is very different from that of the message of 1823. The alarm felt at Washington in December had now largely passed away, for the results of the Polignac interviews had by this time been communicated by Canning to the American minister, and by him transmitted to the administration.[10] Reassuring dispatches had also come from France,[11] and it was possible, therefore, in dealing with the Salazar questions, to act on the assumption that no immediate danger threatened the new states, so far as actual intervention might be concerned. With regard to monarchical intrigues, it would be sufficient to urge upon the Colombian government that it have absolutely nothing to do with them. With regard to Spanish activities, taking place during the French occupation, there was no reason, as Adams declared, why these should be regarded as dangerous. But there still remained the question of a possible danger in the future; and with regard to this the American Secretary of State expressed his views in language that certainly conveys an impression far less militant than did the

---

[9] Washington. State Dept., Notes to Ministers, Colombia, vol. 1.

[10] Rush, *Court of London*, pp. 409–15.

[11] Monroe, *Writings*, vi, pp. 398, 436f. The first of these references is to a reassuring private letter of Sheldon's to Adams, dated October 30, 1823. Sheldon, who was the American chargé at Paris, declared he had been told by Stuart that there would be no isolated action, and that "the subject would be brought forward for mutual consideration." "At all events, no steps are likely to be taken hastily or immediately in relation to those countries," he declared. James Brown, the American minister to France, writing May 30, 1824, declared that all decision of the colonial question or even of a congress was suspended.

declaration of Monroe. It is not that the language of the message is in any sense repudiated; on the contrary, it is expressly declared that the Executive has not altered its opinion, and that in a contingency similar to that mentioned in the President's pronouncement it will seek legislative concurrence for its views. But the emphasis of the dispatch is very far from reassuring. For, not only is no guarantee given — in the strict constitutional sense, none could be given — as to the action of Congress, but conditions are attached to the aid of the United States. It would be given only in case of "a deliberate and concerted system of the Allied Powers to exercise force"; and it would be dependent upon

a previous understanding with those European Powers, whose interests and whose principles would secure for them an active and efficient coöperation in the cause, an understanding preliminary to that of any alliance between the United States and the Colombian Republic, or at any rate coeval with it.

Put in plain and blunt terms this means that the United States, in spite of its brave words, would not act unless Great Britain did, and, to all appearances, would not act except in the event of a "general European intervention." Was not this a good deal like coming in "as a cock-boat in the wake of the British man-of-war"? If the Adams note to Salazar was not the abandonment of the Doctrine, it was, I think it must be conceded, a distinct retreat. It put American policy toward the South American republics on a footing considerably less audacious than did the message of 1823.

The reasons for this comparative caution cannot be definitely assigned; but it is at least interesting to speculate upon the point. Something may have been due, perhaps, to the cool reception which the original Monroe Doctrine had met with in Congress; something may have been due to the fact that Monroe's and Adams's ardor cooled with the passing of what seemed to them a moment of peril. But behind all these things, there is one other that can be more definitely stated. This is the reluctance, the traditional reluctance, of the United States to enter into binding engagements calling for the exercise of armed force. In refusing the Colombian request for a treaty of alliance, the President and his Secretary of State were, of course, acting on principles at least as old as the administration of Washington; in refusing to convert the Monroe Doctrine into a pledge of action contingent on fixed circumstances, they were following a line of policy congenial to the whole diplomatic tradition of the United States.

The position thus assumed, however, did not prevent Monroe from restating the principles of 1823 in his final message to Congress in December, 1824.[12] Here, as in the year before, he set forth American opposition not only to hostile European intervention but to intermeddling with the political forms of the new states. His language, as suits the change of circumstances, is considerably more restrained than that of the Doctrine; but the essential elements remain the same. Monroe did not mean them to be forgotten.

[12] Monroe, *Writings*, vii, pp. 47 f. "With respect to the contest to which our neighbors are a party, it is evident that Spain as a power is scarcely felt in it. These new States had completely achieved their independence before it was acknowledged by the United States, and they have since maintained it with little foreign pressure. The disturbances which have appeared in certain portions of that vast territory have proceeded from internal causes, which had their origin in their former Governments and have not yet been thoroughly removed. It is manifest that these causes are daily losing their effect, and that these new States are settling down under Governments elective and representative in every branch, similar to our own. In this course we ardently wish them to persevere, under a firm conviction that it will promote their happiness. In this, their career, however, we have not interfered, believing that every people have a right to institute for themselves the government which, in their judgment, may suit them best. Our example is before them, of the good effect of which, being our neighbors, they are competent judges, and to their judgment we leave it, in the expectation that other powers will pursue the same policy. The deep interest which we take in their independence, which we have acknowledged, and in their enjoyment of all the rights incident thereto, especially in the very important one of instituting their own Governments, has been declared, and is known to the world. Separated as we are from Europe by the great Atlantic Ocean, we can have no concern in the wars of the European Governments nor in the causes which produce them. The balance of power between them, into whichever scale it may turn in its various vibrations, cannot affect us. It is the interest of the United States to preserve the most friendly relations with every power and on conditions fair, equal, and applicable to all. But in regard to our neighbors our situation is different. It is impossible for the European Governments to interfere in their concerns, especially in those alluded to, which are vital, without affecting us; indeed, the motive which might induce such interference in the present state of the war between the parties, if a war it may be called, would appear to be equally applicable to us. It is gratifying to know that some of the powers with whom we enjoy a very friendly intercourse, and to whom these views have been communicated, have appeared to acquiesce in them."

More extraordinary still, he put forward, though in rather cautious language, the claim that the new doctrines had been accepted by other powers. "It is gratifying to know," he remarked sententiously, "that some of the powers with whom we enjoy a very friendly intercourse, and to whom these views have been communicated, have appeared to acquiesce in them." This language, with regard to Continental Europe, is without a scintilla of justification; Monroe's assumption could be based upon nothing whatsoever but the argument from silence. Even with regard to Great Britain it was distinctly a qualified truth, for the British government had none of the American hostility to a settlement on monarchical principles, and had never signified its approval of the message in any form. But the fact that the President could use such language is interesting and significant. It may be taken as a step in the development of the romantic legend that the United States prevented European intervention in 1823.

Scarcely was the new declaration of 1824 uttered than there was a new occasion for the interpretation of American policy. This time the applicant for enlightenment was the Empire of Brazil. Brazil had been recognized by the United States in May, 1824. There had been some discussion in the cabinet as to whether the acknowledgment of a monarchy was consistent with the principles of the United States.[13] But both the President and Adams were ready for such a step. Monroe, indeed, argued that it might have a favorable influence upon European public opinion, and Adams was concerned only with the receiving of satisfactory assurances that the newly established Empire was independent in fact as well as in name, and would not serve as a focus of European influence.[14] The hope of bringing Brazil within the sphere of American rather than European policy may also have had a part in the decision.

Such a hope was not unreasonable. The desire for an understanding with the American government was keenly felt at Rio de Janeiro, and had been intensified by the President's declara-

---

[13] Adams, *Memoirs*, vi, pp. 281. Only Wirt had opposed recognition.
[14] *Ibid.*, vi, pp. 280–285, 314, 317.

tion. Gonsalves da Cruz, a Brazilian agent in the United States in 1823, had written that Monroe's pronouncement had been generally regarded as opening the way to closer political relations, and that such was "the moral certainty" of a treaty of confederation that "certain diplomatic personalities" had inquired as to the willingness of Brazil to participate in it.[15] Encouraged by such language, the Brazilian Foreign Minister, Carvalho e Mello, in drawing up the instructions for Rebello, who was sent to Washington to urge recognition of the Empire in January, 1824, incorporated in his instructions a reference to the possibility of an offensive and defensive alliance between the two states.[16] In later instructions the desire for such an alliance was frequently reëmphasized, and Rebello was urged to enter into negotiations with the United States.[17] It has been suggested that the interest in a close association with the government at Washington was inspired by hostility to the other South American states, and in particular to La Plata, with whom Brazil had a standing quarrel over the Banda Oriental, the territory now known as Uruguay. But this interpretation of the facts does not accord with the tenor of the instructions of Rebello, in which the emphasis was laid very definitely upon aid against European in-

[15] *Archivo diplomatico da independencia* (Rio de Janeiro, 1922), v, p. 75 (Jan. 1, 1824).

[16] *Archivo diplomatico da independencia*, v, p. 13. Rebello's instructions are here given in full (pp. 10–18), dated Jan. 31, 1824. They are thus the earliest South American reference to the Doctrine. The essential clauses are in sections 6 and 15, and run as follows. (Section 6) "Such are the principles of the policy of those States, which alone were sufficient to hasten our recognition, principles which in the Message of the President to both Houses in December last, assumed a more generic application to all the States of these Continents, since in that Message is clearly enunciated the necessity of our combining for the defense of our rights and our territory." (Section 15) "You will sound the sentiments of the Government as to an offensive and defensive alliance with this Empire, as part of the American Continent, on the supposition that such an alliance should not be based on mutual concessions, but should be deduced only from the general principle of the mutual convenience of such an association." Also in J. M. da Silva Papanhos Rio Branco, *Brazil, the United States and the Monroe Doctrine* (Rio de Janeiro, 1908), pp. 8 f., and in W. S. Robertson, "South America and the Monroe Doctrine, 1824–1828," *Pol. Sci. Quart.*, xxx (1915), p. 94.

[17] *Archivo diplomatico da independencia*, v, p. 24, under date of Sept. 15, 1824; p. 30, under date of Jan. 28, 1825; and pp. 33 f., under date of May 14, 1825.

tervention. The truth of the matter seems to be that the Brazilian government may have been a little nervous as to the European situation. This may seem strange in view of the fact that negotiations had already been opened with the mother country. But these negotiations were not going very promisingly in the summer of 1824, and, moreover, there was a Portuguese expedition preparing in the Tagus for the reconquest of the former colony.[18] As late as January, 1825, Carvalho e Mello speaks of the possibility of reconquest, and, remote though the actual danger may have been, it was sufficiently real to warrant casting an anchor to windward. To this motive there may have been added a genuine interest in an American system, such an interest as had prompted the Abbé Correa to propose a close association between the United States and the Portuguese-Brazilian monarchy, as early as 1820. The references to such a system are not infrequent in the dispatches of Rio de Janeiro, and there is no reason for believing them insincere.

At any rate, whatever the motive, the Brazilian government was interested in a closer accord with the United States, and was, indeed, the first South American government to take notice of the Doctrine, since Rebello's instructions of January, 1824, referred to it.

Rebello, however, seems to have been reluctant to broach the matter at Washington. In his speech to the President on his reception, May 26, 1824, he did indeed hint at a "concert of American powers to sustain the general system of American independence."[19] But he took no step to go further than this until the following January, after renewed instructions from Rio de Janeiro. On January 27 he had an interview with Adams, in which he discussed the possibility of a close accord between the two countries.

The Secretary of State asked that the proposal be put in writing. Accordingly, the very next day, the Brazilian transmitted a note which, like that of Salazar, is based upon the language of

---

[18] See Manuel d'Oliveira Lima, *O Reconhecimento do Imperio* (Rio de Janeiro and Paris, 1901), pp. 98–131.

[19] Adams, *Memoirs*, vi, p. 359.

the Monroe Doctrine, and attempts to secure an interpretation of it. That "honorable, generous and gratuitous declaration," declared Rebello, "is certainly applicable to Brazil." In case of European aid to Portugal, "the government of the United States would be obliged to put into practise the principles of the policy enunciated in the aforesaid message, giving proof of the generosity and consistency which animated it, which could not be done without a sacrifice of men and treasure." Would the United States, therefore, not enter into an offensive and defensive alliance with the Empire of Brazil, the *casus foederis* to apply in case of European aid to Portugal for the reconquest of the colony, or, secondly, in case of the renewed hostility of Portugal herself? [20]

To this appeal John Quincy Adams vouchsafed no reply. He had other things to think of in the winter of 1825, with his own candidacy for the presidency at stake in the House of Representatives. But when, after Adams had become President, Rebello renewed his interrogatory to Henry Clay, the new Secretary of State, Clay replied with considerable promptitude. His language was much like that used to Colombia in 1824, minimizing the danger, and refusing to pledge the aid of the United States in any contingency.

With respect to your first proposition [he wrote — that is, alliance to apply in case of European intervention], . . . as there does not appear at present, any likelihood of Portugal being able to draw to her aid other powers to assist her in resubjugating the Brazils, there would not seem to be any occasion for a convention founded upon that improbable contingency. The President, on the contrary, sees with satisfaction that there is a reasonable probability of a speedy peace between Portugal and the government of Brazil, founded upon the Independence of it, which the United States were the first to acknowledge. . . . If in the progress of events there should be a renewal of demonstrations on the part of the European allies to attack the Independence of the American States, the President will give to that new state of things, should it arise, every consideration which its importance would undoubtedly demand.

With respect to your second proposition of a Treaty of alliance offensive and defensive to repel any invasion of the Brazilian Territories by the forces of Portugal, if the expected peace should take place, that also would be un-

[20] Washington. State Dept., Notes from Foreign Legations, Brazil, vol. 1, Jan. 28, 1825. Reprinted in Rio Branco, *op. cit.*, pp. 12 f., and in Robertson, *op. cit.*, p. 95.

necessary. But such a treaty would be inconsistent with the policy that the United States have heretofore prescribed to themselves; that policy is, that whilst the war is confined to the parent Country and its former Colony, the United States remain neutral, extending their friendship and doing equal justice to both parties. From that policy they did not deviate during the whole of the long contest between Spain and the several Independent Governments which have been erected on her former American territories. If an exception to it were now for the first time made, the justice of your Sovereign will admit that the other new Governments might have cause to complain of the United States.[21]

It is interesting to observe that in the note just quoted Clay recognized by implication the applicability of Monroe's principles to the independent monarchy of Brazil. By the strictest interpretation, the message would not have justified such a construction; but the American Secretary of State was willing to extend it to cover a case not provided for in its terms, and to declare that a European intervention in the affairs of Brazil would raise much the same considerations as an attack upon the new republics formed from the dominions of Spain. At the same time he rejected all notion of an alliance, either against Portugal or against the Holy Allies in general. This did not signify that the Monroe declaration was meaningless; it simply meant that the United States would be free to construe it as in its own judgment it saw fit.

There was not, it must be reiterated, the slightest intention of abandoning the principles laid down in 1823. In fact, Henry Clay was anxious to make them more vividly felt than before, and to secure their acceptance by other nations. He was anxious, too, to claim full credit with South America for Monroe's announcement, and to make it the basis of favoring relations. This is clearly seen in the instructions which he drew up for Poinsett, the newly appointed American minister to Mexico, in the early spring of 1825.

You will bring to the notice of the Mexican government the Message of the President of the United States to their Congress, on the 2nd December 1823, asserting certain important principles of intercontinental law, in the relations of Europe and America. The first principle asserted in that message is that the American continents are not henceforth to be considered as sub-

[21] Washington. State Dept., Notes to Foreign Legations, vol. 3.

jects for future colonization by any European powers. In the maintenance of that principle all the independent governments of America have an interest, but that of the United States has probably the least. Whatever foundation may have existed three centuries ago, or even at a later period, when all this continent was under European subjection, for the establishment of a rule, founded on priority of discovery and occupation, for apportioning among the powers of Europe parts of this Continent, none can be now admitted as applicable to its present condition. There is no disposition to disturb the colonial possessions, as they now exist, of any of the European powers, but it is against the establishment of new European colonies upon this Continent that the principle is directed. The countries in which any such new establishments might be attempted are now open to the enterprise and commerce of all Americans; and the justice, or propriety, cannot be recognized of arbitrarily limiting and circumscribing that enterprise and commerce by the act of voluntarily planting a new Colony, without the consent of America, under the auspices of foreign powers belonging to another, and a distant continent. Europe would be indignant at any American attempt to plant a colony on any part of her shores; and her justice must perceive, in the rule contended for, only perfect reciprocity.

The other principle asserted in the Message is that, whilst we do not desire to interfere in Europe, with the political system of the allied powers, we should regard as dangerous to our peace and safety any attempt on their part to extend their system to any portion of this Hemisphere. The political systems of the two Continents are essentially different. Each has an exclusive right to judge for itself what is best suited to its own condition, and most likely to promote its happiness, but neither has a right to enforce upon the other the establishment of its peculiar system. This principle was declared in the face of the world at a moment when there was reason to apprehend that the allied powers were entertaining designs inimical to the freedom, if not the independence, of the new governments. There is ground for believing that the declaration of it had considerable effect in preventing the maturity, if not in producing the abandonment, of all such designs. Both principles were laid down after much and anxious deliberation on the part of the late Administration. The President, who then formed a part of it, continues entirely to coincide in both. And you will urge upon the government of Mexico the utility and expediency of asserting the same principles on all proper occasions.[22]

This dispatch is closely paralleled by those to Forbes at Buenos Aires and to Condy Raguet at Rio de Janeiro.[23]

The viewpoint thus expressed by Clay certainly marks a step forward in the attitude of the American government toward the

[22] *American State Papers*, Foreign Relations, v, p. 909; also in Monroe, *Writings*, vi, p. 438 ff.

[23] Washington. State Dept., Instructions to Forbes and to Raguet, both dated April 14, 1825.

Monroe Doctrine. In the first place, the two principles of the message, non-colonization and non-intervention, are here for the first time placed in close juxtaposition. In the declaration of 1823, they were separated in the text, and almost certainly not brought together in the thought of the President. But they are here combined into a "system." They are given, not a temporary, but a permanent, significance. They are recommended to the consideration of other governments, as principles to be followed. And, this time more definitely than in the presidential message of 1824, the claim is put forward that they have already been efficacious in preventing hostile action on the part of Europe. In the thought of the Secretary of State, the Monroe Doctrine was to be given, not less, but greater, importance. It was to be elevated into a Doctrine in very truth.

The emphasis placed on the non-colonization principle in this dispatch, and the character of the reasoning by which that principle was justified, seem to point also to the influence of the President. There was, as will be seen, much discussion of this distinctive Adams dogma in the course of 1825 and 1826. But, before adverting to this matter, it will be desirable to call attention to a third occasion on which, as in the case of Colombia and Brazil, the United States was to be called upon to define its attitude with regard to the protection of the states of Latin America from European aggression.

This was in August, 1825, and this time the demand for assistance came from Mexico. The Mexican minister to Washington, Pablo Obregon, accredited in August, 1824, had been instructed by his government to ascertain how far the government of the United States was ready to go in assisting the new states in case of European attack.[24] To all appearances he never made such inquiries, but at Mexico City steps were taken to make more precise the attitude of the administration at Washington.[25] The incidents that led to this step were the movements of French vessels in the Caribbean in the summer of 1825. A French war-

[24] W. R. Manning, *Early Diplomatic Relations between the United States and Mexico* (Baltimore, 1916), p. 25, citing the instructions in the Mexican archives.

[25] There is no reference to any such inquiry in Adams's diary, or in the dispatches from Obregon published in the *Diplomacia Mexicana*.

ship convoyed a fleet of Spanish warships to Havana, and a French fleet appeared off Martinique; and these events naturally led to profound agitation when they were known in Mexico.[26] On August 16, the day after the receipt of these disquieting tidings, Alamán, the Mexican Foreign Minister, showed the correspondence regarding it to Poinsett and to Ward, the British minister. The two diplomats suggested that the Foreign Minister address to them identical notes on the matter, and this Alamán agreed to do. On the seventeenth these notes were sent. They declared that the Mexican government saw in the movements of the French war vessels an act hostile to the independent states of America; they referred to the declaration of President Monroe against the interference of any third power in the conflict between Spain and her dominions; they argued that the conduct of France was certainly such interference, and urged the American minister to bring the matter to the attention of his government, in order that explanations might be demanded of the court of the Tuileries. They also declared that the United States was virtually pledged to action. To this latter assertion Poinsett, very naturally, strongly objected. Though he was later, by the use of the word "pledge," to cause himself serious embarrassment, he was acute enough to see the danger of assuming any binding obligation, and the phrase which created such an implication was stricken from the note before it was finally accepted by the American minister. The note itself was then transmitted by him to Washington.[27] The alarm which was caused by the appearance of the French fleet proved to be entirely unfounded.[28]

---

[26] For fuller discussion, see Manning, *op. cit.*, pp. 117 ff.

[27] *American State Papers*, Foreign Relations, v, pp. 909 f.

[28] This episode of the French fleet is an interesting one. The main purpose of its presence in the West Indies seems almost certainly to have been to bring about a settlement between France and her former colony, Haiti, by means of a naval demonstration. Donzelot, the French admiral, also had orders, *if requested by the Spanish Governor*, to land troops in Cuba to repress internal insurrection. This fact, and the additional circumstance that Donzelot actually convoyed a Spanish force to the island, has led to the suspicion, voiced by Mr. Temperley in his article in the *Eng. Hist. Rev.*, xl (1925), p. 48, and in his book, *The Foreign Policy of Canning* (London, 1925), pp. 169 f., 174, that France may have had sinister designs on the island. But it seems strange that the principal ally of Ferdinand, and the upholder of legitimacy,

Certainly no hostile intent toward Mexico was ever manifested. Moreover, by the time that Poinsett's dispatch had reached the United States, the supposed danger from the French fleet had been dissipated. Part of it had sailed for home, and part of it had returned to its station at Martinique. All possibility of hostile action against Mexico might be considered as out of the question. But it is interesting to note that Henry Clay made an effort to demonstrate to the Mexican government the sincerity of the American attitude with regard to European intervention. In a dispatch to Poinsett of November 9, 1825, he mentioned the appeal of the Mexican government, treating that appeal, however, as if it had regard only to the protection of the island of Cuba against French aggression. What the United States "would have done had the contingency happened," he wrote, "may be inferred from a dispatch to the American minister at Paris, a copy of which is herewith sent, which you are authorized to read to the plenipotentiaries of the United Mexican States." [29] The dispatch in question, transmitted to Brown on October 25, protested against the sending of a large French fleet to the shores of the Caribbean without notice to the United States, and asserted that the United States "could not see with indifference" the islands of Cuba and Porto Rico pass into the hands of any other power.[30]

This effort to win the good graces of the Mexican government was not particularly adroit. It gave no assurance whatsoever that *Mexico* would be protected against the designs of European powers; and its assertion with regard to Cuba and Porto Rico, however sound in principle, was not calculated to gratify the politicians at Mexico City at a time when they were dreaming in a vague sort of way of gaining possession of the islands for themselves. Clay hardly strengthened his country in Mexican favor by such a response.

should have thought of wresting the island from its lawful possessor. See also St. Petersburg, F. O., Reçus, no. 27,484, in which Pozzo di Borgo flatly states that France had no hostile intentions; and London, P. R. O., F. O., Mexico, vol. 9, no. 14, Oct. 14, 1825, in which Canning declares his disbelief in French designs on Cuba.

[29] *American State Papers*, Foreign Relations, v, p. 855.

[30] *Ibid.*, p. 856.

The episode of the French fleet and the flurry over Cuba have another relationship to the Monroe Doctrine which deserves a word of mention. They mark a stage in the evolution of that corollary to the President's declaration which may be described as the no-transfer principle, the principle that the United States cannot see with indifference the transfer of territory in the American hemisphere from one European power to another. This principle, so far as I know, was never enunciated by Monroe. It had been laid down in general terms by Adams, however, in the reply to Tuyll. With regard to a specific territory, it had been stated by both Congress and the Executive as early as 1811, and reiterated — this time with Cuba in mind — by Adams in the instructions to Nelson on April 28, 1823. It was now, in the note to Brown, once more asserted by Henry Clay; again, however, only in specific terms with Cuba in mind. The fact that the Secretary made use of this note, as has just been seen, to prove to the Mexican government the loyalty of the administration to the principles of Monroe's message, shows that the Monroe Doctrine and the no-transfer theory were closely connected in his mind. And in the future, as is well known, they were to be still more closely blended together in the popular notion and in the official statement of the Monroe Doctrine. The warning to France with regard to Cuba has thus its place in the story of the presidential declaration.

There is still another aspect of the Cuban question to be noticed, besides that of French designs on the island. At Washington a fear far more real than that as to the policy of France was felt with regard to the views of Mexico and Colombia. Might they not, in the course of the prosecution of the war with Spain, attempt to seize the most valuable remaining possession of Ferdinand? And how could the United States stand by and see the island riven from the grasp of an effete monarchy, and transferred to one of the rising republics of the New World? To obviate the danger Clay resorted to vigorous measures.[31] He made clear his viewpoint directly to Mexico in his general instructions to Poinsett.[32] He urged peace directly upon Spain.[33] And he sought to

[31] His policy is fully treated in Manning, *op. cit.*, pp. 105–128.
[32] Washington. State Dept., Instructions, vol. 10, p. 225, Mar. 26, 1825.
[33] *American State Papers*, Foreign Relations, v, p. 866.

bring pressure on the obstinate Spanish court by an appeal to the Tsar, through Middleton, the American minister.[34] He sought also to enlist French [35] and British influence to the same end.[36] It is no part of this study to trace these efforts in their details. But there are two things about them that deserve to be pointed out. The Monroe message had drawn a sharp line between the New World and the Old; it had laid down the doctrine of the two spheres in plain and unequivocal language. But this did not prevent an American minister from invoking European aid when it seemed to him that the interests of the United States demanded such a course, nor an American President, who as Secretary had himself urged the making "of an American cause," from sanctioning such an overture. In 1825 there was no doctrinaire attachment to the dogma of the complete separation of the New World from the Old. The second point worth noting about these overtures is their unhappy effect upon our relations with a part of Latin America. They exposed the selfishness of the United States in rather striking fashion. They did not put an end to South American hopes of closer relationships with the great Anglo-American power to the north. But they were not calculated to increase the sympathetic coöperation of the new republics with the American governments, or, at any rate, the friendly feeling of that one of them which lay nearest to this country. The altruism of 1823 was revealed in a different light by the Cuban policy of the United States, two years later.

But whatever illusion there may have been with regard to the American attitude toward closer association with Latin America was soon to be even more fully dispelled. The American attitude toward the Congress of Panama was to mark a great step in the clarification of the viewpoint of the United States. With that Congress as a whole it is not necessary here to deal. The subject has been admirably discussed already.[37] But it is necessary to

---

[34] *American State Papers*, Foreign Relations, v, p. 846.

[35] Washington. State Dept., Instructions, vol. 10, p. 345.

[36] Ibid., p. 356.

[37] See Lockey, especially chaps. vii–x, and also the more intensive discussion of R. F. Arragon in his doctoral dissertation, "The Congress of Panama," in the Widener Library, Harvard University.

call attention to the relation of the Congress to Monroe's famous declaration.

The idea of a general gathering of the South American states was almost as old as the revolution in South America. It began to take more concrete form with the treaties of alliance of 1822 and 1823, and at that time hints were given the American government that its participation might be welcome. But effective measures toward the convening of such a congress did not take place till 1824. One of the motives for inviting the United States was, no doubt, the hope of translating the Monroe Doctrine into a more definite engagement.

This was especially true as regards Colombia. Despite the Adams note to Salazar, the government at Bogotá continued to hope for a closer accord with the United States, as a result of the approaching congress. As early as October, 1824, Gual instructed Salazar on this matter, laying considerable emphasis on the non-colonization principle. At the same time he wrote to Funes, the Colombian minister at Mexico City, suggesting the inclusion of the American government in the projected gathering, and again indicating that the language of Monroe might serve as the basis of a general understanding. Early in the spring of 1825, the Mexican and Colombian ministers at Washington had an interview with Clay in which they sounded the views of the United States. Clay told them that, though the United States could not make itself a party to the war with Spain, such a congress might be useful in "settling several important disputed questions of public law," a phrase which distinctly suggests a new reference to the non-colonization doctrine. He also declared that a more exact view of the character of such a meeting ought to precede its actual assembling.[38] So the matter rested till the following November, when the ministers of Colombia, of Mexico, and of Central America,[39] transmitted to the Secretary formal invitations to the projected gathering. These invitations show that the governments which sent them hoped to use the non-colonization principle to form a more intimate connection with the

[38] *American State Papers*, Foreign Relations, v, p. 835.
[39] *Ibid.*, pp. 836–839.

United States. After adverting to other phases of the matter, Salazar wrote:

The manner in which all colonization of European powers on the American continent shall be resisted, and their interference in the present contest between Spain and her former colonies prevented, are other points of great interest. Were it proper, an eventual alliance, in case these events should occur, which is within the range of possibilities, and the treaty, of which no use should be made until the *casus foederis* should happen, to remain secret; or, if this should seem premature, a convention so anticipated would be different means to secure the same end of preventing foreign influence.[40]

Such an engagement, added the Colombian minister, would be "in accordance with the repeated declarations and protests of the cabinet at Washington." The language of Obregon, the Mexican minister, was much the same:

One of the subjects which will occupy the attention of the Congress will be the resistance or opposition to the interference of any neutral nation in the question and war of independence between the new powers of the Continent and Spain. The Government of the undersigned apprehends that, as the powers of America are of accord as to resistance, it behooves them to discuss the means of giving to that resistance all possible force, that the evil may be met, if it cannot be avoided; and the only means of accomplishing this object is by a previous concert as to the mode in which each of them shall lend its coöperation; for otherwise, resistance would operate but partially, and in a manner much less certain and effective. The opposition to colonization in America by the European powers will be another of the questions which may be discussed, and which is in like predicament with the foregoing.[41]

The language of Cañaz, the Central American, was distinctly more vague, making no definite reference to the Doctrine, but referring to an American system and the necessity of adopting "the best plan for defending the States of the New World from foreign aggression, and, by treaties of alliance, commerce, and friendship, raise them to that elevation of wealth and power which, from their resources, they may attain." [42]

But all these documents again raised the question of the American attitude toward the declaration of 1823, and had Henry Clay been a truly skilful diplomat, he would have seized the occasion to lay down the policy of the United States in definite terms, along the lines which were already becoming clear. He might

---

[40] *American State Papers*, Foreign Relations, v, p. 837.
[41] *Ibid.*, p. 836.　　　　　　　　[42] *Ibid.*, p. 839.

have answered the invitation in the affirmative, as he did; but he would have dispelled, once and for all, South American illusions, in their nature not to be satisfied, as to an alliance with the United States. He had taken the only possible stand in his reply to Rebello; why did he not take it now in answering Salazar, Obregon, and Cañaz? An alliance with the new states was, by this time, clearly out of the question; and the fact might have been, and ought to have been, stated. But it was not. The replies to the South American ministers contained no reference to the principles of the message, but merely indicated that the representatives of the United States to be sent to Panama would be "fully empowered and instructed upon all questions likely to arise in the Congress on subjects in which the nations of America have a common interest." [43]

President Adams himself was more prudent. When he sent to the Senate the nominations of Anderson and Sergeant for the Panama mission, he made it clear that the motive of the commissioners' attendance was "neither to contract alliances, nor to engage in any undertaking or project importing hostility to any other nation." [44] On the other hand, with regard to his own principle of non-colonization, he added that

an agreement between all the parties represented at the meeting, that each will guard, by its own means, against the establishment of any future European colony within its borders, may be found advisable. This was, more than two years since, announced by my predecessor to the world as a principle resulting from the emancipation of both the American continents. It may be so developed to the new Southern nations that they will all feel it as an essential appendage to their independance.[45]

What Adams had in mind, so far as the Monroe Doctrine was concerned, then, was the translation of the principle which he himself had evolved into a rule of American public law. This is further, perhaps, than some Americans of a later day would be willing to go; but it certainly involved no dangerous surrender of independence, and no entangling alliance. It was consistent with everything that had gone before; and it indicates with precision the furthest limit to which the United States would advance, in

---

[43] Clay's answers are to be found in *American State Papers*, Foreign Relations, v, pp. 837 ff.     [44] *Ibid.*, p. 834.     [45] *Ibid.*, p. 835.

forming any engagement upon the subjects treated in the famous message of 1823.

To this idea Adams tenaciously adhered despite violent opposition in Congress to the Panama mission. Nothing daunted by the strictures of the Senate, he reasserted and justified the non-colonization principle in a special message to the House of Representatives.[46] And when at last the weary battle was over, and the way clear for the sending of the American representatives, the general declaration on colonization formed one of the objects of their mission.[47]

Throughout, his conception of such a statement remained the same. There was to be no alliance, no pledge of common action — merely an assertion of principle, the "moral effect" of which was thought to be all that was necessary to prevent the evils of European settlement.

With regard to non-intervention, the President, in his various state papers of the epoch, had much less to say, perhaps because the danger was quite properly deemed to be past. In his message to the Senate there is no allusion to the subject. In the communication to the House there is a suggestion of a joint declaration.

> With respect to the obtrusive interference from abroad [wrote Adams], if its future character may be inferred from that which has been and perhaps still is exercised in more than one of the new States — a joint declaration of its character and exposure of it to the world may be probably all that the occasion would require. Whether the United States should or should not be parties to such a declaration may justly form a part of the deliberation.[48]

This is certainly not very aggressive, nor very far-reaching. And in the instructions to Anderson and Sergeant it fades away again into a language even more general, into an injunction to the American representatives to urge upon the ministers of the South American states that they should not buy European recognition at the price of an alteration in their form of government.[49] Consistent in thus seeking to restrict or to banish European influence,

---

[46] Richardson, *Messages and Papers of the Presidents*, ii, pp. 334 f.

[47] *Register of Debates*, Twentieth Congress, Second Session (Washington, 1830), Appendix, p. 45.

[48] Richardson, *Messages and Papers of the Presidents*, ii, p. 335.

[49] *Register of Debates*, Twentieth Congress, Second Session, Appendix, p. 48.

the Adams administration was not willing to enter into common accord on this matter with the new republics of the New World.

Speaking generally, it may be said that Adams and Clay, in their attitude toward the Congress of Panama and its relation to the Monroe Doctrine, were not anxious to propose any kind of engagement which would enlarge the responsibilities of the United States. They wished chiefly to give the non-colonization principle a general authority and a larger moral force; beyond this they were hardly ready to go.

Before we take leave of the attitude of the Executive at the time of the Panama mission, there is one other matter that deserves examination. It is the Poinsett pledge. On January 4, the Senate, under the resolution of Senator Macon, called for papers bearing on the Panama mission. Among the papers transmitted was a dispatch of Poinsett's of September 28, 1825, describing his negotiations with the Mexican government with reference to a commercial treaty. Earnestly arguing for the right of the United States to be put upon a footing of equality with the nations of South America in matters of trade, Poinsett had, in his ardor, committed a diplomatic indiscretion. He had declared that

the United States had pledged themselves not to permit any other power to interfere either with their independence or form of government; and that, as, in the event of such an attempt being made by the powers of Europe, we would be compelled to take the most active and efficient part and to bear the brunt of the contest, it was not just that we should be placed on a less favorable footing than the other Republics of America, whose existence we were ready to support at such hazards.[50]

The opposition in the Senate made a terrific to-do over this so-called pledge; and when the question of Panama came up in the House, there was a call for further papers, and for Clay's instructions. And, doubtless to the embarrassment of the Secretary, it now appeared that, when writing to Poinsett of the Cuban business on November 9, Clay had himself referred to "the memorable pledge" of 1823.[51] Under these circumstances an explanation was decidedly in order, and the explanation was given. In the

[50] *American State Papers*, Foreign Relations, v, p. 854.
[51] *Ibid.*, p. 855.

very document transmitting these latter papers, the Secretary set
forth his views:

The people of the United States would have stood pledged, in the opinion
of their Executive, not to any foreign State, but to themselves and their
posterity, by their dearest interests and highest duties, to resist to the utmost such an attempt; and it is to a pledge of that character that Mr.
Poinsett alone refers.[52]

This was more ingenious than convincing; and it is, perhaps,
no wonder that, in the House debates on the Panama mission,
Livingston, a friend of the administration, called Clay's use of
the word "pledge" "a solecism in language." And yet Clay
meant exactly what he said. He meant that the United States
could not see European intervention in the New World with indifference, and that it would infallibly find its interests involved
such a contingency. This was a point of view not without support at the time, and not without support since.

So much for the attitude of the Executive in the Panama discussion of 1825 and 1826. It is now necessary to examine the
atttiude of Congress during the same period. As has been already
indicated, from the very moment of the President's nominations
the administration had to contend against a vigorous opposition.
In the Senate the expediency of the mission was warmly debated,
and in the House there was also a long consideration of the measure, centering chiefly, not on the appropriation bill necessary to
pay the expenses of the mission, but on a resolution reported from
the committee on foreign relations in favor of the President's
policy, and on the amendments to that resolution. These various
deliberations throw much light on the attitude of the legislature
with regard to the Monroe Doctrine.

Of the happy effects of the message at the time that it was
enunciated there was, if not unanimity, at least substantial agreement among both friends and opponents of the mission. The
legend that Monroe had warded off a terrible danger found con-
firmation in the debates in the Senate.

[52] *American State Papers*, Foreign Relations, v, p. 908.

This declaration [stated Johnston of Louisiana] was received throughout Europe and America with enthusiasm. . . . On the other side of the Atlantic, it touched every bosom. Every friend of freedom felt his faith and
confidence confirmed. The Powers of Europe paused. England, immediately
after, no doubt in concert with this Government, acknowledged the independence of the Spanish American Republics. The designs of the Holy
Alliance were disconcerted. This memorable declaration has had its effect.
It has resulted in the determination of all parties to leave Spain free to regain
her lost dominions, and they free to defend them.[53]

Johnston was a friend of the administration. But White of Tennessee, an opponent of the mission, admitted that Monroe's
pronouncement had had a good effect, and might have prevented
intervention;[54] and Van Buren, another opponent of Adams's,
declared that it had "rendered efficient service."[55]

Only Dickerson of New Jersey was mean-spirited enough to
suggest that it "produced but little effect, except to induce the
new Republics to give this invitation to join the Congress of
Panama, and will produce but little effect, except to embarrass
our Government hereafter."[56]

In the House of Representatives there were many who eulogized the declaration warmly. In an often-quoted speech, Webster
took up arms indignantly against any attempt to depreciate it.

Sir, I agree with those who maintain the proposition, and I contend
against those who deny it, that the message did mean something; that it
meant much; and I maintain against both, that the declaration effected
much good, answered the end designed by it, did great honor to the foresight
and spirit of the Government.[57]

The American people rejoiced, he added, that there had been
done "something useful, and something effectual, for the cause
of civil liberty." This language was echoed by many others.
Johnson of Kentucky,[58] the vigorous Livingston of Louisiana,[59]
and Hemphill of Pennsylvania,[60] declared their belief in the value
of the message, and a member named Test indulged in a rhap-
sodic and wholly inaccurate description of its effectiveness.[61] The

---

[53] *Register of Debates*, Nineteenth Congress, First Session, i, col. 224.
[54] *Ibid.*, col. 200.          [55] *Ibid.*, col. 242.
[56] *Ibid.*, col. 297.          [57] *Ibid.*, ii, col. 2269.
[58] *Ibid.*, col. 1811.          [59] *Ibid.*, col. 2212.
[60] *Ibid.*, col. 2236.          [61] *Ibid.*, col. 2461.

same language came from some opponents of the mission. Polk
gave cautious adhesion to the theory that the message "probably
altered the disposition of the European powers;[62] and McDuffie
of South Carolina, Calhoun's brilliant lieutenant, declared that
Monroe's declaration "operated with almost electrical power in
every part of Europe where freedom had an advocate." To him
its effect was "decisive," and it would "add a glorious brilliance
to the brightest page of our history." [63] There were, it is true,
others who took a contrary view. Worthington of Maryland [64]
and Campbell of Ohio [65] deemed the message a *brutum fulmen*,
and the former of these two doubted the existence of any danger
whatsoever in 1823, declaring that it would have been a "mad
project" to attempt to reconquer South America, especially in
view of British opposition. But the general view in Congress
undoubtedly was that Monroe had struck an effective blow for
liberty in his famous declaration.

On the other hand, many members were ready to admit the
existence, and the efficacy, of British support for the views of
the United States. Johnston in the Senate,[66] Livingston [67] and
Webster [68] in the House — to cite only the most notable examples
— readily conceded that Canning, as well as Monroe, had done
his part in protecting the new republics. In view of the vigorous
nationalism of American sentiment in the eighteen-twenties, it is
surprising to see with what good grace this British assistance was
conceded.

It was also the general opinion that the message was justified
in its own day and generation. True, in the Senate, Branch of
North Carolina spoke disrespectfully of it as "an unauthorized,
unmeaning, and empty menace, well calculated to excite the
angry passions and embroil us with foreign nations"; [69] and the
sceptics noted above who doubted of its effects doubted also of
its wisdom. But Forsyth declared that he approved of it at the
time,[70] and McDuffie declared that it was "as wise as it was
magnanimous." [71]

[62] *Register of Debates*, Nineteenth Congress, First Session, i, col. 2489.
[63] *Ibid.*, col. 2502.     [64] *Ibid.*, col. 2393.     [65] *Ibid.*, col. 2425.
[66] *Ibid.*, i, col. 224.     [67] *Ibid.*, ii, col. 2212.     [68] *Ibid.*, col. 2268.
[69] *Ibid.*, i, col. 386.     [70] *Ibid.*, ii, cols. 1817 f.     [71] *Ibid.*, col. 2502.

A question of more practical import, upon which there was tremendous debate in the Panama discussion, was whether the Monroe message constituted a pledge, as had been intimated by Poinsett in his conversations on the commercial treaty, and by Clay, in his instructions of November 9, to Poinsett. The opponents of the mission utterly denied the propriety of any such interpretation of the President's language. Monroe's pronouncement, declared Berrien of Georgia in the Senate, was "a mere gratuitous declaration to Congress, of one of the public functionaries of this Government," [72] and Hayne of South Carolina and White of Tennessee echoed this language.[73] Van Buren was rather more moderate in his analysis, but his conclusion was identical. "He asserted, (if you please), correct principles, but left us at liberty to act or not, in enforcing them, as our interest or our policy might at the moment require." [74] The same point of view was again and again expressed in the House of Representatives. Rives thought Monroe's sentences vague and oracular,[75] and Verplanck of New York, Worthington of Maryland, and Campbell of Ohio took much the same view.[76] Forsyth pointed out that there could be no binding obligation in a document which was not addressed to any other power, and naturally enough disparaged Clay's sophistical explanation of the word "pledge." "How strange," he exclaimed, "that vigorous and practised minds should resort to such defenses." [77]

The friends of the message hardly sought to deny the point thus made by the opposition. Johnston of Louisiana in the Senate,[78]

---

[72] *Register of Debates*, Nineteenth Congress, First Session, i, col. 284.

[73] *Ibid.*, cols. 161, 200.　　　　[74] *Ibid.*, col. 242.

[75] *Ibid.*, ii, col. 2072.　　　　[76] *Ibid.*, cols. 1815, 2393, 2425.

[77] *Ibid.*, col. 2319. "The existing generation but too often gives a pledge for posterity, which posterity is called upon to redeem. A pledge to posterity may always be given with perfect security. The party who only has the right to demand the redemption of a pledge, is he to whom it is given. Posterity can never make such demand until the present is united to the future.

"Equally safe is a pledge to ourselves. The party holding the pledge can release it. If we ourselves should ever be so indiscreet as to call, at an inconvenient season, for the redemption of a pledge given by ourselves to ourselves, we ourselves can release ourselves from the obligation to redeem the pledge given by ourselves to ourselves. Could the genius of ridicule itself, by the use of words, produce a more whimsical confusion of ideas?"　　　　[78] *Ibid.*, i, col. 223.

and such able defenders of the administration as Webster in the House,[79] freely admitted the contention of the other side. Far from justifying the notion of a pledge, in almost every instance they expressly disclaimed it. There was, indeed, only one notable exception to this general rule. Livingston of Louisiana, one of the most vigorous supporters of the administration, took the ground that Monroe's declaration was a "pledge to the world that we would interfere, according to our means, to resist" the intervention of Europe in South America. But, he contended, this pledge related only to the state of things that then existed. It was not intended as the foundation of an alliance with Spanish America. This fact should be and could be made clear by the dispatch of the mission to Panama. On the other hand, in the unlikely contingency that the circumstances under which the declaration was made should recur, Livingston declared that he would wish all Europe to understand that our conduct would redeem the pledge then made.[80]

Though none but an obscure Maryland member, whose speech is not reported, echoed this language, in so far as the assertion of the existence of a pledge is concerned, Livingston was not alone in his view that the Monroe Doctrine ought not to be weakened or abandoned. "It neither would comport with our dignity, our honor, or our principles," declared Johnston of Louisiana in the Senate, "to weaken the force of that moral influence which this memorable declaration has had on the European continent." [81] On the other hand, Hayne of South Carolina denied that the United States "is now, or ever was, prepared to go to war for the independence of South America," [82] and Woodbury of New Hampshire eloquently demanded "how many of our gallant sons are to find ignoble graves under the tropical sun of Guatemala, if some petty Hessian Prince should hire a regiment of infantry to Spain?" "Avowals of such principles," he declared, "whether

[79] *Register of Debates*, Nineteenth Congress, First Session, ii, col. 2269.
[80] *Ibid.*, cols. 2211 f. Livingston, however, denounced Clay's explanation as a "subterfuge unworthy a great nation, as well as a solecism in language."
[81] *Ibid.*, i, col. 227.
[82] *Ibid.*, col. 161.

made by Mr. Monroe or others, are very justly, on one occasion, styled by the Secretary, 'uncalculating.'" [83]

In the House the question of standing by the message played a considerable part in debate, and occasioned one extremely interesting vote. There were many who were ready to admit the justice of the general principles laid down by Monroe. Powell of Virginia, Buckner of Kentucky, Wurts and Thomson of Pennsylvania, and Bartlett of New Hampshire, all friends of the mission, took the ground that they could not agree to retract a syllable of the famous presidential declaration.[84] And Markley of Pennsylvania introduced a resolution, which never came to a vote, declaring that Monroe's manifesto

was wise, seasonable and patriotic; that it reserved to this Government an uncontrolled power of deciding or acting, in any crisis, as our interest and policy might require; . . . and that the sentiments of that declaration, if circumstances should, hereafter, unhappily and unexpectedly arise, to make them again applicable, would be strictly conformable to the duty and true policy of the United States.[85]

Nor was this interpretation of the interests of the United States confined entirely to the defenders of the administration. Rives of Virginia, for example, a stalwart opponent of the mission, was ready to admit the possible necessity of American interference in case of intervention.[86] Cambreleng of New York described the principles of Monroe as reviving and dying with the occasion,[87] — an implied admission of their validity, — and Forsyth of Georgia took ground which, while construing the message rather differently from others, conceded its essential justification. In his view, the President was protesting, not against monarchical institutions in the New World, but against intervention as a principle. And he was rightly protesting. "If the crusade began at Patagonia, it would not end at Mexico." But, he added, we should act on the theory of a real danger in such meddling "whenever the emergency may require it, without regard to the message;

---

[83] *Register of Debates*, Nineteenth Congress, First Session, ii, col. 192.
[84] *Ibid.*, ii, cols. 2029, 2096, 2189, 2345, and T. H. Benton, *Abridgment of the Debates of Congress* (New York, 1858), ix, 212.
[85] *Register of Debates*, Nineteenth Congress, First Session, ii, col. 2098.
[86] *Ibid.*, col 2083.
[87] *Ibid.*, col. 2438.

and our mode of action will be precisely the same as if the message had never been sent to us." [88]

On the other hand, in the House as in the Senate, there were those who were not ready to acquiesce even in the general principle that the United States could not see with indifference intervention in South America. Floyd of Virginia declared that he had condemned the principles of the message at its inception,[89] Wickliffe of Kentucky took the same view,[90] and McLane of Delaware, in submitting an amendment to the resolution of the committee on foreign relations, spoke impliedly against Monroe's principles, declaring that they needed explanation and clarification.[91]

A middle ground between the defence of Monroe's principles and the denial of their validity, curiously enough, appeared almost not at all in the debate, as it has, indeed, appeared only seldom in the history of the Monroe Doctrine. It is amazing how rarely publicists have made any distinction, in the application of the President's declaration, between the island republics of the Caribbean and the remote reaches of Patagonia. Only in recent years has a restricted form of the Doctrine suggested itself. In the debates of 1826, only Webster raised any such consideration. He suggested, as he had two years before, that there might be a difference between the intervention of the Holy Alliance in Buenos Aires and its intervention in Mexico. The one case might justify action, where the other would not.[92] But this judicious viewpoint found no echo in the debates in the House or in the Senate.

But what of the non-colonization principle? What was the congressional judgment upon that? In the report of the Senate committee on the Panama nominations, the favorite dogma of the President was gently dealt with. The theory that the American continents were wholly appropriated was reaffirmed, and the non-colonization doctrine ranked by implication among the "high, just, and universally admitted rights of all nations." [93] In the Senate itself there was little opposition to the abstract principle

---

[88] *Register of Debates*, Nineteenth Congress, First Session, ii, col. 2321.

[89] *Ibid.*, col. 2446.    [90] *Ibid.*, col. 2043.    [91] *Ibid.*, col. 2013.

[92] *Ibid.*, col. 2269.    [93] *Ibid.*, Appendix, p. 94.

laid down in 1823. In the House the situation was different. Forsyth, in a brilliant speech, declared that the thesis of the President was

based upon assertions of fact, which I trust we shall never be called upon to establish, and of principles that are fallacious. Can we prove [he asked], and if we could, is it our business, either to prove or assert, that, with the exception of the existing European colonies, the territories of the independent Nations of North and South America cover the whole surface of the two continents, if, by "existing colonies," it is intended to exclude territorial claims, not accompanied by an actual colonial possession?

As for the notion that colonial dominion and monopoly were inseparable, and that this afforded justification of the non-colonization doctrine, the Georgian was unwilling to admit any such contention. If we have a right to freedom of commerce at all, we have such a right no less against colonies than against independent states, and no more against independent states than against colonies.[94] Rives of Virginia opposed the Adams doctrine on grounds, not of logic, but of expediency. He pointed out that it had been, from the beginning, contested by Great Britain. An attempt to maintain it would, he believed, involve us in a war with that power. It was a dangerous principle to assert.[95] And, finally, Worthington denounced the declaration as "rash and inconsiderate, and utterly incompatible with the pacific and unambitious spirit of our Republican institutions." [96]

In general, however, the members of Congress quarrelled, not with the tenets of the message of 1823, but with the administration's effort to extend them. If one turns from abstract discussion of the Monroe declaration to discussion of Adams's concrete proposals for a new assertion of them, one finds a striking lack of sympathy for the President. His suggestion that the powers at Panama reassert the non-colonization dogma, each in relation to its own territory, was savagely attacked. To take a pledge to other nations to preserve our own territory inviolate was to Hayne, to White of Tennessee, and to Forsyth, nothing short of "degrading." [97] Hamilton of South Carolina thought such a

---

[94] *Register of Debates*, Nineteenth Congress, First Session, ii, col. 2317.

[95] *Ibid.*, col. 2075.　　　　　[96] *Ibid.*, col. 2394.

[97] *Ibid.*, i, cols. 164, 206; ii, col. 2316.

pledge would be "a miserable retreat" from the language of 1823.[98] The Senate report stated that such a declaration would be either futile or a departure from America's established policy of no entangling alliances.[99] Adams's idea, of course, had been to bind the new republics to the observance of his cherished principle. Webster and Wurts of Pennsylvania emphasized this fact in the course of the debate.[100] But no one defended the proposal vigorously. Everett was typical of the friends of the administration in declaring that he saw no harm in it, though it was not particularly desirable.[101] There was not the slightest genuine interest in the President's proposition, nor any indication that even his supporters saw its possible significance, in the largest sense.

As for a declaration with regard to European interference, the enemies of the administration were vigorous in their denunciation, and its friends virtually silent. Rives declared that it would commit to the use of force, and Ingham, echoing this viewpoint, asserted such a step to be "the worst form which the proposed political connection with the Southern American Governments could assume." [102] Forsyth thought it futile, and Cambreleng of New York thought it positively dangerous.[103] To these strictures the friends of the mission did not respond. Not one of them defended the President's suggestion. The mission itself had its defenders, its advocates, and the event was to prove them in the majority; but the attempt to give wider force to the message of 1823 received little or no commendation.

There is a final aspect of the Panama debates, in their relation to the message, which must now be examined. It is that of the votes in the House on the amendments to the report of the committee on foreign affairs endorsing the mission. These votes have a relation to the Monroe Doctrine, and may further serve to illustrate the attitude of at least one of the Houses of Congress. The House debate began on March 25, and continued to April 22. As early as April 3, McLane of Delaware submitted an amend-

---

[98] *Register of Debates*, Nineteenth Congress, First Session, ii, col. 2148.
[99] *Ibid.*, Appendix, p. 94.   [100] *Ibid.*, cols. 2189, 2271.   [101] *Ibid.*, col. 2431.
[102] *Ibid.*, col. 2359.   [103] *Ibid.*, cols. 2318, 2438.

ment to the committee resolution, endorsing the mission, asserting it to be the settled policy of the United States to abstain from entangling alliances, and declaring that the ministers sent to Panama should not

be authorized to discuss, consider, or consult, upon any proposition of alliance, offensive or defensive, between this country and any of the South American Governments, or any stipulation, compact, or declaration, binding the United States in any way, or to any extent, to resist interference from abroad with the domestic concerns of the aforesaid Governments.

The next day McLane added the following words:

Leaving the United States free to adopt, in any event which may happen, affecting the relations of the South American Governments with each other, or with foreign nations, such measures as the friendly disposition cherished by the American people, toward the People of those States, and the honor and interests of this nation, may dictate.[104]

This amendment never came to a vote in the form proposed by its sponsor, but a substitute was brought forward, by Buchanan, on which the House took action. The Buchanan amendment went beyond the limits of that brought forward by McLane; it declared against any compact for the purpose of preventing colonization upon the continents of America, no less than against any alliance or binding agreement with regard to European intervention in South America; and it also banned not only any agreement or declaration pledging the United States to resist interference, but even any declaration "for the purpose of preventing" such interference — a form of words that would have excluded even the mild proposal of the President himself, for common action in the form of an exposure of European designs. The Buchanan amendment reads as follows:

The House, however, in expressing this opinion, do not intend to sanction any departure from the settled policy of this Government, that, in extending our commercial relations with foreign nations, we should have with them as little political connexion as possible; and that we should preserve peace, commerce, and friendship, with all nations, and form entangling alliances with none. It is, therefore, the opinion of this House, that the Government of the United States ought not to be represented at the Congress of Panama, except in a diplomatic character, nor ought they to form any alliance, offensive or defensive, or negotiate respecting such an alliance, with all or any of

---

[104] *Register of Debates*, Nineteenth Congress, First Session, ii, cols. 2009, 2011.

the Spanish American Republics; nor ought they to become parties with them, or either of them, to any joint declaration for the purpose of preventing the interference of any of the European Powers with their independence or form of Government, or to any compact for the purpose of preventing colonization upon the continent of America; but that the People of the United States should be left free to act, in any crisis, in such a manner as their feelings of friendship towards these Republics, and as their own honor and policy may at the time dictate.[105]

Against this amendment the friends of the administration vigorously contended; and one of them, Mallary of Vermont, moved to strike out most of the second sentence, leaving only the declaration that the United States ought to be represented only in a diplomatic character, and the final clause. Mallary put his proposal on the explicit ground that by accepting the Buchanan amendment the House would seem to disavow the celebrated declaration of Monroe in 1823, and pleaded against such a course. Referring to the message, he said: "Let nothing be done to impair it. Let it remain where it is. Let it stand before the world as the declared feeling of the Executive of the nation, to be exercised as emergencies may, in the opinion of the Government, demand." [106]

Mallary's motion was voted down 56 to 112,[107] and a proposal to strike out the reference to the colonization compact was also defeated.[108] When it came to the vote on the Buchanan amendment *in toto*, in Committee of the Whole, the vote was 93 for, 94 against, a defeat by a single vote.[109] But when the Committee reported back to the House, and Buchanan's motion came up again, it was adopted by the close vote of 99 to 95.[110] The friends of the administration now combined with the out-and-out opponents of the mission to defeat the resolution of the committee on foreign relations as it now stood, and the vote was 54 to 143.[111] Thus the resolution failed.

How may one interpret these various votes from the standpoint of the Monroe Doctrine? The task is not an easy one. Far

---

[105] *Register of Debates*, Nineteenth Congress, First Session, ii, col. 2369.

[106] *Ibid.*, col. 2409.          [107] *Ibid.*, col. 2452.

[108] *Journal of the House of Representatives*, Nineteenth Congress, First Session (Washington, 1825), p. 452.

[109] *Register of Debates*, Nineteenth Congress, First Session, ii, col. 2453.

[110] *Ibid.*, col. 2457.          [111] *Ibid.*, col. 2490.

more members than the vote shows probably sympathized with the point of view expressed in the Buchanan amendment. The real question was as to the expediency of going on record, of qualifying the declaration of 1823, by a gloss which would appear to be representative of the views of the American people. Should all misapprehension be ended as to the purport of Monroe's language? Should any intention of closer connection be unequivocally disclaimed? There was, it has been seen, a bare majority in favor of such a course, and an even larger majority rejected Mallary's plea to save the Doctrine by weakening the amendment. Parliamentary reasons may explain the vote on the Mallary amendment; that is, some of the administration supporters may have reasoned that the thing to do was to make Buchanan's proposal as unpalatable as possible, in order to secure its defeat later; but the fact remains that, on a direct appeal not to weaken the force of the presidential declaration, only fifty-six members responded. Whatever the reason, the argument that the Buchanan amendment would diminish the authority of the Monroe Doctrine does not seem to have had much weight. Congressmen were more intent upon preventing a too-extended interpretation of Monroe's language than upon maintaining its sanctity.

But, after all, an analysis of the Panama debate is not dependent on the resolutions just examined. The vote on these resolutions was, it is well known, colored with faction; and to weigh the force of this perverting element is an impossible and a fruitless task. The essential facts stand out above and beyond the counting of the votes: the disinclination of virtually all members of Congress to admit the existence of any pledge of future action implied in Monroe's declaration; a general aversion to an alliance with any or all of the South American states; and a lukewarm attitude, even among the administration's friends, toward its own proposals for joint declarations on colonization and European interference. However much they may have eulogized Monroe's message, and praised its effectiveness at the time, they were far from wishing to extend its scope. The Panama debates contribute nothing to the positive development of the Monroe Doctrine.

But they do, of course, define the limits of the Doctrine, as, for the matter of that, does the language of the Executive. Even so, a fourth appeal for aid under the Monroe declaration was made by La Plata in 1828, in the war between that country and Brazil.[112] This episode, however, I do not intend to examine. The Panama discussion may set the limits of this study. It properly marks the end of the first epoch in the development of perhaps the most influential of all American state papers. One might have thought at the time that it marked the eclipse of the Doctrine itself. For, though Monroe's language was certainly not retracted, there was little or no indication in the debates at Panama that his words were to be the basis of a fundamental and lasting principle of American policy. The politicians who debated so heatedly in the House of Representatives and in the Senate could hardly have suspected the long future. They could hardly have suspected, any more than Monroe did in 1823, that they were dealing with a document that was constantly to give evidence of its vitality, and exercise an immense influence on American foreign policy. They did not treat the President's declaration as if it were meant for all time. It has been only with the years that Monroe's words have been invested with something like sanctity, and become a shibboleth to which American politicians of our own day can make confident appeal.

[112] See W. S. Robertson's article in *Pol. Sci. Quart.*, xxx (1915), pp. 101–104.

# CHAPTER VII

## THE AFTERMATH OF THE MESSAGE IN EUROPE

In the comment of European statesmen upon the famous declaration of December 2, 1823, there is considerable evidence that the power and policy of the United States were not a very important element in the formation of the plans of the Holy Alliance. But the real measure of the influence of the American government and of the effects of Monroe's message must be found in an analysis of the policy of the European courts toward South America in the years immediately following the President's manifesto.

It has already been seen that the European powers, far from regarding the message as a check to the projected congress on South American affairs, were inclined to believe that it would actually stimulate Great Britain to take part in the councils of the allied powers. Not only was this view frequently expressed in the diplomatic correspondence of the time, but it was urged upon the British government itself.

> Can the government at London longer blind itself [wrote Chateaubriand to Polignac] to the policy and desires of the United States, whose interests lead it to work with all its power to isolate America from Europe? It is important for England as for France to preserve as many ties as possible between Europe and the New World, and not to leave the latter wholly under the empire of the policy and system of the United States.[1]

Ofalia at Madrid held much the same language to A'Court, apparently taking the message as his text. If a separation took place, declared the Spaniard, as reported by the British minister,

> Mexico, at least, if not the greater part of the other American colonies would fall under the dominion of the United States; that old England would do well to reflect that a new England was rising on the other side of the Atlantic, which, ere a Century elapsed, would probably exceed her in population in the proportion of at least three or four to one. He said that we should do well to bear this constantly in mind, and to recollect that in lending

---

[1] Paris. Aff. Étr., Corr. Pol., Grande Bretagne, vol. 618, fol. 20, Jan. 12, 1824.

ourselves to the separation of the colonies from Spain, we were only hastening the arrival of that day when the Star of our prosperity must fade before that of our powerful, ambitious, and enterprising descendants.[2]

Metternich, too, sought to use the attitude of the American government to influence Great Britain, remarking to Wellesley that if Canning refused the invitation to a congress it would be imputed to him that he meant to follow the course taken by the United States.[3] And that the Austrian Chancellor really felt that the message afforded an additional reason for European solidarity is clear enough from the impressive, even portentous, tone in which he pleaded with the British Foreign Secretary. The question was one of "life or death," [4] of "ruin or safety for the cause of the whole civilized world." [5] The extravagance of this language is probably in a measure explained by the language of the American manifesto.

On all sides, it is clear from the utterances just quoted, the hope remained that a congress might be held, despite the interposition of the United States in the colonial problem. And not only this, but it is also to be noted that the publication of the message did nothing to alter the prevalent opinion among Continental statesmen as to the undesirability of including the American government in their deliberations. Chateaubriand reiterated to Polignac his previously expressed views on the matter,[6] and also told Stuart that Monroe's language struck at the principle of mediation by peremptorily deciding the question of South American independence, without listening to the concessions which either of the parties at issue might be disposed to admit.[7] Metternich took much the same tone, declaring it impossible to admit to the deliberations of the European cabinets "a power revolutionary in its principles, and persisting in declaring itself such in the face of the world."[8] The President's message did nothing what-

[2] London. P. R. O., F. O., Spain, vol. 285, desp. 5, Jan. 4, 1824.
[3] Ibid., Austria, vol. 182, desp. 16, Jan. 21, 1824.
[4] Ibid., Austria, vol. 7, desp. 182, Jan. 21, 1824.
[5] Vienna. Staats-Archiv, France, Weisungen, Jan. 21, 1824. Cf. note 46.
[6] Paris. Aff. Étr., Corr. Pol., Grande Bretagne, vol. 618, fol. 20, Jan. 12, 1824.
[7] London. P. R. O., F. O., France, vol. 305, desp. 8.
[8] St. Petersburg. F. O., Reçus, no. 21,224, Jan. 19, 1824. "If we have expressed an absolute veto [on the admission of the United States to a congress] our action is

soever to secure for the views of the United States a respectful hearing in the chancelleries of the Old World.

On the other hand, it did not have the effect which so many Continental statesmen seem to have anticipated, of securing British adhesion to the plans of the allied powers. For, on January 30, in one of the ablest of his diplomatic papers, George Canning refused the invitation to the congress, and, by his action, gave the death-blow to the whole project of such a gathering.[9]

To what degree, if at all, was this action of Canning's influenced by the previous declaration of the United States? It was, it may be confidently asserted, in no sense directly dependent upon the language of Monroe. In the Polignac interview, it is true, the British Foreign Secretary had not flatly refused to participate in a congress on the colonial question.[10] Toward the end of October, to judge from the instructions sent to Stuart, his mind was still open as to the final decision.[11] But, on the other hand, by the end of November, the determination of the British cabinet not to enter into any conference that might be held at Paris seems to have been wholly definite.[12] There was by no means unanimity as to the general policy to be pursued toward South

justified, not only on principle, but by the rules of sound policy. The grave question which will occupy the conference is not, in the light in which it is desirable to consider it, an American question; it is, and will remain in the first period of the discussion, entirely European. In the beginning of the discussion the aim will be to prevent the children of Europe from becoming the adults of America.

"To think of drawing the United States into the council occupied with this important inquiry, to admit even the possibility that they should intervene in it by virtue of any right whatsoever, this would be to commit a great error, to renounce the security which is still found in a principle even when the question of fact is no longer under one's influence."

[9] Published in *British and Foreign State Papers*, xi (1823–24), pp. 58–62.

[10] *Ibid.*, pp. 49–53. Canning had merely declared that "England could not go into a joint deliberation upon the subject of Spanish America, upon an equal footing with other Powers." This language, though suggestive of refusal, left the door open for a contrary policy.

[11] London. P. R. O., F. O., France, vol. 285, no. 82, Oct. 28, 1823. "It will be quite time enough to decide on the course to be taken by your Government when, if ever, that suggestion [*i. e.*, of a Congress] shall be renewed in the shape of an informal proposal either from the Court of the Tuileries, or from the Allied Courts jointly, or from the Court of Madrid." See also no. 84, Nov. 9, 1823.

[12] *Ibid.*, Austria, vol. 179, no. 18, Nov. 28, 1823. See also Berlin, Staats-Archiv, England, 69, Nov. 30, 1823.

America. Canning and his friend Huskisson were anxious to press on toward recognition. The Duke of Wellington, on the other hand, the Premier, Lord Liverpool, and the great majority of the ministry were in favor of a cautious policy. But on the question of entering into a congress there was apparently no division. The ineptitude of Sir Charles Stuart, the British ambassador, and the shifty character of Pozzo di Borgo, so Canning told Lieven, would make any such meeting highly undesirable, from Great Britain's standpoint.[13] These views were echoed by Wellington.[14] It is clear, then, that the President's message was by no means the decisive influence which determined Great Britain's refusal of the direct invitation of Spain.

On the other hand, its influence must not be wholly disregarded. In the first place, though Canning repudiated the idea of a *congress*, he was ready, so he told Lieven and Vincent, to enter into *conferences* on the colonial question.[15] At the end of November, he made a rather jingoistic speech at Plymouth which brought down upon him the condemnation of the moderate members of the cabinet.[16] Thereafter, his tone began to change. He was, in December, 1823, ready to accept the idea of friendly discussion with the Continental powers. The message swung the balance back toward an independent policy. Such, at least, was Baron Werther's interpretation of its effect.[17] And this seems entirely reasonable. For Canning, from his own point of view, could not afford to have the United States take all the tricks in the pack. He had to adopt a tone and pursue a policy that would maintain and extend British influence in the New World. That tone certainly became increasingly definite again in the period after the message was published in England. We hear no more of conferences with the allied powers.

[13] Berlin. Staats-Archiv, England, 71a, Jan. 9, 1824. See also ibid., Bernstorff's instructions of March 9, 1824.

[14] Ibid., England, 71a, Jan. 9, 1824.

[15] Ibid., Frankreich, 191, II, Jan. 27, 1824. See also ibid., Jan. 12, 1824.

[16] Ibid., Oesterreich, I, 96, II, Dec. 13, 1823. See also Paris, Aff. Étr., Corr. Pol., Autriche, vol. 404, Dec. 18, 1823.

[17] Berlin. Staats-Archiv, England, 71a, Feb. 3, 1824. See also St. Petersburg, F. O., Reçus, no. 21,385 (encl.), Feb. 7, 1824.

Furthermore, though Monroe's declaration may not have been the reason why the British Foreign Secretary refused the invitation to the congress, it afforded him excellent grounds for justifying his decision. Canning was, of course, too good a politician to put any reference to the United States into his official answer to Spain, for to do so would be to increase the prestige of the American government, and to increase it entirely unnecessarily. But, in his conversations with the various members of the diplomatic corps at London, he made adroit use of the President's manifesto. He told Polignac again what he had told him in October, that it was useless to hold a congress without the participation of the United States, and that he knew that the United States would not participate.[18] And to Werther he emphasized the fact that Great Britain, confronted by the danger of American supremacy in the New World, could counteract that influence only by an independent policy directed at winning the favor of the new states, an argument more interesting than convincing to a Continental statesman whose solution of the colonial problem was common action against the perils of republicanism.[19] The attitude of Monroe thus helped to justify Canning's stand, if it did not actually shape it in the fullest sense of the word.

With Canning's action, the proposal for a formal congress on the Spanish colonial question comes to an end. But this does not mean that the discussion of South American affairs was suspended, or that Continental Europe abandoned all interest in the problems involved. For more than two years the European chancelleries continued to concern themselves more or less actively with the whole matter, and their deliberations, in more than one respect, throw light on the influence of the President's declaration, and on the place which the United States occupied in the diplomacy of Europe in the third decade of the nineteenth century.

Perhaps the most interesting aspect of these deliberations is the raising of the question of intervention in 1824. In 1823, prior to the message, as we have already seen, there was no coherent

---

[18] Paris. Aff. Étr., Corr. Pol., Grande Bretagne, vol. 618, fol. 17, Jan. 8, 1824.
[19] Berlin. Staats-Archiv, England, 71a, May 31, 1824.

plan for dealing with the new states, certainly no plan of reconquest; one might even say, no discussion of reconquest. But the
case is different in the period following the President's declaration. Despite the defiant language of Monroe and the aloofness
of Canning, the Russian statesmen, throughout the year 1824,
seem to have nourished the hope that Spain might be assisted,
perhaps directly assisted, in the reëstablishment of her authority
over her revolted subjects in the New World, and that she ought
more than ever to be encouraged in a policy of reconquest of her
former dominions.

The first hint of such a policy is to be found in the activities of
Pozzo di Borgo, immediately after the publication of Canning's
note of January 30. That energetic diplomat seems, on his own
initiative, to have called a conference of the representatives of
the Continental powers, which met on February 9; and before
this conference he set forth the vital necessity of some form of
action on the colonial question. The enthusiasm of his fellow
ministers appears to have been but tepid, for no action was
taken.[20] A week later the representatives of Russia, Prussia, and
Austria held a new consultation, and agreed to instruct their respective ministers at Madrid to discuss what the Allies might do
to bring to an end the differences which had arisen between the
colonies and the mother country.[21] But action so moderate as
this could hardly be expected to satisfy the Corsican, and in his
own instructions to Bulgari, Russian minister to Madrid, Pozzo
di Borgo went on to urge the preparation of a Spanish force to
attempt the subjugation of the colonies, and the flotation of a
commercial loan which might be used to finance such an expedition.[22] Such a proposal did not involve any sacrifices on the
part of Russia herself, but it was clearly intended to encourage
Spain's extravagant dreams of reconquest; and, equally clearly,
it was influenced by the situation created by the declaration of
the President and the policy of Canning. The reception of these
ideas of Pozzo's at Madrid was not, as we shall see, a very favorable one; but it is interesting to note that his interest in an active

[20] Berlin. Staats-Archiv, Frankreich, 101, II, Feb. 10, 1824.
[21] Ibid., Oesterreich, 97, Feb. 26, 1824.          [22] Ibid.

colonial policy was not, on that account, abated. Bulgari, under his direction, assumed an interventionist tone at the court of Ferdinand.[23] And Pozzo di Borgo himself wrote to Nesselrode that, having encouraged Spain to demand intervention, "in the hope of a just reciprocity of aid and of good offices, it would neither be honorable nor generous in the Allies to abandon her to her fate and expose her to throw herself in desperation into the arms of England."[24]

This viewpoint seems also to have been cherished at St. Petersburg. The possibility of actual armed intervention was certainly discussed at the court of the Tsar. Lebzeltern tells us that the Russian government nourished the hope that a series of allied conferences would lead to "furnishing the King of Spain with the material aid to pacify and reconquer his colonies,"[25] and La Ferronnays describes Alexander as "more than ever disposed to sacrifice every other interest to the maintenance of his theories."[26]

Why [said Nesselrode, laughingly, to the French minister] should not the Allies give some aid to Spain? What could England say, or rather what could she do, if an army composed of Spaniards, Frenchmen, Russians, Prussians, and Austrians, embarked upon ships lent and paid for by all the allies of the King of Spain, and sailed for America to reinstate him in his rights?

"This idea, extraordinary as it is," commented La Ferronnays, "is amongst those which may seduce the Emperor, and which he would be very much inclined to follow up."[27] Through the summer of 1824, this mood seems to have continued. Villèle declared in July that Russia was still talking at Madrid of the submission of the colonies;[28] and in September the Tsar stated frankly to

[23] Paris. Aff. Étr., Corr. Pol., Espagne, vol. 727, fol. 36. "On the other hand, Russia presents herself to Spain as wishing to give her effective aid in the reconquest of her colonies, despite France and England." London. P. R. O., F. O., Spain, 285, desp. 45, March 9, 1824. "M. de Bulgari's language upon the subject is singularly changed; nothing short of the full sovereignty of Spain, over Mexico, at least, will satisfy him."

[24] St. Petersburg. F. O., Reçus, no. 21,814, March 14–26, 1824.

[25] Vienna. Staats-Archiv, Russland, Berichte, P. S. ad Num. 73, April 14–26, 1824.

[26] Paris. Aff. Étr., Corr. Pol., Russie, vol. 166, fol. 81, March 10, 1824.

[27] Ibid., fol. 187, May 14, 1824.

[28] Villèle, *op. cit.*, v, p. 91.

the French minister that only aid was needed to bring victory to the cause of Ferdinand.[29] In December the Russian government apparently sought through La Ferronnays to sound France on the possibility of granting some kind of assistance to Spain, and on its attitude in case Russia should take up the cudgels for the cause of legitimacy.[30] Pozzo di Borgo was still speaking hopefully of expeditions at the close of the year.[31] Had wishes been policies, it does not seem at all unlikely that Alexander might have attempted, in the course of 1824, to apply to the New World the principles of action which he had championed in the Old.

But the Russian autocrat, though he thus considered the possibility of intervention, was hampered by the distinctly frigid attitude of his Continental allies. Russia could not act in the colonial question alone; and France, Austria, and Prussia all took a very different view of the matter from Alexander's. No one of the other powers can be said to have been at all enthusiastic about the giving of any actual aid to Spain.

The policy of France, in the winter and spring of 1824, certainly did not look toward intervention. It may be that for a brief moment the volatile Chateaubriand, despite the Polignac pledge, thought of some aggressive action with regard to Latin America. At any rate, he seems to have been turning over in his mind the possibility of war; and, at the beginning of March, instructions were sent out to Rear-Admiral Jurien, the commander of the squadron of the Antilles, directing him to secure information on the naval forces of other powers in those waters, and to examine all the elements of the situation, taking into account the chance, "not very probable," of an outbreak of hostilities.[32] But these instructions to Jurien are very cautiously phrased, and they would be a slender basis upon which to erect any hypothesis whatsoever; and, as an offset against them, may be cited the instructions of the latter part of the month, emphasizing the continued neutrality of France, the amicable relations with the new

[29] Paris. Aff. Étr., Corr. Pol., Russie, vol. 167, fol. 56, Sept. 11, 1824.
[30] Ibid., fol. 118.
[31] St. Petersburg. F. O., Reçus, no. 25, 333, Jan. 19–31, 1825.
[32] Paris. Archives Nationales, Minist. de la Marine, BB⁴, vol. 457, À M. le contre-amiral Jurien, Très secrette, March 1, 1824.

states, and the necessity of promoting the interests of French commerce,[33] and the assurance sent to Chassérieu that the sending out of any new vessels would be purely for the protection of trading interests, and for no other purpose.[34] Judged by subsequent events, the policy of France was caution itself. Chateaubriand would not, as a matter of fact, even consent to further conferences on the colonial question in either Paris [35] or Madrid.[36] He would not consent to give any assurances to the other Continental powers as to the non-recognition of the new states.[37] Spain's request, made in July, for the sale of one or two frigates was flatly refused.[38] The French government would take absolutely no action in behalf of Ferdinand.

It must not be imagined, however, that the reason for this caution is to be found, in any important measure, in the message of President Monroe. Fundamental, in the first instance, was the interest of French commerce, that interest which was recognized by the sending out of agents to the New World, and by Villèle's conversations with the agents of the new states in Paris. "France," wrote Tatischev, "has subordinated the considerations of policy which we follow to the counsels of mercantile cupidity." [39] The viewpoint herein expressed was the common explanation of the trend of French policy.[40]

Of perhaps equal importance was the fear of the French ministers that Great Britain would recognize the republics of South America. To prevent such a step was a primary aim of Chateaubriand's. It was frankly avowed in his correspondence, as it had been in 1823.[41] It was recognized by the ministers of the other powers at Paris.[42] An active policy on behalf of Spain would

---

[33] Paris. Archives Nationales, Minist. de la Marine, BB[4], vol. 457, À La Farge, Hugot-Derville, et Sorel, March 30, 1824.

[34] Paris. Aff. Étr., Méms. et Docs., Amérique, vol. 39, fol. 93, March 18, 1824.

[35] St. Petersburg. F. O., Reçus, no. 21,814, March 14–26, 1824.

[36] Ibid., no. 21,816 (encl.).

[37] Ibid., no. 22,337, April 26–May 6, 1824.

[38] Paris. Aff. Étr., Corr. Pol., Espagne, vol. 727, fols. 130 and 171.

[39] St. Petersburg. F. O., Reçus, no. 21,874, April 6, 1824.

[40] See, for example, Pozzo di Borgo in ibid., no. 25,689, March 2–14, 1824.

[41] Paris. Aff. Étr., Corr. Pol., Espagne, vol. 726, fol. 397, March 31, 1824.

[42] St. Petersburg. F. O., Reçus, no. 21,814, March 14–26, 1824.

almost surely precipitate such recognition. The views of London on the colonial question, it may be readily admitted, were a matter of great concern to the ministers of Louis XVIII. But there is little evidence to support the belief that the views of Washington were deemed of much significance. In February and March of 1824 there are a number of letters or dispatches of Chateaubriand's which discuss the possibility of war. In only two of these is there any reference to the United States, and these references are only passing ones.[43] We know that the French minister's estimate of the material power of this country was not a very high one.[44] We know, too, that he did not, after the middle of March, take the prospect of an Anglo-American entente very seriously. For when Rush made the approaches to Polignac to which reference has been made, Chateaubriand drew the conclu- sion from these approaches that the two English-speaking powers were not in harmony, and even spoke of the United States as "the natural Ally" of France.[45] A statesman who could make such a comment in the winter of 1824 must have had but slight comprehension of the viewpoint of the United States. French policy on the Spanish-American question must certainly be traced to other causes than the declaration of Monroe.

With regard to Austria and Prussia, much the same things are to be said that have just been noted in the case of France. The policy of both the German courts was essentially conservative. Metternich, as we have already seen, had never believed at all in the possibility of active intervention, and had not even been a very warm advocate of a congress on colonial affairs. His views in 1824 were precisely the same as his views in 1823. He set them forth at great length in a masterly memorandum of February 7, 1824, addressed to St. Petersburg and Berlin. Once again he

[43] Chateaubriand, *Congrès de Vérone*, ii, pp. 275, 284. The first of these references is as follows: "Mr. Canning has made it clear, as well as the President of the United States that he denies to the Continental powers the right to intervene by force of arms in the affairs of the colonies" (Feb. 17, 1824). The second is: "If she [Great Britain] declares the colonies independent, and allies herself with the United States, will all the Continental powers draw the sword?"

[44] See *antea*, p. 174.

[45] Paris. Aff. Étr., Corr. Pol., Angleterre, vol. 618, fols. 135 and 161.

emphasized the division of the colonies into three classes, the enormous areas of the New World in which the struggle had virtually ceased, the necessity of Spain's coming forward with proposals of a concrete character, her own impotence to accomplish anything by force, and the remote possibility of the assistance of the allied powers. The Continental powers, he declared, could never act without the coöperation of one or another of the great maritime states. England would certainly undertake no such coöperation. France, even supposing her ready to spend hundreds of millions in an enterprise whose success and advantages would be alike doubtful, had bound herself to a contrary course of action. In taking up arms in the cause of Spain, she would run the risk of a quarrel with Great Britain and the United States, both of which governments had taken so definite a stand against intervention. Under such circumstances, the action of the powers must inevitably be limited to measures of conciliation.[46] The Prussian Foreign Minister, Count Bernstorff, took the same view. The colonial question, he wrote to Schöler, his ambassador at St. Petersburg, must be judged by what was practicable, not by what was desirable. The Continental powers are without the means of applying the force of which they dispose, and the measure of their means of action must be the measure of their obligation. Any other course would compromise their dignity, and risk the enfeeblement of sound principles by carrying these principles to an extreme. Austria, Prussia, and Russia may sway the Continent, but not the destinies of the New World. France, it is true, has naval power, but a naval force just beginning to come into its own again. She ought not to be asked to make further sacrifices in a gigantic enterprise which is beset with terrible obstacles. Her commercial interest leads her to desire peace with Great Britain. In the face of the opposition of England and the United States, no forcible intervention in the provinces of South America could be adjudged to be practicable.[47]

In the winter of 1824, then, both the Austrian and Prussian courts were urging a moderate course upon the Tsar Alexander.

[46] Vienna. Staats-Archiv, Russland, Weisungen, Feb. 7, 1824.
[47] Berlin. Staats-Archiv, Russland, I, 83, Feb. 19, 1824.

They drew an argument in favor of their viewpoint from the language of President Monroe. But they did not shape their policy differently on account of the presidential declaration, but merely reiterated their already clearly expressed opposition to the armed reconquest of the colonies.

In the face, then, of the attitude of all the Continental powers, and the almost certain opposition of England, the Tsar Alexander, despite the possible desire to go crusading in the New World, was compelled by the force of circumstances to adopt a restrained policy. This fact was, after all, pretty clearly recognized at St. Petersburg. Side by side with the references to the possibility of intervention, which have already been called to the attention of the reader, go indications of a much more moderate viewpoint. The instructions of Nesselrode to Lieven and to Pozzo di Borgo are, in every case, extremely cautious documents. In his dispatches to the former, the Russian minister contented himself with maintaining the theoretical right of the allied powers to intervene in the colonial question.

> If Spain possesses rights [he wrote] she possesses the right to make them prevail, she does not weaken the justice of her cause by borrowing aid from the Allies, and all opposition, any hostile measure, caused by their aid, would seem to us not to conform to the maxims of justice which ought to constitute the basis of the code of nations, and which England herself has so honorably defended.

But, "the remark we have made," he hastily added, "relates simply to a point of abstract theory on which we have thought it necessary to explain ourselves with candor." [48] In his instructions to Pozzo di Borgo, after all the best index of what was seriously intended, Nesselrode never went further than to urge the preparation of a purely Spanish force, to be sent to Mexico or Peru, and the flotation of a loan.[49] A month and a half later, he sought to check the Corsican's ardor with the following chilling sentence:

[48] St. Petersburg. F. O., Expédiés, no. 9322, March 17, 1824. Originally the latter part of this dispatch read, "The English Government knows that our intentions are pacific as well as disinterested, and the remark we have made hides no design for the future." This was struck out, perhaps as expressing too definite a disclaimer, but it is interesting none the less.

[49] Vienna. Staats-Archiv, Russland, Berichte, communicate, March 17, 1824.

Though the Allies, by a strict interpretation of their doctrines, might be bound not to refuse a direct assistance in men and ships to Spain, that power will readily see that so rigid a construction of their engagements will serve no useful purpose while England maintains its present attitude.[50]

"While England maintains its present attitude." Here was the essence of the situation from the Russian viewpoint. In not a single despatch from St. Petersburg to the ministers of the Tsar is there the slightest emphasis on the position of the United States. It was the attitude of Canning which held Alexander back from the active policy which he might otherwise have favored.

All things considered, there was little actual danger of the re-conquest of the colonies by the allied powers in 1824. The project was, no doubt, discussed; but having regard to all the facts of the situation, it is difficult to see how it could ever have come very near fulfilment. Only Russia had any enthusiasm whatever for such a line of action; and even Russia never made any concrete proposals for direct action on the part of the Continental powers either to Spain or to any of her associates of the Holy Alliance.

This does not mean, however, that with the definition of England's attitude the statesmen of the Old World ceased to concern themselves with the colonial question. It was an active subject of discussion during the next two years, and there are aspects of this discussion which, either directly or indirectly, may reasonably attract the interest of the student of the Monroe Doctrine.

With one interesting project in connection with South American affairs, the President's message has only the most incidental connection. In order to prevent English action, and to strengthen the diplomatic position of Spain, Chateaubriand, acting apparently upon the suggestion of Polignac,[51] urged upon the Spanish government that it throw open the colonial ports to the commerce of the whole world. Such a proposal was also shrewdly calculated to put French commerce in the colonies upon a more justifiable footing, and is an interesting evidence of the strength of the eco-

[50] Paris. Aff. Étr., Corr. Pol., Russie, vol. 167, fol. 169.

[51] Ibid., Grande Bretagne, vol. 617, fol. 273, Dec. 12, 1823. This is the first reference to the idea that I have seen.

nomic factor in French policy. It was endorsed by the representatives of the other Continental Powers at Paris early in the winter of 1824, and a decree was actually extorted from Ferdinand on February 9.[52] Such a decree was, of course, a matter of entire indifference to both of the English-speaking powers. They had traded with South America for years. It cannot, to be sure, by any stretch of the imagination, be regarded as the consequence of Monroe's declaration, or as intended in any way to counteract it. But it is interesting to note that Chateaubriand used the message as an argument in favor of the opening of colonial ports,[53] and that the Spanish government, as fatuous as usual, resisted such action for a time on the ground that it would be advantageous to the United States.[54]

Of far more importance, however, is the vitality of the project of Bourbon monarchies in 1824 — perhaps one ought to say the vitality of the monarchical idea in general. The antagonism of political systems, expressed in the famous American declaration, comes out again and again, and, despite the warning of the President, European statesmen continued to dream of, and to work for, the establishment of kingdoms in the Spanish colonies, and the consolidation of the monarchical system in the New World. We have already seen that the French policy in 1823 aimed at the sending out of Infantes to the new states. In the discussions of November and December, this idea seems to have been in a measure subordinated to the possibility of actual recognition. But in 1824, despite the attitude of the United States, it assumes a new importance in French diplomacy. Chateaubriand urged it upon the Spanish court in a diplomatic dispatch of January 3,[55] in which he specifically mentioned the message, and the danger of Anglo-American understanding, as reasons for the reopening of

---

[52] The decree is published in José María Céspedes's *La Doctrina de Monroe* (Havana, 1893), p. 137. It was really hardly more than a promise of action in the future, sketching out a general policy, but leaving the essential details for future action. For the negotiation on this subject see the article by François Rousseau in *Revue des Questions Historiques*, xc (July, 1911), pp. 86–116, entitled "L'ambassade du marquis de Talaru en Espagne, juillet 1823–août 1824."

[53] Paris. Aff. Étr., Corr. Pol., Espagne, vol. 726, fol. 28, Jan. 8, 1824.

[54] Ibid., fol. 158, end of Jan., 1824.

[55] Ibid., fol. 13.

the plan of Bourbon monarchies. At the same time he undertook to persuade Canning of the feasibility and desirability of the project by playing on the latter's jealousy of the United States.[56] Toward the end of March, he broached the idea again at the court of Ferdinand,[57] and in July, Villèle sounded Stuart, as he had a year before, as to its practicability.[58] Even as late as the beginning of 1825, the project was still considered as at least possible by the French premier. Both Sheldon, the American chargé,[59] and his successor, Brown, the American minister,[60] were of the opinion that the ultimate aim of France would be the foundation of European monarchies in the former dominions of Spain.

In her zeal for the preservation of the monarchical system, and in her indifference to any American opposition to such a plan, France did not stand alone. Metternich now favored the project;[61] and, whatever may have been the views of the Russian government, it is interesting to note that Oubril,[62] who succeeded Bulgari at Madrid, attempted to persuade his court of its feasibility. The Prussian government also inclined toward some such solution of the colonial problem. In the instructions sent out by Count von Bernstorff, the monarchical principle figures very largely from the beginning of the discussion. The social order, he wrote to Royer in November, 1823, would be exposed to the greatest dangers or else consolidated by the treatment of the South American problem.[63] Revolution would find asylum and succor in the new world if republican governments were established there.[64] These ideas seem to have taken deeper root in the

[56] *Revue politique et littéraire*, Nov. 2, 1912, "Supplément au Congrès de Vérone," p. 548. "Mr. Canning has a clear interest in every moderate plan. Can the cabinet of London longer blind itself to the policy and desires of the American government, whose interests lead it to work with all its might to isolate America from Europe? . . . We believe that constitutional monarchies established in America would be a very good result, both for England and for us."

[57] Paris. Aff. Étr., Corr. Pol., Espagne, vol. 726, fol. 397, March 31, 1824.

[58] London. P. R. O., F. O., France, vol. 310, no. 315, June 24, 1824.

[59] Washington. State Dept. Despatches, France, vol. 22, no. 18, Jan. 18, 1824.

[60] Monroe Papers, Library of Congress, Brown to Monroe, June 12, 1824.

[61] London. P. R. O., F. O., Austria, vol. 182, no. 10, Jan. 21, 1824.

[62] St. Petersburg. F. O., Oubril to Pozzo, Encl. in Reçus, April 10, 1824.

[63] Berlin. Staats-Archiv, Spanien, 50, Nov. 5, 1823.

[64] Ibid., Spanien, 50, Nov. 16, 1823.

mind of the minister after the reception of Monroe's declaration. The fear of an American federation, clearly expressed in his instructions to Werther at London, led him to reflect upon the precise policy which ought to be adopted to frustrate such a dangerous alignment of the New World against the Old.[65] The solution of the matter, in his opinion, must be a personal union between the colonies and the mother country.[66] A Bourbon monarchy in Mexico might also be a wise and reasonable expedient.[67] By hook or by crook the monarchical principle must be preserved.

Thus the notion of a settlement of the colonial question on the basis of independence, but with the preservation of some kind of bond with Europe, with full regard to the maintenance of the dogma of legitimacy, found current acceptance in most of the Continental courts in the first months of 1824, despite the attitude of the United States. The directing statesmen at every European court, with the exception of St. Petersburg, were in favor of such a settlement. Russia, of course, was even more extreme in its legitimist view, and therefore even more directly opposed to the standpoint of the American government.

But what is still more striking is the interest which the British government, prompted by much the same motives as the Continental courts, displayed in the project of Bourbon monarchies. Despite the resentment with which Great Britain regarded the negotiations of 1819 between France and La Plata, there was a considerable body of sentiment in the ministry in favor of the preservation of the monarchical principle by some kind of arrangement between Spain and her colonies.[68] Castlereagh was almost certainly favorable to some such arrangement,[69] and in 1821 and 1822 it seems entirely probable that the British minister at Madrid was actually pressing it upon Spain.[70] In the latter

---

[65] Berlin, Staats-Archiv, England, 71a, March 10, 1824.

[66] Ibid., Spanien, 54, II, April 19, 1824.

[67] Ibid., Spanien, 54, II, March 31, 1824.        [68] See *antea*, pp. 56–57.

[69] On this interesting subject see C. K. Webster's *The Foreign Policy of Castlereagh*, pp. 431–436.

[70] Washington. State Dept. Despatches, Spain, vol. 20, May 20, 1822. "From Mr. Hervey I understand that the Infante Don Francisco is anxious to be sent to

year, the revolutionary Spanish Cortes had under consideration a project for semi-independent kingdoms under Bourbon princes; and the relations of Hervey with the proponents of this scheme suggest that it was far from distasteful to the British government.[71] In 1823, when Canning sent out agents to the new states, the same viewpoint again appears, though this time it is restricted to a single Spanish province, to Mexico. "The constitution of Mexican Society," wrote the British Foreign Secretary, "favors the notion" of a disposition toward monarchical government.

> It does not seem unlikely that the views of the Mexicans should be turned with pretty general concurrence to the restoration of monarchy in the person of one of the princes of the Spanish race, but on the basis of Mexican independence. To any proposal for your coöperation to bring about such a settlement you will not hesitate to avow your full readiness to accede, with the certainty of obtaining the cordial approbation of your Government. I need not add that while you accept such a proposal, if submitted to you, you are not to attempt to prescribe to the Mexican authorities this or any particular course of action. Nor need I repeat that to your acceptance of the proposal, it is an essential and indispensable condition that the negotiation is to be conducted with Spain and alone, and that no foreign force should be employed to conduct the Spanish Prince to Mexico.[72]

At a date a little later than that of this significant dispatch Wellington was avowing to Werther his strong predilection for the monarchical system in the New World.[73]   No sufficient emphasis has yet been placed upon the conservative forces that operated in the Liverpool cabinet on the colonial question, or even upon Canning's own preference for the establishment of kingdoms, rather than republics, on the other side of the Atlantic. The British government was not, of course, as appears from the above instructions to Hervey, ready to make any particular sacrifice for the monarchical idea, but its natural bias was distinctly in that direction.

That bias was even more pronounced in 1824 than at any other

Mexico, and is intriguing to effect it; and that, though he now thinks it too late Mr. Hervey advised Spain twelve months since to send out one of the Princes. The Russian chargé assures me that such was the wish of the English government only five months since."

[71] Villanueva, *Fernando VII y los Nuevos Estados*, p. 89.
[72] London. P. R. O., F. O., Mexico, vol. 3, no. 5, Oct. 10, 1823.
[73] Berlin. Staats-Archiv, England, 71a, June 11, 1824.

time. Indeed, though the fact does not appear from the formal instructions to Sir William A'Court preserved at the Record Office in London, it seems indubitable that, in the months immediately following the enunciation of the Monroe Doctrine, there was a very serious discussion of the plan for Bourbon monarchies. Sir Charles Lamb, British ambassador to Spain in 1825 and 1826, says that the idea was perfectly understood, and there is ample evidence to support this view.[74] Chateaubriand wrote to Talaru at the end of March that Canning was favorable to the sending of an Infante to Mexico.[75] At Madrid the language of A'Court to his colleagues was distinctly encouraging. Oubril declared that the British minister had told him that some such project was necessary "to prevent the United States from incorporating this vast and rich kingdom in their confederated republic" and "to oppose the establishment of a confederation of American republics, of which the United States would inevitably become the regulators."[76] Talaru[77] and Royer[78] reported the same kind of observation from the British minister. It is even possible, as Tatischev informs us, that the British government would have been ready to guarantee Cuba, if Spain would come to some arrangement with her colonies, as a part of which a monarchy might be set up on the borders of the United States.[79] Brown, the American minister at Paris, and Erving, whose letter on the Doctrine has been already quoted, were of the opinion that Great Britain was decidedly favorable to monarchical government in the New World.[80] This general attitude was, of course,

[74] London. P. R. O., F. O., Spain, vol. 30, no. 5, June 20, 1825.

[75] Paris. Aff. Étr., Corr. Pol., Espagne, vol. 726, fol. 398, March 31, 1824.

[76] St. Petersburg. F. O., Reçus, no. 22,941 (encl. B), March 10–22, 1824. See also London, P. R. O., F. O., Spain, vol. 285, no. 23, Feb. 8, 1824.

[77] Paris. Aff. Étr., Corr. Pol., Espagne, vol. 726, fol. 297, March 2, 1824, and fol. 324, March 10, 1824.

[78] Berlin. Staats-Archiv, Spanien, 54, Feb. 18, 1823.

[79] St. Petersburg. F. O., Reçus, no. 22,249.

[80] Monroe, *Writings*, vi, p. 436. "Of her wish to see the new American States independent," wrote Brown to Monroe, May 30, 1824, "I have little doubt. I have as little doubt of her wishing them to establish monarchical governments, although I believe this wish is subordinate to that for their independence." "As to the forms of government under which they shall be settled . . . ," wrote Erving, "I should suppose that even now there can be no great difference between the views of England and France." (*Ibid.*, p. 433.) Cf. antea, p. 237.

strictly subordinated to Great Britain's desire to see the new states independent. No British minister would have advocated the restoration of Spanish sovereignty, which was, for the matter of that, entirely impracticable. But the majority of the cabinet would doubtless have preferred the establishment of kingdoms rather than of republics across the sea, and Canning must have realized, and probably acted on the realization, that the recognition of the South American governments by Great Britain would be easier to bring about if those governments assumed a monarchical form.

Behind this interest in political form there lay, beyond a shadow of a doubt, a very clear antagonism to the United States. We have already seen that it cropped up in the language of A'Court. It appears also in the language of Canning.

The great danger of the time [Canning wrote to Frere in 1825, after British recognition of the colonies], a danger which the policy of the European System would have fostered, was a division of the World into European and American, Republican and Monarchical; a league of worn-out Govts. on the one hand, and of youthful and strong Nations, with the U. States at their head, on the other.[81]

The interest of the British government in the project of Bourbon monarchies was a phase of a general antagonism to and jealousy of the United States which we shall have occasion, a little later, to examine.

Before taking leave, however, of the project of Bourbon monarchies, it may be worth while to examine its feasibility as matters stood in 1824. Was there a solid basis for the hopes of European statesmen? Or were those hopes, as a matter of fact, entirely illusory? There can, of course, be no doubt that, for a considerable period after the outbreak of the Spanish-American revolutions, monarchical sentiment still existed in some of the new states. Even in Colombia this sentiment existed in a measure. In Buenos Aires there was, for a time, a strong royalist faction favoring a European connection, as the negotiations of 1819, already mentioned, amply attest. Indeed, most of the earlier revolutionary leaders in La Plata were monarchists, and the great

[81] Gabrielle Festing, *John Hookham Frere and his Friends* (London, 1899), pp. 267 f.

rival of Bolívar, San Martín, was, through most of his active career, in favor of the foundation of independent kingdoms in the New World. What was true of La Plata was doubly true of Mexico. The treaty of Córdoba, of 1822, signed by a Spanish viceroy with the leaders of the Mexican revolution, was based upon the acceptance of the monarchical idea. The episode of the rule of the Emperor Iturbide is additional evidence of the strength of the anti-republican spirit in this section of the former dominions of Spain. And, in the case of both states, and, indeed, of Chile as well, the powerful influence of the clergy was often cast in favor of the doctrines of the old régime. In view of such facts as these, it is not strange that European conservatives were hopeful of the possibility of saving the New World, or at least a section of it, from the invasion of the pernicious doctrines which distinguished the United States of America.

But the existence of monarchical sentiment and the acceptance of an Infante are two different matters, and the existence of the one does not imply acquiescence in the other. Especially, as late as 1824, would the sending of Bourbon princes to the New World have been an enterprise of doubtful character. With regard to the territories controlled by Bolívar, the chances of success were so slight that the project was never discussed, at least after 1822. With regard to Chile, the circumstances were the same. In Buenos Aires, by the end of 1821, the monarchists had been driven from power, and the republican régime was definitely established.[82]

In Mexico the chances may have been better. Though the Emperor Iturbide had been driven out in 1823, and the republicans had come into power, there was a strong monarchical sentiment which might have been utilized. Canning seems to have been of the opinion that the project of a Bourbon monarchy might have been carried through in 1824.[83] Polignac was equally hopeful.[84] But, on the other hand, the agents of the European

[82] Adolfo Saldias, *La Evolución republicana durante la revolución argentina* (Buenos Aires, 1906), pp. 181–199.

[83] E. J. Stapleton, *Some Official Correspondence of George Canning* (London, 1887, 2 vols.), i, p. 247.

[84] Paris. Aff. Étr., Corr. Pol., Angleterre, vol. 617, Dec. 12, 1823.

governments actually on the spot were far from optimistic. Hervey wrote that while it might be possible for the Duke of Lucca with French aid to make some impression, it was hopeless to believe that any one of the Spanish princes could expect success alone.[85] The French agent, Schmalz, believed that an unconditional recognition of independence was a condition antecedent to any settlement of the Mexican status.[86] Samouel, another French agent, reported that a European prince would have to overcome the strong anti-European feeling and that, in the opinion of the Mexicans most favorable to monarchy, he would have to be sustained by the will of united Europe.[87] Even in this case, therefore, the best-informed opinion regarded the project of the Infantes as distinctly outside the bounds of practical politics.

But, whatever may have been the case so far as the Spanish Americans are concerned, the real impracticability of the whole project of Bourbon monarchies is to be found in the attitude of Spain herself, and in the character of the princes of the Spanish House. There never was a time when Ferdinand VII could have been brought to accept such a compromise. There were Spanish ministers, now and again, who could be persuaded to discuss it, but never was there any real chance of its adoption by the Spanish government. The soundings of 1818 had produced absolutely no favorable reaction at Madrid.[88] The French offers of 1821 and 1822, actually involving the use of some measure of naval aid, were hardly given a hearing. The effort in the extraordinary Cortes of 1821 to carry through a project for the crowning of the Infantes broke down in abject failure.[89] The treaty of Córdoba with Mexico, drawn up in 1822, was rejected in the course of the next year by the overwhelming vote of the revolutionary, and assumedly liberal, parliament.[90] The King, on his release from

[85] London. P. R. O., F. O., Mexico, vol. 4, no. 12, Feb. 21, 1824.
[86] Paris. Archives Nationales, Minist. de la Marine, BB4, 405 bis. Schmalz to Samouel, May 4, 1824, cited in Villanueva, *La Santa Alianza*, p. 57.
[87] Ibid., BB4, 456. Samouel to Clermont-Tonnerre, Aug. 13, 1824. This dispatch is given in full in Villanueva, *La Santa Alianza*, pp. 60–72.
[88] See *antea*, p. 107, and Villanueva, *Bolívar y el general San Martín*, pp. 79 f., 83 f., 87 f.
[89] Villanueva, *Fernando VII y los Nuevos Estados*, pp. 111 ff.
[90] Villanueva, *La Santa Alianza*, p. 83.

the control of the revolutionists in the fall of 1823, repudiated the whole project.[91] Though Ofalia may have had some slight interest in the idea in 1824,[92] he could never have secured the consent of his sovereign. Ferdinand, Talaru reported, regarded the project with an extreme personal repugnance.[93]

Consider, too, the character of the Infantes themselves. It would hardly have been practicable to send out to the New World Don Carlos, the legitimate and only heir to the Spanish monarchy in 1824. Of the other three princes of the House of Bourbon no one was fitted for the task that would have had to be entrusted to him. The youngest, Don Sebastián, was a youth of only thirteen years. The next, the Duke of Parma, was in actual possession of a prosperous sovereignty, and was effeminate and timid in character. The third, Don Francisco, was almost unknown, and had never been on very cordial terms with Ferdinand. A policy that rested upon individuals of this type could have had, in any case, very little chance of success.[94]

All things considered, the project of Bourbon monarchies must be viewed as largely chimerical. Yet it showed an enormous vitality. There are still references to it in 1825 and 1826.[95] And at no time, in the various discussions of the project after 1823, is there any evidence that the attitude of the United States was counted as a serious obstacle, or that the message of President Monroe had any discouraging effect. On the contrary, that message seems to have stimulated a more intense interest in this solution of the colonial question. Not only chronology, but the language of the statesmen themselves in 1824, points to this conclusion.

There is another collateral question in which the desire of Europe to maintain the monarchical principle comes out in 1824 and 1825. Just as the project of the Infantes was based upon the

---

[91] Paris. Aff. Étr., Corr. Pol., Espagne, vol. 724, fol. 308, Dec. 5, 1823.

[92] Ibid., fol. 49, Jan. 11, 1824. By March 22, however, Ofalia refused to discuss the project. St. Petersburg. F. O., Reçus, no. 22,041, March 10–22, 1824, encl.

[93] Ibid., fol. 372, March 24, 1824, and vol. 727, fol. 31, April 7, 1824.

[94] Paris. Aff. Étr., Corr. Pol., Espagne, vol. 734, fols. 247–250, Nov. 29, 1825. This dispatch of Moustier, the French minister at Madrid, contains much interesting information, information equally applicable to the situation in 1824.

[95] See Villanueva, *La Santa Alianza*, pp. 211–279.

desire to preserve monarchical institutions in the New World, and to counteract the republican influences that were rising into power there, so, too, the policy pursued by Great Britain and Austria toward composing the differences of Portugal, and its revolted colony, Brazil, was directed by the same considerations. The problem in this case is not precisely of the same character as that involved in the question of the Spanish colonies. In Brazil, the movement of colonial revolt, following hard on the return of John VI of Portugal and Brazil to Lisbon in 1821, had culminated, not in the establishment of republican government, but in the foundation of an independent empire under John's son, Dom Pedro. In this widely extended empire monarchical institutions continued to endure, and the maintenance of monarchy in Brazil, where it had never been overthrown, was a very different matter from the setting up of monarchy in those parts of the New World which had more or less definitely repudiated it. The challenge to the United States was far less apparent. In the case of Spanish America, the opposition of the government of the United States to the reinstitution of a Bourbon régime was perfectly clear, and perfectly understood; in the case of Brazil, on the other hand, no such assumption could fairly be made. In the course of the year 1824, indeed, the United States definitely recognized the independent Brazilian monarchy. It is very evident, therefore, that the interests of the United States, as conceived by its statesmen, did not demand the extinction of a kingdom already established in the New World if that kingdom were a wholly independent one.

The friendly attitude of Canning and Metternich toward the Empire of Brazil, their efforts to arrange a settlement between Brazil and Portugal, and the solicitude of the British Foreign Secretary for the interests of the Brazilian state in its relations with its neighbors, need not be regarded, in the light of the facts just stated, as in any sense a direct challenge to the United States or to the Monroe Doctrine. Canning and Metternich may, of course, have believed that they were following a course which would reduce the influence of the United States, but their policy never met with the slightest criticism from the American government.

Since this was the case, any detailed consideration of the Brazilian question can be dispensed with.[96] But inasmuch as the problem illustrates the importance which even Great Britain attached to monarchical forms in the New World, a brief explanation of the salient facts may be desirable. Canning's direct interest in bringing about a settlement between the new kingdom and the mother country dates from the fall of 1823, when he offered his mediation to the two contending parties.[97] It will be observed that it antedates the American declaration. But it is noteworthy that, only ten days after the arrival of Monroe's message in London, the British Foreign Secretary wrote to his representative at Lisbon:

> I lose no time [to suggest that you] press upon the Brazilian Government the propriety of an immediate relaxation of several measures of rigor which they have taken against Portuguese persons and property, of proclaiming a cessation of hostilities, and of accrediting any Agent they may send to Europe to the Court of Portugal, as well as to his Majesty's Government.[98]

A later dispatch of August, 1824, shows the reason for his position:

> The effect of keeping the dispute open will be, not to get better terms for Portugal, but to overthrow monarchy in Brazil. Such, I confess, is my entire conviction. I believe an arrangement on something like the enclosed project to be the only chance of saving Brazil from anarchy, and I am further satisfied that the example to be set by Portugal may have the most beneficial effect upon any arrangement between Spain and her colonies, and (even failing that Result) that the conservation of a monarchy in any part of South America will tend to break the shock of the veritable divorce by which the New World is about to be divided from the Old.[99]

The interest of the British Foreign Secretary in the subject is further attested by the zeal with which he pressed the negotiation. Sir Charles Stuart was sent first to Lisbon and then to Rio de Janeiro, on a special mission intended to bring the two parties together; and it was due primarily to British diplomacy that a

---

[96] For a detailed analysis of this question, based on the documents in the Brazilian Foreign Office, see Manuel d'Oliveira Lima's *O Reconhecimento do Imperio;* also, from the British viewpoint, A. G. Stapleton's *The Political Life of the Right Honorable George Canning* (London, 1831, 3 vols.), ii, pp. 250–372.

[97] *Ibid.*, ii, p. 270.

[98] London. P. R. O., F. O., Portugal, vol. 284, no. 1, Jan. 6, 1824.

[99] Ibid., Austria, vol. 181, Aug. 13, 1824.

treaty was at length signed at the Brazilian capital on August 29, 1825. Nor did Canning's solicitude for the Brazilian monarchy end with the establishment of its independence from Portugal. When, in the same year, hostilities threatened between Dom Pedro and the great republic of La Plata to the south, Great Britain urged moderation. To Parish, at Buenos Aires, the British Foreign Secretary wrote:

> You will express the confident expectation of your Government that the independence of Brazil will be looked upon with a friendly eye by the other new states of America, with whom Great Britain has entered into relations of amity. Having respected in them the form of government which they have thought proper to establish, we feel that we have a just right to require in return a similar consideration and respect for the independent monarchy of Brazil.[100]

Finally, with a view to fostering the influence of monarchy, Canning used all his efforts to persuade the Brazilian government to send delegates to the Congress of Panama.[101]

These examples may readily serve to illustrate the rôle of Great Britain. Associated with Great Britain in the Portuguese mediation was Austria. John VI had requested Austrian mediation in October, 1823.[102] For five months the suggestion seems to have gone unheeded. But in March, 1824, Prince Metternich expressed himself as ready to take a hand in the matter,[103] and in April he assured the British minister that he would give Neumann full powers to treat on the subject in the conferences then being held in London. Though the British government played the major rôle throughout, the influence of Austria was exerted, not only with the disputants, but with the other Continental powers, in behalf of a reasonable settlement.[104] Metternich, in this as in the Spanish colonial problem, was far removed from the legitimist doctrinaire in which guise he has sometimes appeared. And though he had no love for Canning, he was willing to coöperate with him for the preservation of monarchy in the New World.

---

[100] London. P. R. O., F. O., Buenos Aires, vol. 7, no. 16, Nov. 3, 1825.
[101] St. Petersburg. F. O., Reçus, no. 28,369. Nov. 23, 1825.
[102] London. P. R. O., F. O., Brazil, vol. 182, no. 31.
[103] Ibid.
[104] London. P. R. O., F. O., Brazil, vol. 182, no. 34, March 14, 1825.

The gulf that separated Great Britain from the Continental powers was less wide than has sometimes been assumed.

But it is necessary to turn back from the Brazilian question, which, as already stated, only touches upon the subject of this study, to examine, from still another point of view than those already treated, the policy of the powers in the Spanish-American question. It has been seen that the Monroe Doctrine did not affect very profoundly the question of intervention in the colonies, and that it stimulated rather than checked consideration of the plan for Bourbon monarchies. In projecting our examination of European policy a little further, it will likewise be found that it did nothing to check the discussion of the colonial question in any one of the European chancelleries, and that in the case of Great Britain, at least, it actually stimulated a more active policy, designed to counteract the influence of the United States in the New World.

There can be no question that George Canning, who had wished to recognize the independence of the colonies from the very beginning of his incumbency in the Foreign Office, saw in the action of the United States an additional reason for moving in that direction. But the cabinet could not be persuaded to take such action, which might reasonably have been considered an affront by Spain. Under these circumstances the British Foreign Secretary made every effort to persuade Spain herself to recognize the new states. The dispatch of January 30, in which Great Britain refused the invitation to a congress on the colonial question, also contained a suggestion of possible British mediation.[105] When this suggestion met with no response, when Spain, acting on the advice of the conference of ambassadors at Paris, completely ignored it, Canning made a new offer, on March 1,[106] and still another on March 31.[107] And the last of these offers was accompanied by bait of a kind rarely offered by the British government. If Ferdinand would come to some arrangement with his revolted

---

[105] *British and Foreign State Papers,* xi (1823–24), 61.

[106] Seville. Archivo General de las Indias, Estado, América en General, legajo 4, sheet 135.

[107] Ibid., sheet 143.

subjects, Great Britain would guarantee the island of Cuba.[108]
In a sense, of course, such an arrangement was entirely consistent
with British interests, and with the attitude which England had
always assumed with regard to the most important of all Spain's
possessions in the Caribbean. And yet the danger to the island,
if any existed, might come from the newly formed states on the
mainland; and the employment of British influence and, if necessary, of British naval force to make good the pledge given to
Ferdinand might very easily have led to serious embarrassment.
The fact that Canning was thus ready to pledge his government,
no less than his repeated offers of mediation, shows clearly his
great anxiety and impatience to effect a settlement of the colonial
question. That the message of President Monroe contributed to
this attitude of mind is, I think, beyond question. Indeed, in discussions with the Continental powers, the British Foreign Secretary more than once spoke of the growing power of the United
States, of the danger of its establishing its hegemony over the
New World, and of the necessity of British action to prevent such
a contingency.[109] Such an argument for recognition was more
than a merely ingenious one, addressed to the prejudices of Continental statesmen: it was one which had its roots in sincere
apprehension. Steadily, throughout 1824, he pressed for the recognition of the new states. If he did not write, he could certainly

[108] London. P. R. O., F. O., Spain, vol. 284, no. 14 (secret), April 2, 1824. "It
is most important that the Spanish Government should be made to feel that the
state of their Possession in Cuba requires their utmost vigilance. . . . So far is the
British Government from looking with Indifference at any possible contingency by
which that Magnificent Colony should be separated from Spain, that if the Spanish
Government conceive that the tenure of Cuba will be strengthened by a formal engagement on the part of Great Britain to employ when called upon her maritime
power to defend that Colony for Spain against any external aggression, unwilling as
this country is, generally, and upon principle, to undertake any engagement in the
nature of a Guarantee, His Majesty's Government would consider this as a case in
which they might be justified in departing in a certain degree from their accustomed
cautious policy. They would not hesitate to contract such an engagement, as soon
as Spain shall have adopted the suggestions of my other Dispatch [that concerning
mediation] with respect to her Provinces on the continent of South America."

[109] See note 19, antea; also Berlin, Staats-Archiv, England, 71a, Werther to
Bernstorff, May 31, 1824, in which Canning expressed his views to the representatives of the three eastern courts; and ibid., April 22, 1824, in which he uttered the
same sentiments to Werther alone.

have subscribed to, the often-quoted memorandum of December, in which a principal motive for action was found in the "ambition and ascendancy" of the United States. He was nervously anxious over the possibility of a general trans-atlantic league of the governments of the New World, of which the United States would have the sole direction. His jealousy of the American government is beyond question.[110]

In the perspective of a century, that jealousy, like many other jealousies, appears to have been without solid justification. In December, 1824, there was not the slightest evidence that the United States would seek a closer political connection with the new states, and the course of events in the next two years, culminating in the Congress of Panama, and the abortive mission sent thither by President Adams, was to prove how little dreams of Pan-American hegemony appealed to the population of the United States. And, on the economic no less than on the political side, events were to demonstrate the secure ascendancy of British trade in the late colonies, and to refute any fears that might have been aroused on this score.[111] Canning was, as it turned out, fighting spectres in his later American policy. Yet he is, perhaps, hardly to be blamed for fearing the increased influence of the United States, and it is easy to understand the basis for his policy. Moreover, he is to be credited with seeing, more clearly than

[110] The memorandum here alluded to is in the Vansittart papers in the British Museum, Ad. MSS 31,237, fol. 238. Mr. Temperley thinks it is in the handwriting of Vansittart, with some corrections by Canning. That it represents Canning's views is clear from the letter to Frere from which we have already quoted.

[111] The figures for British and American exports to the former Spanish colonies follow:

|  | Exports | |
|---|---|---|
|  | British | American |
| 1822 | 19,432,975 | 3,698,996 |
| 1823 | 28,257,868 | 4,913,108 |
| 1824 | 38,266,570 | 8,219,912 |
| 1825 | 42,282,123 | 11,257,312 |
| 1826 | 22,066,427 | 10,754,961 |
| 1827 | 33,152,534 | 7,562,365 |

The British statistics are drawn from L. A. Lawson, *The Relation of British Policy to the Declaration of the Monroe Doctrine*, p. 84. Pounds are translated into dollars at the rate of 4.87 to 1. The American statistics are to be found in Watterston and Van Zandt, *Tabular Statistical Views*, pp. 98–103.

most men, the possible implications of the Monroe Doctrine, and with working more tenaciously than any other to counteract its effects. In the years following its enunciation, he never lost an opportunity to limit its action, and, if possible, to discredit the United States.

We have already seen this in his encouragement of the monarchical idea in the spring of 1824, in his Brazilian mediation, and in his repeated efforts at a colonial settlement. It is equally obvious at a later date. When, for example, the American government, fearing an attack upon Cuba by Mexico and Colombia, made representations to those states, and invited Canning to do the same, the British minister used the proposal to prejudice the South American governments against this country.

The British Government [he wrote to Dawkins, the agent sent out to Panama] is so far from denying the right of the new states to make an hostile attack upon Cuba, whether considered simply as the possession of a power with whom they are at war, or as an Arsenal from which expeditions are fitted out against them, that we have uniformly refused to join with the United States in . . . remonstrating against the supposed intention or intimating that we should feel displeasure at the execution of it. We should, indeed, regret it, but we arrogate to ourselves no right to control the operations of one belligerent against another. The Government of the United States now professes itself of a different opinion. It conceives that the interests of the United States would be so directly affected by either the occupation of the Havannah, or by the consequences which an attack upon Cuba, even if unsuccessful, might produce in the interior of the island, that the Cabinet of Washington hardly disguises its intention to interfere directly or by force to prevent or repress such an operation.[112]

Certainly no words could have been more cunningly calculated to widen the rift between the new republics and the United States. No wonder that the man who wrote the above lines was indignant when he learned that his minister at Washington, Vaughn, had actually suggested an "interference by the United States of America" with the freedom of action of the Colombian and Mexican governments! No wonder that he disavowed that minister, and in scathing terms declared:

You will not find in your instructions any authority to hold such language. If it had been intended that you should treat in a matter so delicate as the proposed interference of neutral powers to control the legitimate operations

---

[112] London. P. R. O., F. O., Colombia, vol. 50, March 18, 1826.

of belligerents against each other you would not have been left without instructions upon a point of as much novelty, as delicacy and importance.
The general maxim that our interests and those of the United States are
essentially the same is one that cannot be too readily admitted, when put
forward by the United States. But we must not be dupes to the conventional
language of courtesy. The avowed pretensions of the United States to put
themselves at the head of all the Americas and to sway that confederacy
against Europe (Great Britain included) is *not* a pretension identified with
our interests, or one that we can countenance or tolerate.[113]

The same temper reveals itself in the willingness of the British
government to send a representative to Panama, and in the language of his instructions:

> Any project for putting the United States of North America at the head
> of an American Confederation as against Europe would be highly displeasing
> to your Government. It would be felt as an ill return for the services which
> have been rendered to those states, and the dangers which have been averted
> from them by the countenance, and friendship, and public declarations of
> Great Britain, and it would, too, at probably no very distant period, en-
> danger the peace both of America and Europe.[114]

It is useless to multiply the evidences of Canning's attitude in
the light of language so clear.[115]

And yet we must, of course, avoid attributing too much influence in the formation of Canning's fears and prejudices to a
single state paper, to the message of 1823. The rivalry between
the United States and Great Britain rested on a broader basis
than any one diplomatic document, and the British Foreign
Secretary was never precisely an enthusiastic friend of the United
States. We have seen that jealousy, as well as a sense of common
interest, was behind the overtures to Rush in 1823. The policy of
1824, aside from the Monroe Doctrine, was a consistent expression
of British interests, and of the views of the British cabinet. Trade
rivalry would have inevitably arisen, with the growth of American
relations with South America. The suspicions of American influence at Panama might have been no less real had there been no

---

[113] London. P. R. O., F. O., America, vol. 209, Feb. 18, 1826.

[114] Ibid., Colombia, vol. 50, March 18, 1826.

[115] For this whole subject, see the able article, "The Later American Policy of
George Canning," by H. W. V. Temperley in *Am. Hist. Rev.*, xi (July, 1906), pp.
779–797.

presidential declaration. Too much emphasis in the formation of British policy must not be put upon the language of Monroe. Especially is this true as the message recedes into the distance. It was, no doubt, pretty definitely in Canning's mind in the spring of 1824. But would it bulk so large later? It seems difficult to answer this question in the affirmative, all the more so since direct allusion to the presidential declaration is not to be found in any of the state papers of 1825 and 1826. On the other hand, there can be no doubt that Monroe's message nowhere made so profound an impression, or exerted a more real influence, than upon the policy of Great Britain.

In examining the policy of the Continental courts in 1824 and 1825, it is difficult, indeed, after the Bourbon monarchy flurry of early 1824, to establish any connection at all between European action and the American manifesto. The allied powers certainly did not disinterest themselves in the colonial question as a result of the attitude of the United States; that we have already seen. The fact is further emphasized by the course of allied policy for some time to come. In March,[116] and again at the end of April, new efforts were made by Spain to engage Great Britain in a general conference of the powers.[117] The diplomatic action of the Continental powers was exerted to the same end.[118] These negotiations, of course, came to no result. Canning firmly refused the successive invitations of Ferdinand, and in his note of May 17, 1824, went so far as to declare that Great Britain reserved the right to take such independent action as she might think proper in the question of the colonies.[119] Even so, however, the Continental powers did not desist from their activities. The language of Canning, and still more the language of the Duke of Wellington, encouraged the belief that if a detailed plan of reconciliation were presented *by Spain*, the British would give it consideration,

[116] Seville. Archivo General de las Indias, Estado, América en General, legajo 4, doc. 138.

[117] The note of April 30 is published in *British and Foreign State Papers*, xii (1824–25), pp. 958–962.

[118] Seville. Archivo General de las Indias, Estado, América en General, legajo 5, unnumbered.

[119] Vienna. Staats-Archiv, Russland, Berichte, no. 77, Litt. B; Berlin.

and might even help to carry it out.[120] How seriously these assurances were meant it is difficult to say, but the notion of British coöperation certainly died very hard indeed.[121] And the tenacity with which that coöperation was urged is a measure of British, as compared with American, influence. In the spring of 1824, as in the winter and the previous autumn, the allied powers were entirely willing to assume to settle the colonial problem without the United States.

Even the final collapse of all hope of Canning's coöperation by no means put an end to Continental interest in the colonial question. So long as Chateaubriand was Foreign Minister a real accord of the Continental powers was difficult to arrive at, for the Frenchman had a nervous fear of British recognition of the colonies, and was afraid that conferences on South America, if they became known to the British government, might precipitate recognition. But in June, Chateaubriand fell from office, and in his place stood the Comte de Damas, far more ready to coöperate with the allied powers. There begin, then, shortly after this time, a series of ambassadorial conferences which deal, at least in part, with the Spanish colonial question.[122] They extend from August 14, 1824, to July 17, 1825, and consist chiefly of platonic advice tendered to Spain, and, in the first instance, an incitement to Spain to attempt the reconquest of Mexico.[123] They have an interest for us only as they indicate that European statesmen were far from accepting the American doctrine that the affairs of the New World were the exclusive concern of the United States, and of the new nations of South America.

[120] Berlin. Staats-Archiv, England, 71a, Werther to Bernstorff, June 8 and June 11, 1824; also ibid., Russland, 83, Bernstorff to Schöler, July 22, 1824.

[121] Some hope was still entertained in Bernstorff's instructions to Schöler, just cited in note 119, in the Tsar's instructions to Pozzo di Borgo of June 19, 1824 (St. Petersburg. F. O., Expédiés, 9555), and in Nesselrode to Metternich (Vienna. Staats-Archiv, Russland, Weisungen, July 26, 1824).

[122] The minutes of these conferences are reprinted in *Am. Hist. Rev.*, xxii (April, 1917), 595–616. They are taken from Paris. Aff. Étr., Corr. Pol., Espagne, vol. 727, fols. 323–327 v.; vol. 728, fol. 111; vol. 731, fols. 55–58 v., 95–98 v., 163–164; 331–332, and 368–369 v.; vol. 732, fols. 141–144 v., 399–404 v.; and vol. 733, fols. 99–103 v.

[123] See especially ibid., p. 599.

It seems safe to say, in summing up the influence of the Monroe Doctrine on the policy of Continental Europe, that it was of the most transient and unimportant nature. The message may have stimulated discussion, and quickened the desire for action in the winter of 1824, but it is difficult to see how the policy of the allied powers would have been very different from what it was, had Monroe never issued his famous manifesto.

But did the message, perhaps, influence the general attitude of the Continental powers toward America? We have already seen that it roused a considerable measure of resentment; did this resentment express itself in the attitude of the chancelleries toward the United States? The question is worth a brief consideration.

With regard to France, the Continental power with which this country had, perhaps, the closest relations, it would be very difficult to find any evidences of bad feeling. Indeed, there is, only two months after the reception of the message, an episode that indicates a contrary sentiment. The interviews which took place between Rush and Polignac in March, 1824, have already been mentioned. In these interviews the American minister did not disguise his fear of the enormous increase in the power and prosperity of Great Britain, and his conviction that, if it were not checked, Great Britain, combined with the states of the New World, would dictate laws to America and Europe.[124] He spoke, too, of the common interest of France and the United States. These observations Polignac received with real cordiality, and Chateaubriand began to talk of the United States as of a natural ally.[125] Both were willing, apparently, to forget the threatening language of the message, and enter into the most friendly relations with the American government. Rush, as we have seen, received a mild rebuke from the French ambassador, but it was a rebuke framed in terms of patronizing friendship. In the later development of French policy, there appears no settled hostility to the United States. When, in 1825, the possibility of guaranty of Cuba by Great Britain, France, and the United States was under discussion, and when, by a misunderstanding, it was

---

[124] Paris. Aff. Étr., Corr. Pol., Grande Bretagne, vol. 618, fol. 130, March 2, 1824.
[125] Ibid., fol. 161, March 15, 1824.

thought in Paris that the American government favored such a guaranty, there was in the French ministry, so Granville wrote to Canning, a feeling that

the interference of a state of the New World, with respect to the Policy to be adopted by an antient Monarchy of the Old World, is repugnant to the feelings of those who hold high the principle of legitimacy, and the communication of the sentiments of the American Government, will, I am told, retard rather than accelerate the object it has in view.[126]

But, on the other hand, France in the same year urged Spain to accede to the unfulfilled demands of the United States, under the treaty of 1819, the surrender of the documents relative to the cession of Florida;[127] approved of the augmentation of the American squadron in Cuban waters for the protection of commerce against pirates; and was even ready to acquiesce in the blockading of such pirates in Cuban ports.[128] As a matter of fact, French policy was again tending toward colonial recognition in the summer of 1825, and the hopes of any accommodation between Spain and the new states was rapidly fading.

As for the Tsar, he had always had a friendly feeling toward this country. Russian policy was almost uniformly considerate of the United States. It is true that the efforts of Clay, in 1825, to enlist Russian influence in persuading Spain to recognize her colonies were not particularly successful. But, on the other hand, there was no diplomatic rebuff, and Alexander even commended the American policy of warning off Colombia and Mexico from an attack on Cuba. Furthermore, Russia associated itself with France in the decisions referred to above, with regard to the Florida treaty and the pirates of the Caribbean.

Of Austria and Prussia, it is hardly necessary to speak. They had, of course, few relations with the United States. Austria had no diplomatic representative at Washington. Prussia was unrepresented during most of 1824. In the state papers of neither power are there any evidences that the Monroe Doctrine produced any effects on their general policy.

The truth is that Monroe's famous declaration was of tempor-

[126] London. P. R. O., F. O., France, vol. 330, July 11, 1825.
[127] Paris. Aff. Étr., Corr. Pol., Espagne, vol. 731, fols. 368 f., March 6, 1825.
[128] Ibid.

ary, rather than enduring, interest to most Europeans. The action taken by the President in 1823 ought, from the standpoint of his own time, to be regarded as a significant episode, and as little more than that. In general it may be said that it left no lasting impression. Of this there is interesting evidence in the fact that the message is ignored more frequently than not, in the historical works and political pamphlets of the time,[129] and is

[129] Of six pamphlets published at Paris on the South American question in 1824 and 1825, only two mention or even hint at the Monroe Doctrine. The work of A. Schefer, *Histoire des États-Unis de l'Amérique Septentrionale* (Paris, 1825), speaks of Monroe's pronouncement as having prevented intervention, and the Abbé de Pradt, in *Le Congrès de Panama* (Paris, 1826) mentions the American attitude approvingly. An anonymous work, entitled *The United States as They Are* (London, 1828), speaks in commendation of Monroe's stand. Of ten works published in Europe in the dozen years following the Doctrine, and dealing with Monroe's administration or the South American question, not one mentions the message. A list of titles follows.

### PAMPHLETS

Anon. *Considérations sur l'état présent de l'Amérique du Sud, et sur l'arrivée à Paris de M. Hurtado, Agent de Colombie.* Paris, 1824. Not a word on the United States.

Anon. *De l'état actuel de l'Espagne et de ses Colonies.* Paris, March, 1824. Treats of the British attitude, but does not mention the American standpoint.

Anon. *De l'Angleterre et de la Sainte Alliance.* Paris, 1825. Ardent for intervention in America. Does not allude to Monroe's stand.

Guillermin, M. de. *Considérations sur l'état moral et physique de l'Amérique espanole, et sur son indépendance.* Paris, 1824. A savagely reactionary pamphlet, which mentions the American attitude only to cover it with contempt. See p. 174, antea.

M. E. M. *Encore un mot sur l'Espagne.* Paris, 1825. Discusses the British attitude on the colonies without mentioning the United States.

Mauviel, J. *Lettre à M. le Vicomte de Chateaubriand, Ministre des Affaires Étrangères.* Paris, March, 1824. Advocates the recognition of the colonies, and eulogizes the stand of the United States, without, however, specifically mentioning the message.

### OTHER WORKS

Anon. *Résumé de l'histoire des revolutions de l'Amérique Septentrionale depuis les premières découvertes jusqu'au voyage du Général Lafayette.* Paris, 1824. Deals with Monroe's administration, but does not mention the message.

Anon. *General History of North and South America.* London, 1834. No word on the message.

Barberoux, C. O. *L'Histoire des États-Unis d'Amérique.* Paris, 1832. No specific reference to the message, though the general attitude of the United States is mentioned. No assumption that Monroe prevented intervention.

given no very great weight in the reports of the European diplomats at Washington on the Panama debates, in the American
congress in 1826, in which it was again to figure.[130] The presidential declaration aroused discussion for a brief time; but it soon
faded from the picture, and was for the time being forgotten.

Nor was it ever influential in the sense in which its authors expected it might be. It did almost nothing to check European
policy. In the case of the project of Bourbon monarchies, and in
its effects on the attitude of Canning, it stimulated rather than
prevented a course of action inimical to the interests of the United
States. The notion that it struck fear into the hearts of the diplomats of the Old World is legend, and nothing more; and as legend
it deserves to be recorded.

But in the final estimate of the Monroe Doctrine we must not,
turning aside from the exaggerated estimates of its importance

Buchholz. *Historisches Taschenbuch.* Berlin, 1824. Deals with Monroe's administration, but not with the message.

Hinton, J. H. *History and Topography of the United States.* London, 1830. Nine
pages on Monroe's administration; no mention of the Doctrine.

J. M. B. *Lettres sur les États-Unis d'Amérique.* Paris, 1835. Gives political
sketch, without a word on the Doctrine.

Lardner, Rev. Dionysius. *Cabinet Encyclopedia.* London, 1830. No word on
the Doctrine in brief summary of Monroe's administration.

Phillippi, Ferdinand. *Geschichte der Vereinigten Staaten von Nord Amerika.*
Dresden, 1826. No word on the message in summary of Monroe's administration.

Politz, K. H. L. *Die Staatensystem Europas und Amerikas seit dem Jahre 1783.*
Leipzig, 1826. Not a word on the message.

Rich, O. *A General View of the United States of America.* London, 1836. A short
sketch of foreign policy, with no mention of the message.

[130] There is *no* comment on the Monroe Doctrine in the correspondence of the
French and British ministers at Washington in 1826. In the Spanish correspondence
the Panama debates are said to have revealed the message as "pure braggadocio,"
"teaching all Europeans and Americans to receive with more caution and less confidence the apparent promises and threats of the government of this union." (Seville.
Archivo General de las Indies, Estado, América en General, legajo 7, doc. 16,
May 12, 1826.) Wallenstein, the Russian secretary of legation, wrote at this time,
"It was more or less clearly indicated that the declaration of Mr. Monroe was only
*in terrorem;* that its language was sufficiently involved to leave many expedients to
avoid embarrassments; and that to resist European intervention did not imply an
alliance or coöperation with the new states. (St. Petersburg. F. O., Reçus, no. 1794,
March 30, 1826.) These are the only direct references to the message that I have
seen.

that have been so commonly expressed, even by the scientific historians, err on the side of too complete a depreciation of its place in the history of American foreign policy. A study such as this, the general tendency of which might seem to be to write down the value of the President's declaration, may properly end with an attempt to estimate its positive significance. In at least three respects, Monroe's message was of high historic import.

In the first place, it is an interesting, if not a decisive, episode in the clash of two opposing principles — intervention, on the one hand, based on the theory of absolutism; non-intervention, on the other, based on the rights of peoples to determine their own destiny. Both of these conceptions were, no doubt, sound, provided one accepted the premises on which they were based. To Pozzo di Borgo and to Nesselrode nothing seemed clearer than the fact that if the King of Spain possessed rights, rights of which no revolution could divest him, he possessed equally truly the right to call other powers to his aid in the defence of his legitimate sovereignty. This point of view they were not ready to apply in practice; but they held it always to be incontestable in theory, and so it surely was — always granting their initial assumption. To Monroe and Adams, on the other hand, believing in the right of peoples to determine their own form of government, nothing could be more odious than the doctrines of the Holy Alliance. They may have accomplished very little practically by the glowing sentences of the message, and the dispatch to Tuyll; but the principles which they stated have a place in the democratic evolution of the nineteenth century. In its protean forms, the Monroe Doctrine has not always been a doctrine of liberty, and non-intervention has seemed perilously like intervention in actual practice; but it is, I think, fair to state that it was not so that Monroe and Adams intended it. They made no attempt to force any particular form on the states of the New World, at no time exerted more than a moral influence in favor of republicanism; they were really, in their own day, the champions of principles of liberty. However little this may have meant in practice, it meant something from the standpoint of the history of ideas, and ought so to be regarded.

In the second place, the technique of the message gives it a certain importance. We have heard much, in these latter years, of open diplomacy. One might think that such diplomacy was a novelty. But, as a matter of fact, for more than a century statesmen have known how to make the appeal to public opinion serve the purposes of their policy. And never was that appeal more cleverly and vigorously used than in 1823. Grant the premises on which Monroe and Adams acted, and what could have been more skilful? From their own standpoint, how much more effective the declaration to Congress than an unostentatious diplomatic protest, how much more gratifying to the national pride, how much more productive of prestige in South America, how much more disconcerting to Europe! If the principles stated failed of effect, it surely was not due to any lack of skill in choosing a form in which to enunciate them.

Thirdly, it is so obvious as hardly to need to be stated, that the language of Monroe's message has had a great effect, in the long run, upon American foreign policy. There are no indications that the President expected this. If, in the paragraph on non-colonization, John Quincy Adams may have been consciously laying down principles for a long future, the same cannot be said of Monroe in penning his warning to the Old World. He was thinking of an immediate danger. The language of the original message was directed toward an existing situation. There is no sign that he meant to enunciate maxims of foreign policy for many years to come. Nevertheless, this was precisely what he did.

This is the paradox of the message of 1823. From the standpoint of its immediate results, it was close to a futility. It did not even raise American prestige appreciably or for long in South America, and hardly altered the politics of Europe. But, as James Monroe could hardly have suspected would be the case, it became in later years an American shibboleth, powerful in its appeal, and far-reaching in its influence. It is more important for its ideas than as a piece of practical statesmanship. Nor is this the first or only time in history that words powerless to alter the course of immediate events have lived beyond the moment of their utterance, and played their part in the wide developments of the future.

# BIBLIOGRAPHICAL NOTE

# BIBLIOGRAPHICAL NOTE

## MANUSCRIPT SOURCES

THE principal manuscript sources for the study of the Monroe Doctrine are the collections of diplomatic correspondence in the archives of the various powers. At Washington, in the Division of Publications in the State Department, is the American correspondence, classified, as regards the most important series, into Instructions to Ministers, Dispatches, and Notes to and from Foreign Legations. Deserving of mention, also, though of relatively slight value, are the Prevost and McRae papers, in the Special Agents file. At London, in the Public Record Office, are the Foreign Office manuscripts, classified by individual countries, instructions and dispatches bound together. At Paris, in the Ministère des Affaires Étrangères, are the French sources, divided into two grand divisions, Correspondence Politique, and Mémoires et Documents, of which the first is the more important. The documents are subdivided by individual countries, and instructions and dispatches bound together. The Archives de la Marine, in the Archives Nationales, also contain important materials, especially the instructions to French naval officers in the Antilles. At Berlin, in the Staats-Archiv, the Prussian correspondence is classified by countries, without other distinction. In Vienna, at the Staats-Archiv, the arrangement is by countries, with instructions and dispatches separately collected. In St. Petersburg, in 1912, the Russian diplomatic papers were divided into two grand divisions, Reçus and Expédiés, and numbered. There was no classification by countries. In Seville, in the Archivo General de las Indias, there is important material in the first five legajos, or packets, under the heading América en General. In Madrid, the archives of the Ministerio del Estado are arranged by countries, with no other distinction.

Of these various collections the most important are those of the major Continental powers. The material at Washington and London has been so often worked over as to reveal little that is new. There are some interesting materials in Seville, but of relatively slight extent. The French and Russian correspondence is very useful, and there is, in the Prussian and Austrian archives, a great amount of material which illuminates the policy of the other Continental courts.

Outside of the diplomatic dispatches, there are few important manuscript sources. The Monroe manuscripts in the Library of Congress, in so far as they relate to the Doctrine, have all been published. The Adams papers, of which the most important parts have been published, are no longer available for research. There is in the Manuscript Division of the New York Public Library an important document known as Mr. Adams's Sketch, with Monroe's notes upon it. These practically cover the field.

## PUBLISHED SOURCES

On the American side of the Monroe Doctrine, there are copious and important published materials. Of first significance is John Quincy Adams's diary, edited by his son, Charles Francis Adams (Philadelphia, 1874–77, 12 vols.). Volumes iv to vii cover the period of the evolution and early interpretation of the Doctrine. Though it is necessary to remember the harshness of Adams's judgment of others, and his own egocentricity, the diary is invaluable, especially for its account of the crucial discussions of November, 1823. Mr. W. C. Ford is publishing an edition of Adams's *Writings* (New York, 1913–17) of which seven volumes have appeared, extending to the middle of 1823. This collection contains much useful material, and, in particular, the more important of Adams's diplomatic papers, especially instructions to American diplomats abroad.

Monroe's correspondence has been edited by S. M. Hamilton in seven volumes (New York and London, 1898–1903). This edition of his works is valuable not only for numerous letters, but also for the well-selected collection, in volume vi, of diplomatic papers bearing on the Doctrine. Most of these papers are to be found elsewhere as well, but nowhere else, except perhaps in Mr. Ford's articles, to be separately noted, are materials for the study of American policy more suggestively brought together.

Of less importance are the works of other statesmen of the time. The *Works* of John C. Calhoun (New York, 1853–55, 6 vols.), the *Life and Speeches* of Henry Clay, compiled by Daniel Mallory, 4th ed. (New York, 1844, 2 vols.), the *Writings* of Thomas Jefferson, edited by A. A. Lipscomb (Washington, 1903, 20 vols.), and the *Writings* of James Madison, edited by Gaillard Hunt (New York, 1900–10, 9 vols.), all contain some materials bearing on the South American policy of the United States. Clay's speeches are interesting as a presage of the message; Jefferson's and Madison's correspondence, because of their part in the deliberations of 1823; and Calhoun's work, as bearing on the authorship of the non-colonization principle.

Worthy, however, of separate mention is the volume by Richard Rush, *Memoranda of a Residence at the Court of London* (Philadelphia, 1845). As is well known, this contains a first-hand account of the important negotiations with Canning in the summer of 1823, and also sheds light upon the reception of the Doctrine, and the northwest controversy.

Turning from collections of this kind to collections of published diplomatic correspondence, bearing on American policy, the following may be noted. The *Proceedings of the Alaskan Boundary Tribunal* in Senate Executive Documents, Fifty-eighth Congress, Second Session, vol. ii (Washington, 1904), contain most of the essential correspondence on the northwest controversy. See also the *American State Papers*, Foreign Relations (Washington, 1832–59, 6 vols.), v, 432–471, for the same question. Highly important documents bearing on the Doctrine, in particular Adams's replies to Tuyll and to Rush, with many others, are to be found in *Proceedings* of the Massachusetts Historical Society, 2d series, xv, 373–436. Some, but not all, of these documents are found in Mr. W. C. Ford's two articles on "John Quincy Adams and the Monroe Doctrine," in the *American Historical Re-*

*view*, vii (July, 1902), 676–696, and viii (Oct., 1902), 28–52. In T. B. Edgington, *The Monroe Doctrine* (Boston, 1905), is much of the correspondence of Rush with his government. Mention must also be made of the *Diplomatic Correspondence of the United States Concerning the Independence of the Latin American Nations*, edited by W. R. Manning (New York, 1925, 3 vols.), and Alejandro Alvarez's *The Monroe Doctrine* (New York, 1924), both of which contain much useful material.

The *Annals of Congress*, and, for the period after 1824, the *Register of Debates*, naturally afford much information on the congressional reaction to the Monroe Doctrine. T. H. Benton's *Abridgment of the Debates in Congress from 1789 to 1856* (New York, 1857–61, 16 vols.) is an extremely useful summary, especially for the Panama debates.

So much for American policy. The principal published sources for the British attitude are the *Correspondence, Despatches, and other Papers* of Viscount Castlereagh, edited by his brother, Charles Vane, Marquess of Londonderry (London, 1848–53, 12 vols.); *Supplementary Despatches and Memoranda* (London, 1858–72, 15 vols.), and *Despatches, Correspondence, and Memoranda* of Field Marshal Arthur, Duke of Wellington, edited by his son, Arthur Richard, Duke of Wellington (London, 1867–80, 8 vols.); *Some Official Correspondence of George Canning*, edited by E. J. Stapleton (London, 1887, 2 vols.); and A. G. Stapleton's *Political Life of the Right Honorable George Canning* (London, 1831, 3 vols.), and *George Canning and his Times* (London, 1859). Of these the first two are illuminating for the early period down to the Congress of Verona; the others, for Canning's South American policy. Although not wholly accurate, and marred by the tone of eulogy, Stapleton's works, as those of one close to Canning, cannot be neglected. Of less importance than any of these is Captain Josceline Bagot's *George Canning and his Friends* (London, 1909, 2 vols.), containing few letters not published elsewhere.

For important diplomatic documents there is the invaluable collection, *British and Foreign State Papers*, which, for the years 1818 to 1826, contains not only much of the most important British correspondence, but other interesting materials as well. Hansard's *Parliamentary Debates*, New Series, x (London, 1824), contains two or three significant speeches on the colonial question, with passing reference to American policy.

For French policy in the colonial question the most fundamental published sources are René de Chateaubriand's *Le Congrès de Vérone* (Leipsig and Paris, 1838, 2 vols.), and the *Mémoires et correspondance* of Comte Jean de Villèle (Paris, 1888–90, 5 vols.). Chateaubriand's account of his policy is marred by both egotism and inaccuracy, but cannot be neglected. Villèle's *Mémoires* are particularly useful for French policy in the fall of 1822 and the summer of 1823. Of much less importance are the *Mémoires et souvenirs* of Baron Hyde de Neuville (Paris, 1888–92, 3 vols.), some unedited letters of Chateaubriand printed as the "Supplément au Congrès de Vérone" in the *Revue politique et littéraire*, Nov. 2, 1912, pp. 545–551, and the work of Adhémar, Comte d'Antioche, *Chateaubriand, ambassadeur à Londres* (Paris, 1912).

For Russian policy, by far the most important published sources are Сборникъ Русскаго Историческаго Общества, (St. Petersburg, 1904), cxix, 228–231, printed separately as A. A. Polovtsov's *Correspondance diplomatique des ambassadeurs et ministères de Russie en France et de France en Russie* (Paris, 1902–07, 3 vols.) and the notable "Correspondence of the Russian Ministers at Washington," in the *American Historical Review*, xviii (Jan. and Apr., 1913), 309–345 and 537–562. The former deals with the formative period down to 1820; the second, with the whole period from 1818 to 1825, and is particularly valuable in connection with the northwest controversy. Of little value are the *Lettres et papiers du Chancelier Comte de Nesselrode* (Paris, 1904–12, 11 vols.).

On the side of the German powers there is very little that is worth noting. The sole significant source is Friedrich von Gentz's *Schriften*, edited by Gustav Schlesier (Mannheim, 1838–40, 5 vols.), especially the "Ungedrückte Denkschriften, Tagebücher, und Briefe," in volume v. Gentz had much to do with shaping Austrian policy in the colonial question. Of minor importance, from the Prussian side, is the *Briefwechsel* of Varnhagen von Ense and Oelsner (Stuttgart, 1865, 3 vols.).

On the South American aspects of the Doctrine, the most important sources are the great collections of the correspondence of leading figures in the revolutionary struggle, and some diplomatic series. In the first class must be mentioned especially the *Cartas de Bolívar*, edited by Rufino de Blanco-Fombona (Madrid, 1921), covering the years 1823 to 1825; and, carefully done, the *Archivo Santander*, edited by Ernesto Restrepo Tirado (Bogotá, 1913–26, 22 vols. to date), and the *Memorias* of General O'Leary, edited by his son, S. B. O'Leary (Caracas, 1879–88, 32 vols.), a collection destitute of indexing, but containing a mass of correspondence of Bolívar and his associates. In the second group must go the very useful *La Diplomacia Mexicana*, edited by Enrique Santibáñez (Mexico, 1910–13, 3 vols.) which, however, stops with the year 1825, the *Documentos para la historia Argentina*, xiv, edited by Emilio Ravignani (Buenos Aires, 1921), which contains the foreign correspondence of the years 1820 to 1824, and the *Sesiones de los cuerpos lejislativos de la República de Chile*, edited by Valentin Letelier, (Santiago, 1887–1908, 37 vols.), which contains, not only debates on foreign affairs, but drafts of instructions to Chilean diplomatic representatives, as well. Mention must also be made of J. F. Blanco's and Ramon Azpurúa's *Documentos para la historia de la vida publica del Libertador de Colombia, Peru, y Bolivia*, (Caracas, 1875–78, 14 vols.). For Brazil there is the recently published *Archivo Diplomatico da Independencia* (Rio de Janeiro, 1922), especially volume v, containing the correspondence of the Brazilian Foreign Office with the Brazilian agents and ministers in the United States.

## CONTEMPORARY NEWSPAPERS

The newspaper press of the period covered by this work contains, of course, many references to the general trend of events which concern the Monroe Doctrine. Inevitably, however, it supplies little or no direct information that is not better and more accurately given elsewhere. On the other hand, the reaction to the message is worth following in the papers of the time. Of papers consulted the most important are here listed. On the American side, the Albany *Argus, Albion,* or *British, Colonial and Foreign Weekly Gazette, Connecticut Courant, Eastern Argus, National Gazette and Literary Register* (Philadelphia), *National Intelligencer, New England Palladium,* New York *Advertiser,* New York *Evening Post,* New York *Spectator,* Norwich *Courier,* Richmond *Enquirer,* Pittsfield *Sun,* Providence *Gazette,* Salem *Gazette,* and Troy *Sentinel;* in Great Britain, the London *Times,* the *Courier, Bell's Weekly,* the *Morning Chronicle,* the Liverpool *Advertiser,* and the *British Monitor;* in France, the *Constitutionnel, Courier Français Étoile, Quotidienne,* and *Tablettes Universelles.* All of these have some comment, apart from a mere conventional notice, on the famous declaration.

The familiar *Niles' Register* deserves a word apart, as the most convenient and useful paper of the time.

## SECONDARY MATERIALS

It is obviously undesirable to present here a complete list of works on the Monroe Doctrine. For such a list reference may be made to H. H. B. Meyer's *List of References on the Monroe Doctrine* (Washington, 1919), which contains all but the most recent titles, without critical comment or evaluation. Attention may also be called to the bibliography in Dr. Herbert Kraus's *Die Monroedoktrin in ihren Beziehungen zur amerikanischen Diplomatie und zum Völkerrecht* (Berlin, 1913). I give here as indeed in my list of published sources only those works which have had a direct and positive value in the preparation of this book.

Of books written directly on the subject of the Doctrine by far the best for the years 1823 to 1826 is W. F. Reddaway's *The Monroe Doctrine,* 2d ed. (New York, 1905). Though without references or adequate bibliographical notice, it is one of the few treatments of the President's manifesto that rises above mere conventional narrative. Of less value is the account in J. B. Henderson's *American Diplomatic Questions* (New York, 1901), pp. 289–359, but written from a standpoint more critical than the average. T. B. Edgington's *The Monroe Doctrine* (Boston, 1905) is chiefly valuable, as already mentioned, for the documents it contains. There is a sprightly and suggestive account of the origins of the Doctrine in W. P. Cresson's *Diplomatic Portraits* (Boston and New York, 1923), pp. 341–371.

Of articles in periodicals there are several of high quality. First in the list must come Mr. W. C. Ford's two significant articles on "John Quincy Adams and the Monroe Doctrine" in the *American Historical Review,* vii (July, 1902), 676–696, and viii (Oct., 1902), 28–52. These are fundamental in their positive contribution, and, despite their bias in favor of Adams, of great scholarly value. A more recent discussion of the origins of the Doctrine, also very suggestive, is to be found in Mr. S. E. Morison's article, "Les origines de la doctrine de Monroe," in the *Revue des sciences politiques,* xlvii (1924), 52–84. Important, though not on quite the same level, are the various contributions of Mr. W. S. Robertson, one in the *American Historical Review* on "The United States and Spain," xx (July, 1915), 781–800; one in the *American Political Science Review,* on "The Monroe Doctrine Abroad in 1823–24," vi, 545–564; and one in the *Political Science Quarterly,* on "South America and the Monroe Doctrine," xxx (1915), 82–105. These articles are pioneer work in the broader interpretation of Monroe's message. On the European side, dealing directly with the Doctrine, attention must be paid to Mr. H. W. V. Temperley's suggestive discussion in the *American Historical Review*, xi (July, 1906), 779–797, on "The Later American Policy of George Canning," and the brief note on "Documents illustrating the Reception and Interpretation of the Monroe Doctrine in Europe," in the *English Historical Review*, xxxix (1924), 590–593. An article of my own, "Europe and Spanish America, and the Monroe Doctrine" appeared in the *American Historical Review*, xxvii (Jan., 1922), 207–218.

Turning from works bearing directly on the Doctrine to those which illuminate the colonial policy of the various European powers, mention must first be made of Mr. C. K. Webster's *Foreign Policy of Castlereagh* (London, 1925) and Mr. H. W. V. Temperley's *Foreign Policy of Canning* (London, 1925). Both of these are works of the first order in the field of diplomatic history. Mr. Temperley has also two interesting articles in the *English Historical Review*, one in volume xxxviii (1923), on "Canning, Wellington, and George the Fourth," pp. 206–225, and one in volume xl (1925), pp. 34–53, on "French Designs on Spanish America." The second of these seems to me, however, to exaggerate the danger from France. Much of the argument has to do with Cuba, rather than with the South American states, and, even there, is not wholly convincing. In connection with Canning, mention must also be made of the able article by Colonel E. M. Lloyd, "Canning and Spanish America," in *Transactions of the Royal Historical Society*, xviii, 77–105, and of L. A. Lawson's *The Relation of British Policy to the Declaration of the Monroe Doctrine* (New York, 1922), (Columbia University Studies, ciii, no. 1). On the side of the Continental powers, by far the most important contribution is the four works of the Venezuelan historian, Mr. C. A. Villanueva, published collectively under the title, *La Monarquía en America* (Paris, 1912–13). Though the material is somewhat ill-digested, the books are the result of careful research in the French archives, and contain much valuable documentary material. Stimulating and judicious are the comments on French colonial policy in Christian Schefer's *La France moderne et le problème colonial* (Paris, 1907). Of less importance is the article by François Rousseau, in the *Revue des questions historiques*, xc, 86–116, on "L'ambassade du Marquis de Talaru en Espagne, juillet 1823–août 1824." Outside of the comments of Villanueva, there is very little on the policy of the eastern powers toward Spanish America. For the early period, there is an interesting treatment in W. P. Cresson's *The Holy Alliance* (Washington, 1922) and an article of my own on "Russia and the Spanish Colonies, 1817–1818," in the *American Historical Review*, xxviii (July, 1923), 656–672.

When one comes to South American policy in connection with the Doctrine, mention must be made of J. B. Lockey's *Pan-Americanism*, especially chapter vi, "Hispanic America and the Monroe Doctrine." This work, published in New York in 1920, is valuable for its use of the published source material. It does not appear that Professor Lockey had made much use of the archives at Washington or elsewhere. Professor R. F. Arragon's

*Congress of Panama*, a doctoral dissertation in Widener Library, Harvard University, is a piece of sound scholarship, very useful on South American policy, but not venturing upon the Monroe Doctrine, or completely analyzing its relationship to the Panama debates. Mr. W. T. Manning's *Early Diplomatic Relations between the United States and Mexico* (Baltimore, 1916) is extremely useful, especially since it is based upon Mexican as well as American sources. An important periodical article bearing upon a little-noticed episode is that attributed to J. M. da Silva Paranhos Rio Branco, on *Brazil, the United States, and the Monroe Doctrine* (Rio de Janeiro, 1908), reprinted from *Jornal do Commercio* of Rio do Janeiro, Jan. 20, 1908. There is very little in the standard histories of the South American states such as Diego Barros Arana's *Historia jeneral de Chile* (Santiago, 1884–1902, 16 vols.), or Lucas Alamán's *Historia de Mejico* (Mexico, 1849–52, 5 vols.), or V. F. Lopez's *Historia de la Republica Argentina* (Buenos Aires, 1883–93, 10 vols.), or in any of the lives of Bolívar.

On the northwest question, which stands a little aside from the main trend of the narrative, attention should be called to J. C. Hildt's *Early Diplomatic Negotiations of the United States with Russia* (Baltimore, 1906), (Johns Hopkins University Studies in Historical and Political Science, Series xxiv, nos. 5, 6), to R. G. Cleland's *History of California: The American Period* (New York, 1922), in which the Russian settlement at Bodega Bay is for the first time related to the Monroe Doctrine, and to H. H. Bancroft's *California* (San Francisco, 1885), volumes ii and iii, which are volumes xiv and xv of his *History of the Pacific States of North America*.

# INDEX

# INDEX

A'Court, William, British envoy to Spain (1822–24), 181, 223, 240, 241.

Adams, John Quincy, American secretary of state (1817–25) and President (1825–29), 6, 7, 126, 166, 203, 259; his doctrine of non-colonization, 8–39, 260; conservative view on the Spanish American question, 43 f., 47 f.; on recognition of the new governments, 49–69; aids Monroe in warning Europe against intervention, 70–103; his diary, 149; his Americanism not due to self-seeking, 170 f.; Salazar correspondence, 186–192, 205; Rebello note, 196 f.; Congress of Panama, 207–221.

Addington, Henry Unwin, British diplomatist, 32, 68 f., 83, note, 144, 185.

*Advertiser* (Boston, Mass.), 146.

*Advertiser* (Liverpool), 161.

*Advertiser* (New York), 146.

Africa, 10.

*Aguila Mexicana*, 156.

Aix-la-Chapelle, Congress of (1818), 47, 49, 57, 73, 107, 124, 126, 128, 137, 140, 176.

Alamán, Lucas, Mexican foreign minister, 151, 155, 156, 201.

Alaska, relation of, to the non-colonization principle, 4–39.

*Albion* (New York), 16.

Alexander I, tsar of Russia (1801–25), 7, 9, 29 f., 35, 47, 50, 56, 70 f., 76, 81, 85–90, 96, note, 107, 108, 109, 126–135, 138, 140, 141, 142, 143, 168 f., 175, 204, 229–235, 256.

Allen, Heman, American minister to Chile (1823–27), 160.

Alvear, Carlos María, Argentine minister to the United States, 159, note, 160.

Anderson, Richard Clough, American diplomatist, 185, 207 f.

Andes, the, 42.

Angoulême, Louis Antoine de Bourbon, Duc d', eldest son of Charles X of France, 53, 153, note.

Antilles, the, 105, 175, 230.

Argentine, the, 107 f., 159 f. *See* Buenos Aires, La Plata.

*Argus* (Albany, N. Y.), 145.

Arragon, Reginald Francis, discusses the Congress of Panama, 204, note.

*Asia*, the, 188.

Astoria, 6, 21.

Austria, 30, 51, 52, 135–143, 228, 230, 232 ff., 256.

Bagot, Sir Charles, British minister to the United States, 47, 50; ambassador to Russia (1820–24), 34, note, 35, 36, 181, note, 182.

Banda Oriental, the, 126, 195.

Barbé-Marbois, François, Marquis de, French statesman, 165.

Barbour, James, United States senator from Virginia (1815–25), 146.

Behring, Vitus, Danish navigator in the Russian service, 3.

*Bell's Weekly Messenger* (London), on the non-colonization principle, 32; on the Monroe Doctrine, 161.

Bernstorff, Christian Günther, Count von, Prussian minister of foreign affairs (1818–31), 52, 179, 180, 233, 237.

Berrien, John Macpherson, American senator (1825–29), 213.

Bodega Bay, Russian post at, 5 ff.

Bolívar, Simon, Venezuelan general and statesman, 42, 44, note, 48, 150, 152–155, 157 f., 177, note, 186, 242.

# 276 INDEX